DANCING
in the Fire

STORIES OF AWAKENING
WITHIN THE HEART OF
COMMUNITY

Compiled and edited by Bob Valine
Introduction with Sanial Bonder and Linda Groves-Bonder

Second Edition

ISBN 1-4392-4394-8

Cover Design by Gaelyn Larrick,
Book Design by Kathie Lambert

An Institute of Awakened Mutuality Publication

IN LOVING MEMORY

Bill Trout
Art Pierce

WITH GRATITUDE

To the writers who share their intimate stories
so others will know, "Yes, it's possible."

To Saniel Bonder and Linda Groves-Bonder
for their love, support, enthusiasm, and wisdom.

To the Waking Down Community
for being who you are.

Saniel Bonder and Linda Groves-Bonder

Introduction: This Amazing Blaze of Life

A Conversation on Waking Down in Mutuality with Saniel Bonder and Linda Groves-Bonder By Bob Valine

Saniel Bonder and Linda Groves-Bonder are Senior Teachers of Waking Down in Mutuality. Saniel, the founder of Waking Down, is the author of many books, including Healing the Spirit/Matter Split, Great Relief, Waking Down, *and* The White-Hot Yoga of the Heart. *In addition to their ongoing Waking Down in Mutuality work, Saniel and Linda offer teachings under The WholeHEART Way™ and a more publicly accessible transmission and teaching called HEARTgazing™. They travel around the world sharing their empowerments, teachings, and blessings with the "Take HEART! Tour." Saniel and Linda are both Founding Members of Ken Wilber's Integral Institute and Charter Members of its Integral Spiritual Center, and are featured as masters of awakening in Bill Harris's online program, "Mastering the Power of Now." They live outside Sonoma, California. You can find them online at* www.sanielandlinda.com, www.heartgazing.com, *and* www.TakeHeartTour.com.

Bob Valine: *Dancing in the Fire* is a collection of stories and poetry by women and men sharing the experience of awakening into "a second birth." What is a Second Birth? Is it something new?

Saniel Bonder: Sacred cultures all over the world have used this kind of language to point to dramatic shifts in a person's condition, but we do feel we're referring in some ways to a new bio-spiritual evolutionary development.

To try to summarize briefly, what happens in the Second Birth is that the conscious nature we bring into life becomes self-aware in a way it never has been before. At the same time, it fundamentally recognizes its inherent unity with our whole personal, bodily presence, with our mind and psychology, and with all other beings and things. This new awareness is simultaneously infinite and finite. There are the natural limits we experience as local, mortal, concrete creatures. Yet there is also a feeling of limitlessness, union, or complete connectedness that is an identification with everyone and everything. The title you chose, Bob, *Dancing in the Fire*, gives a feeling for the simultaneous joy and challenge of this awakening.

Linda Groves-Bonder: Some traditions really give a lot more import to the actual awakening of Consciousness itself, more of a transcendental awakening, where they, in some ways, create a split between material existence and that conscious nature that we all are. In this work, though, to put it really simply, there is the marriage or "only-ness" between Matter and Spirit. One is not more divine than the other. They are equally integrated in the awakening of the Second Birth and co-exist in a paradoxical way. So it's really quite juicy and wonderful, an amazing shift and stage of life for people.

Bob: Saniel, you coined the term, "seamlessness," to describe this awakened state. What is seamlessness?

Saniel: People chronically experience the sense of a split between the spiritual realm and our material, ordinary, everyday existence. When I was going through my own awakening process, the instant that the Second Birth took place involved a simple, essential recognition. It wasn't a blowout spiritual experience. I was sitting at a table in a restaurant one morning, waiting for breakfast and working on my laptop. Something caught my eye and prompted me to look outside. Seeing the trees, a building, and the cloudy sky out that window, I also suddenly "saw" that my own consciousness was not different from the consciousness of everything. It wasn't just a mental perception. Maybe we could call it a whole-being perception or knowing. My hair didn't stand on end. I didn't cry or laugh or experience rushes of energy and blinding light. Yet the essence and totality of my whole sense of existence radically shifted from the very roots. In that instant, the first word that came to mind was "seamless." What happened was, somehow, a very fundamental sense of separation between the sense of my own being and the being-ness, the existence of everything and everyone, just vanished. So there was a sense of instantaneous, boundless expansion to include everything and everyone being one. There was no fundamental seam or division left that somehow was cutting a "me" off or separating me out from all that is. That was where the word came from.

But it was a very subtle, sheer transition. The ordinary distinctions and apparent separations remained. My sense of "I," "me," the ego of Saniel the individual man, was still there. And it, I, was still quite different from the table, the computer, the trees and the sky outside, and also from the "I" or "me" of the waitress who soon brought over my eggs and blueberry pancakes! It was also immediately self-validating. I had the immediate feeling, "Ah! Okay. So this is what I've been struggling for all these years. This is the awakening I've been seeking all along." I didn't just know it in my mind. The cells of my body knew it too.

It's also important to say that there is no language that does proper justice to this kind of shift—and that doesn't raise as many issues as it resolves. First of all, we're talking about naming the Ineffable. So right there we've got serious limitations. Then, specifically, many of us who teach this work have found that the phrase "the Second Birth" connotes for some people a necessarily dramatic moment of transition that they are then constantly looking for. Or, later, wondering if they ever had to begin with!

My awakening of this kind, and Linda's also, did take place in specific moments. But we've found over the years that quite a number of people—maybe a third or more of all those who awaken—basically "ooze" into it. They don't notice a definitive, stark transition. So there is a fundamental *passage*, whether momentary or prolonged, into this quality of embodied, awakened consciousness that people do typically go through in this work. But it's not necessarily anything like a "pow!" instant that can be identified in one's experience.

Bob: You've named your work Waking Down in Mutuality. Why "waking down" instead of "waking up"?

Saniel: As Linda was saying a minute ago, many, if not most, spiritual traditions concerned with spiritual liberation or self-realization tend to propose that we need to extricate our spiritual awareness from body, emotions, mind, and all the rest of the psycho-physical world that we're constantly engaged with. We've got to "wake up" to get up and somehow out of being mired in all this karmic illusion and suffering.

We hold that profoundly transcendental awakening is also very possible in the Waking Down approach. This is not a "low rent," consolation-prize, second-rate awakening that doesn't conclusively take people into transcendence of their ordinary suffering and sense of limitation. But, paradoxically, here the "waking" liberation coincides with an equally profound falling into deep identification with our entire psycho-physical life, ego, and the world.

From the moment the process really started to kick into gear for me—and this was in the fall of 1992—even before that awakening that I later called The Second Birth, there was a preliminary awakening of Consciousness, of that dimension of being that is impersonal, transcendent awareness. People often use the term, "the witness," to pointing to it.

When the Witness awakening happened in my process, there certainly was a revelation of that which is simply witnessing my body-mind and ego life. Yet, with the Second Birth, there was also a simultaneous landing in and deeper becoming of that body-mind and ego life, the personal "me." I've often said that if there had been a sound, it would have been something like a thud or a thunk. Later that same day I told a mentor, "I feel like I've landed in my own shoes!" Sometime in those early years, I began to say, "This is about waking down rather than waking up and out."

Bob: And what about "mutuality"? What is it? How is it important in the Second Birth process? Is it a more modern, democratic approach?

Saniel: The mutuality part of the work also came in from very early on. As you know, for many years I had been with a very powerful guru who was a master of spiritual transmission. But once I left that community and suddenly, in a few months, blazed through the Second Birth awakening process myself, I knew I wanted to create a much more democratic approach not only to spiritual practice, but also to living an awakened life. Over the years, the mutuality aspect of the work became as obviously crucial as the waking and the down aspects.

Linda: We talk about the Second Birth Condition and the Second Life Disposition, which I think is important to mention here as well. Saniel beautifully described what the Second Birth Condition is: the non-dual realization of Consciousness in and as every part of who we are—matter, everything—our broken zones, our places where we have difficulties, all equally divine in the Second Birth awakening. After the awakening, that is the condition in which we live. We live it consistently. We move through the world from that ground of being, embodied. I tell my own story of that awakening, which was quite different from Saniel's in many ways, later in the book, so I won't go into it here.

The Second Life Disposition brings in the mutuality aspect. That is usually something that comes much more strongly into play for individuals after they have lived the Second Life for a while and have done some integrating. They feel themselves moving more toward relationship and not away from it. There's often a very organic, natural impulse to relate to others in many ways, and, for some people, a desire to help others land in their own awakenings. The teachers and mentors in the Waking Down in Mutuality work have this natural impulse in their being to help individuals in whatever forms the work takes for them.

So the Second Birth Condition is one thing, and the Second Life Disposition of mutuality, of bringing the awakened condition into relationship, is another, and is really important.

Bob: Could you say a little more about how mutuality works in relationships?

Linda: As we all know, in relationship, as we continue to encounter each other, sometimes there are places where we can really hear and meet each other, and sometimes there are difficult places where it feels like we can't. I always like to tell people I'm working with that it's really impossible to encounter and embrace every single human being from a place of understanding and befriending them. That's just not realistic.

In the real practice of mutuality, when individuals resonate with each other, they do want to continue to relate and evolve and grow within the context of that relationship. And that desire can show up in many different ways. If there's a conflict in relationship, people practice mutuality by trying their best to be authentic and true to themselves and at the same time by working to be authentic and true to the other in their communication, even if they're having a dispute. So there is a willingness to lean in a little deeper with each other.

Now we're not perfect at this. It's not a hundred percent guaranteed that you'll come to an ideal resolution when you're in conflict. But if you have two individuals who, from their hearts, really want to resolve a conflict, then they will work together. And sometimes, in that mutual working together, there may be a time when the individuals hit up against a stumbling block that they can't quite penetrate or get beyond or work through. In our approach to mutuality, in those situations it's really okay to say, "Wow, you know, we're not meeting each other right now. Let's take a breath. Let's just go our separate ways for the time being and then re-engage when the appropriate moment arises." So that is another way of holding being, our own real self, and also holding the tensions of relatedness. Again, it's not a perfect scenario.

Outside conflict situations, mutuality is a beautiful way for individuals to support, hold, and greenlight each other. "Greenlighting" is another term that we use in this work a lot. It means really supporting each individual's own process in a non-judging way, holding them in and from your heart, and helping them address things in their life or in their spiritual process. So that's another form or aspect of mutuality.

Saniel: Bob, you mentioned the democratic aspect. This is something of great concern to a lot of people. It's been a huge movement in the human spirit for hundreds of years. The ideas had been percolating for even longer, but starting with the American Declaration of Independence, humanity has been working intensely with the revolutionary idea that all human beings are fundamentally equal.

Our work takes that dramatically into real life in the realm of spirituality, which in many traditions and cultures has been one of the last bastions of non-equality in human relationships. We hold that at the level of being, in our spiritual essence, everyone is the equal of everyone else. There aren't fundamental, existential hierarchies where some people are, by their very nature, superior to others.

At the same time, in Waking Down in Mutuality, as in democratic political systems, it's also acknowledged that people have functional degrees of superiority to one another in a whole variety of ways. Some people can teach guitar and other people can't play a note. Some people become much more skilled in the management of an awakened life and are able to help others replicate it in themselves, where other people are still in the stage of trying to awaken. So our mutuality in the Waking Down in Mutuality community and network is a complex process that's always moving between existential equality and functional hierarchy.

So mutuality is not about assuming that everybody is the same as everybody else and no one fundamentally is in a position to offer superior or more developed wisdom and understanding.

We have hierarchies in our work and our worldwide community. We have mentors; and beyond mentoring, we have teachers at different stages, from beginning or "interning" teachers to senior teachers. All those distinctions are very real. But we don't just take that for granted, and we work very hard not to have it become exploitive or manipulative of anyone else. One of the definitions I came up with early on that still works pretty well is, "Mutuality is being as true as you can to your own true and total self, your whole self, all the parts of you, while participating with others who are doing the same thing as best they can." So everybody is attempting to be authentic and, at the same time, to have as much empathy, true consideration, and receptivity to one another as possible. Finally, I'll just say, it's messy business, Bob, as you well know.

Bob: Of course. We're human beings.

Saniel: We're human and we're changing. In this process, people often tend to be changing so fast that it's hard to keep up with what's going on in ourselves sometimes, never mind all the details of everybody's shifts and transitions.

Bob: The cover on the book has a feminine figure of fire blossoming from a flower. What about the divine feminine? What role does the primal feminine force play in this awakening and embodying process?

Linda: It plays a major piece. Obviously, in the awakening itself and then the awakened living, there is an integration more and more over time between the masculine and the feminine; there's an equanimity between both parts. But the feminine really is that divine Mother Nature which holds and listens deeply and embraces from the heart all of who we are. As we move through the world as teachers and helpers, the divine feminine is an important aspect of the teaching because there is a deep holding from that source of Being that enables us to hold others as we do. This helps others land more fully in that integrative process of not just the feminine, but the masculine as well.

Saniel: That's beautiful. And you, Linda, as a woman, are a very profound embodiment of that deep holding, mother-accepting, embracing and blessing quality.

First of all, to go back to the roots of this process itself, I think it's important to say that the work coming alive in and through me was the product of my having spent more than twenty years of my early adult life intensively involved in transformational studies and practice, especially coming out of the Oriental yoga traditions of India. There was a combination of the consciousness side, which in Indian spirituality is considered to be the more masculine force, and the energetic, material, and psychic transformations and changes, which are more on the feminine side.

In the culmination of my own search, this mysterious feminine force came alive and awake in my life. The way I awakened wasn't just by doing some questioning of consciousness inside my own mind and being. There was this dance with the Goddess or, as I like to say, the "She-Mystery." Words have all kinds of meanings or lack of meaning for people, and "She-Mystery" at least indicates nobody really knows what we're talking about, yet you can't help but acknowledge the presence, reality, and power of something very female! I certainly can't, and wouldn't want to. So there is a kind of a dance going on in this work that is part of the great empowerment of each and every one. Matter is so amazingly diverse. All forms are different. Every single cell is unique in some way. So matter—from the same word root as "mater," "mother"—is an important aspect of the feminine and is traditionally considered in many circles to be antithetical to our spirituality.

Here, that's not the case at all. Many people involved in Waking Down in Mutuality don't have a mysterious opening to feminine divine archetypes like Linda or I did. But in everyone's ongoing transformation here, the esoteric essence of that dance, its real energetic, is active and crucial, even if that particular person doesn't use the language of feminine/masculine to describe what's going on with them.

Linda: Yes, the divine and spiritual archetypes can be a very mysterious aspect of a person's unfolding in their awakening process, even after awakening. They can show up in mysterious ways through dream time, through visions, through energetic feelings. For me, initially, right around the time of my awakening, I was having Quan Yin appear quite often to me in various dream forms. This was many years ago. Now she continues to be the seminal deity that I most resonate with as far as my own personal spiritual process goes. I have several statues and images of her around our home. So this kind of thing can happen for individuals. It's obviously not a prerequisite or necessary for anyone, but it's something for people to pay attention to as they move in their process of awakening if mysterious revelations like this come to light.

Bob: I think of Quan Yin as an image of holding and compassion.

Saniel: Right. And that capacity for compassion, for empathy, for non-judgmental acceptance plays a crucial role in the whole awakening process. One of the main ways people get empowered to really start actually awakening is by being invited by their teachers not to constantly judge and make themselves wrong. Initially, peoples' minds get thrown because they've been so used to and taught to, in one way or another, judge, control, and fix all the parts of themselves that are supposedly less than spiritual. So that's the promise of Waking Down in Mutuality. And it's also important to say that the divinely human spirit is driving toward this kind of wholeness and integration in many, many circles, not only ours.

Bob: Saniel, you've written in *The Tantra of Trust*, "If we want an end to war, end the unconscious violence at the core of our own heart. And if you want harmony among all peoples and nations, learn and practice the delicate dynamics of trust with every body." How does spiritual awakening of the kind we're exploring, which is so wonderful for the individual, help solve or alleviate the crises of violence, intolerance, disease, poverty, injustice, and environmental disaster we're facing now?

Saniel: Obviously there's a lot of complexity to the myriad of the challenges that confront us. In some ways I would say that the really practical answer to this is not that all humanity needs to awaken because, developmentally, that's not what the soul-journeys are going to be about for everybody. Not any time soon. Not everyone, by any stretch, is ready to go through such a radical shift in who they know themselves to be and what their lives are really all about. So, to me, what's more significant is what can happen among those who are most ripe for growth, self-development, and change, which is a relatively small percentage of humanity. Among these people who are getting very sensitive in self-development, there are some who sooner or later begin to notice that even while they're doing all their spiritual practices, they are in some ways perpetuating that "unconscious violence at the core of your own heart."

That prompts what is for many a very uncomfortable transition, because suddenly they can't just go at this situation and fix it. We talk about that transition as "the Rot." It's a falling away of the whole "hi, ho, hi, ho, it's off to work I go" premise that nearly all traditional and contemporary spiritual practice is built on. It can feel like complete failure as a worthy spiritual practitioner, or just boredom with the whole prospect of seeking; it can take many forms.

However, if they find their way into our work, where that "Rot" is not only okay, but is honored as evolutionary progress, a transformative dark night of the whole being, well, that can lead to this whole cycle of awakening and transformation, and a different, divinely human foundation for living, including embracing all kinds of practices. That's how the Second Birth awakening gets underway, this radical unification, this miracle of the sense of seamless unity between our spiritual and material sides, between our infinite and finite qualities, between the godness of our being and all of our ordinary personal, even egoistic stuff.

One way to speak of it is, it's as if all of the major parts of ourselves, the major shareholders in our being, come to a table and sign a peace treaty in our heart of hearts. So not only the personal ego and the impersonal transcendental God Self, but also some of the more prominent qualities of our psychological nature that are traumatized, wounded, all these primary parts wind up becoming integrated. With that "peace treaty" there is an essential ending to the fundamental, stressful inner conflict that I describe in *The Tantra of Trust* as that "unconscious violence at the core of your own heart." It's really just a beginning of an ongoing process of healing and integration. The Second Birth is just a beginning. Then we have many further degrees and kinds of healing and development ahead in the maturing of a Second Life.

Well, from my perspective, something like that kind of subjective shift is going to be necessary for a whole lot of key people if we humans are to begin to solve the other problems you mentioned. One way or another, that unconscious self-conflict and violence, that Spirit/Matter split, is going to have to go through profound healings in peoples' hearts and in the very cells of their bodies and in their minds so that they become renewed, refreshed. Call it Second Birth, call it what you will, only on that basis are we going to be able to really do what it's going to take to create "harmony among all peoples." Otherwise, we remain governed by the split, the violence stays unconscious, and we won't be able to help but keep projecting conflict outwardly into life and our relationships with one another, with other species, and with Nature and life altogether.

I believe that creation of true harmony, real peace, is going to come through spiritual leaders who are able to help facilitate these changes in others and temporal leaders who go through such transformations and have political, financial, and other kinds of social and cultural power and influence. It will manifest over time as a huge shift in how societies conceive themselves and how individuals, families, communities and nations live.

Linda: I encourage every single body on the planet to realize their fullest potential and most authentic way of living. Serve the planet to help heal some of these deeply wounded places, not only within our individual psyches, souls, and bodies, but in our cultures and societies. I invoke healing for life on this planet, all the way around.

Bob: We need a lot of that. Thank you. Do you have a vision of how Waking Down in Mutuality may evolve in the future?

Linda: Well, I think through what is actually in place in the work now with our teacher and mentor groups, and people who are aspiring to be mentors and teachers in the future, as well as to offer awakened help in other ways, there is a great foundation for taking Waking Down in

Mutuality out into the world to touch a lot of bodies, hearts, and souls. The unique thing about this work, as I always like to say, is that it's not a cookie cutter process. Each individual who engages with a teacher or a mentor will start to discover their own unique means of Self-realization, of showing up in the world as authentic human beings and helping others do the same.

Saniel: This democratizing and making room for innovation is something that has been characteristic of how the work has unfolded all through the years. Part of what's really great about the vision of the future of Waking Down in Mutuality is that many people are already collaborating to further develop the vision itself.

Also, people have to be ready to stand on their own feet. The idea that this is not a cookie cutter process is, on one level, very exciting, inspiring, and liberating, but on another it's challenging. You've got to learn to think for yourself. You've got to be willing to stand up to people, even sometimes your teachers, which takes courage and daring. You've got to be able to make your own discernments and your own choices in the midst of life.

Also, what really makes this whole work tick, as I said back at the beginning, is a transmission of this awakened, integrated condition that is itself a kind of primal nurturance or nutrition. And that can be appreciated by all kinds of people, even people who are not hungry to awaken or for whatever reasons are not inclined to go into Waking Down in Mutuality. Maybe they're very committed, dedicated practitioners of another system of meditation and spiritual practice. Maybe they're devout religious believers. Maybe they're simply looking for a deeper connection to life, to Nature, to others, to the Ultimate.

The other thing I would just say briefly about the future is that the "down" aspect of becoming more embodied in material life, relationships, and activities is central while you're young in your divinely human, Second Life and also, most likely, still fairly young chronologically, not beyond early middle age. It remains a primary focus while you're growing and moving into your divinely human adulthood and early maturity, evolving in ways that find, express, and elaborate your purpose and your contribution to life. But there are other stages of the awakeness and the mutuality that will coincide with refinements in your psycho-spiritual awareness and capacities and with your greater eldership and eventually your passage out of this life. So our work and transformational sequences are not all just about embodiment and waking down into life, and we'll see that more and more in our spiritual culture together.

Bob: If someone is interested in learning more about Waking Down in Mutuality, they may not know why but they're drawn or curious, what would you suggest as first steps for someone like that?

Linda: I would say access the websites to learn a little bit about the foundation aspects of the work you can explore, see the teachers on their teacher pages, maybe read a couple of the books that Saniel has written. In particular *Healing the Spirit/Matter Split* is a wonderful communication, and there's a new edition of that out now in paperback and also an e-book that has updates and extra information Saniel added on. And there's also a four CD set of *Healing the Spirit/Matter Split* in a spoken version.

Those are great things to initially plug into just to get a basic sense of what the teaching is about. Then what you might do is connect with a teacher to explore the teaching and also experience the transmission more personally. There are many wonderful teachers in this work, and if someone is working with a teacher, then you also have access to working with a mentor. So that's also great. Various workshops are offered around this country and in other places too. Saniel and I travel a lot and offer different workshops, and other teachers do the same. Telephone conversations with teachers and others involved in the work is also another good idea for new people.

Saniel: What people will find is that there are a number of different ways to get into this, and you're welcome to find your own way. In the back of the book, *Healing the Spirit/Matter Split*, CC Leigh, one of the senior teachers of the work, and I wrote a little essay called, "How to Explore Waking Down in Mutuality."

To summarize, we came up with one basic attitude, two essential practices, and three tracks of exploration you can follow.

The attitude that we recommend is, do your due diligence. In other words, find out if this really is a match for you. Those working with you from within the Waking Down in Mutuality network will also help you consider that. So there's this orientation of due diligence in the sense of, don't believe anything at face value. In fact, we don't want you to merely believe. We want you to question and clarify and ask what you have to and figure out if this is really right for you.

Then there are two basic practices for starters. One is to "tank up" on this transmission that we talk about, this conscious energy that really is a force field that the individual teachers are responsible to manage and radiate in their relationships with individuals. Get in touch with that transmission because it's going to stimulate and activate these very changes that we're talking about.

The other main practice is listening. Both of these are really mutual. Give of yourself to others in terms of sharing who you are and also take in these teachings because they communicate, in some ways, a radically different view from nearly everything else of this kind. I don't even like to use the word "spiritual" to describe it anymore because it's not just spiritual. It's extraordinarily holistic. The spiritual side is extremely important, and yet it's only a part of the total picture. Find out what we mean by that. It will entail some confusion, which we say is a good sign, because it's the first stage of the appearance of a truly different and deeply sustaining kind of understanding.

Third, there are three different directions or tracks you can explore, which include publications, online courses, and media presentations; events and courses where you can work face to face with teachers and meet others in the work, get to know how it functions; and, as Linda was pointing out, relationships. We like to say to people, "If you're really hungry to get into this work, find a teacher to work with sooner rather than later. They can, in fact, help guide you in terms of which books to read, which courses to take, what events to attend. So create relationships with people, which can be done from all over the world through email and telephone." In fact, a number of people have gone through the Second Birth awakening who, to this day, haven't met any of us. One of our clients in the U.K. did just that.

So, if you're attracted—and we certainly hope the incredibly varied stories of awakening, plus those pictures of clear-eyed human beings that grace this book, will appeal to you—then whether you just want to dip a toe in the water and take your sweet time, or want to jump in and go for it, well, keep your eyes wide open. Yes, let your heart be touched, but also use your mind. Ask the questions you need to, even the ones you're afraid might not be acceptable. Don't assume anybody's requiring you to bow down and have belief systems about it all. Find your own way. And welcome!

Linda: I'd like to add in closing that, no matter where anyone's process leads them, Saniel and I bless each and every one on their journey. May each Divinely Human Being find their heart's passion, grow and serve, and continue to dance in this amazing blaze of life!

Bob Valine

Welcome to This Book

A Foreword by Bob Valine

Inviting you into this book is like welcoming you to a party where I've asked a wonderful mix of people from many different spiritual backgrounds and life adventures to join us. I'm hoping you'll meet one or more you'll feel drawn to, whose story, successes and failures, resonate with your own. I've welcomed every writer to share as vulnerably as they feel comfortable with. They're looking forward to meeting you and sharing from their hearts. May you enter these pages and wander as you please, spend time with whomever, make new friends. My hope is that you enjoy yourself and make a connection that changes your life.

The people gathered here have two things in common: one, they are, or have been, members of a school and community called Waking Down in Mutuality, founded by Saniel Bonder in Marin, California, in 1992. A growing and ever-changing community with members in the United States, Canada, and Europe, Waking Down is dedicated to serving others in personal growth and spiritual evolution. There's further information at the end of this book.

However, they share a second, very uncommon ingredient: what we call "A Second Birth," a profound personal transformation. I don't know that you can truly understand a Second Birth until you experience it. I know I didn't. Even afterwards it was as though I'd been hit by a mysterious, unexpected, undeserved miracle. Beforehand, I'd heard about it, read about it, memorized it, and I still didn't have a clue. I knew there was something I was drawn to: a human realness, a grounding, a force. For whatever reason, I was willing and able not to have to "know" and to let what needed to happen, happen.

That said, I'm grateful I had words, a special Waking Down language, to guide me. For example, the term "greenlighting" was critical. It gave me permission to go into my feelings deeply in the moment. That was my doorway. If you're attracted to the Waking Down process, you'll find your own doorways. That's the way it works. And you'll use the Waking Down language in a way that's right for you.

If you'd like to explore Waking Down terms beforehand, there's a glossary at the back of the book, and I recommend reading Adam's story because he does a wonderful job of describing the stages of his awakening and applying the appropriate term after he has the experience. However, I believe you can read and feel and experience the stories of these beautiful people through the simple, everyday language they use. You can be like Adam and me: learn the words after the experience!

The subtitle of this book is "Awakening Within the Heart of Community." The key word is "Heart." In Waking Down there is a loving compassion for everything you are–the good, the bad, and the really ugly. This community has found a way, with Saniel's leadership, to hold you, welcome you, celebrate you in all your human and divine complexity. It's a powerful, loving, catalytic embrace.

If you pursue Waking Down, you'll learn to tune into yourself and find your own landing place. I don't want to make this process sound simple or easy. The transformation can happen quickly or not, but it's always a heroine's or hero's journey. There are dark forests of your being to enter at some point, and dragons and other terrifying monsters to embrace. For me (and I believe for most) it is the journeys into the darkness of our souls that lead to more and more compassion, wisdom, and strength.

In conclusion, I want to emphasize that this is a "birth," the beginning of a new life. After my Second Birth I felt like an infant. I didn't "know" anything. As a totally new divine human being, I had to learn to crawl, walk, and talk in a new reality. Now, after more than five years, I'm beginning to appreciate that this learning and growing goes on and on. I'm in the middle of an evolutionary process that is a wondrous mystery. Also, with this new life comes, to most, something we call the Wakedown Shakedown. It's at times a tremendously demanding process of integration of the dark, unconscious parts of our being. Therefore, do not enter into Waking Down lightly. It's not therapy. It's not going to help you feel blissful and peaceful forever. What it will do is lead you more and more into who you are and who you're becoming. Welcome to divinely human evolution. Welcome to this book.

Bob Valine
Ashland, Oregon
September 22, 2005

THE SECOND EDITION

New title. New cover. New fire.

Around two years after the publication of the first edition of this book, I met Jalal-ud-Din Rumi in a new way through Andrew Harvey's *The Return of the Mother.* A sudden blaze and the need to redo this book. I've kept the majority of the stories from the previous edition, a few have additions about the years that follow the Second Birth, and among the new pieces a few speak directly of the transforming fire of the Mother, the divine feminine, and the role She plays in awakening us into our hearts, into our human lives. Thus, this book is a wonderful mix, as it's been from the beginning, of our individuality and the oneness of the transforming fire that leads us more and more fully into all that we are and all that we can be on this beautiful and fragile planet. Welcome, again, to the dance of life and the transforming fire of love's mystery.

Bob Valine
Ashland, Oregon
June 14, 2009

"The time has come to turn your heart into a temple of fire.
Your essence is gold hidden in dust.
To reveal its splendor you need to burn in the fire of love."

–Rumi

Contents

"What is realized and lived is not the absence of duality, but the unity of duality and non-duality as Onlyness."

Krishna

Krishna Chris Gauci was born in Monterey, California, and was raised in New York City. Eighteen years ago he settled in the Pacific Northwest. He presently lives in Portland with his beloved Vivian and their cat, Orca. You can learn more about Krishna and his teaching work at krishnasatsang.com. *His email:* goodlucknow@comcast.net

BEYOND NON-DUALITY

When I first came into contact with Saniel Bonder, I was already a veteran of spiritual life, and I was quite sure that there was no point in seeking any further. I had been involved with Eastern spiritual traditions for twenty years, including study and practice in the oldest forms of Tibetan Buddhism and the non-dual teachings of Advaita Vedanta. While pursuing my spiritual endeavors I also had worked as (among other things) an auto assembly line worker, a New York City taxi cab driver, a cabinetmaker and a Seattle bus driver.

PAPAJI

After hearing the teachings of HWL Poonja (also known as Papaji) in 1992, I spent five years traveling back and forth to India to be with him. The kindness and personal attention that he extended to me were beyond intimate. This amazing being effortlessly blessed me in a way that is still with me. I carry him in my heart even now. One could say that he IS my heart. Through his grace I realized my nature as unchanging awareness and discovered the source of peace within. I came to know myself not as a body or a personality but as pure Consciousness. My living relationship with him gave my life profound meaning. Out of great love and respect, I happily visited him as often as possible, drinking in his powerful presence while receiving his darshan. Papaji gave freely of himself and he delivered the goods as promised, and for this I will always be thankful.

And yet after his passing it began to dawn on me that without his physical presence, the written teachings and techniques left me feeling empty of meaning. It wasn't that they were not effective–they certainly put me in the formless reality. But I began to wonder about the rest of me. What about living my daily life? Was there a purpose to my existence in form?

Incorporating Eastern culture into my world was helpful, but I didn't have a sense of how to live my truth. What I received from Papaji was my Self as Consciousness Itself. Other than that, I was more or less on my own. It was clear to me that while ancient Dharma could put me in touch with my Buddha-nature, it didn't necessarily help me (a 21st Century Westerner), to get a grasp of how to live an authentic life in modern America. It wasn't designed to do that.

SANIEL

So how to live an Awakened Life? After realizing my nature as freedom from definitions and limits, I was not about to follow rules or ideals that came from the conditioned minds of other people. I wanted to be plugged into my own unique, individual life's guidance.

When I first began to check into the teachings of Waking Down in Mutuality, I was intrigued, but to be perfectly honest, upon my first meeting with Saniel Bonder I was not impressed. I had read his book, and while I did not disagree with much of what he taught, it did not seem to be anything that I had not heard before. I found one aspect of what he was saying particularly annoying: Saniel seemed to be implying that most if not all forms of teaching in the more ancient schools led to a realization that was not altogether "embodied." In fact his claim to having a unique teaching seemed rather grandiose to me.

So upon attending one of his sittings in 1998 (there were about six people present), I mentioned to him that I felt there were many Indian spiritual schools (like the schools of Tantra) that taught embodied awakening exactly as he did, and it was simply that there were cultural factors and language that made for the appearance of difference. He answered me, explaining that while it was true that culture played a part, it didn't account for all the differences in the embodied realization that he and his friends were living. I was not satisfied with his reply.

It's pretty likely that would have been our last meeting, except for one thing: after the sitting he invited me to lunch with his students. He asked me to sit next to him and we had a very friendly, rather down to earth meal together in which he was totally available to me, not simply as a "teacher," but as a fellow traveler and human being. In the conversations we had it was plain he was actually interested in my life and background and listened to my story attentively. I found him to be sincere and very interesting.

MY FIRST WAKING DOWN WEEKEND (1998)

Within months I found myself (in spite of my doubts) attending one of the Waking Down Weekend intensives. Two things happened there that opened me up to the possibilities in this teaching that I hadn't glimpsed before.

To begin with this was not like any weekend I'd done. From my previous spiritual background, I was used to satsangs, retreats and intensives where there was one teacher and usually anywhere from 30 to 80 participants. In fact in some gatherings there could even be as many as 500 in attendance. At the Waking Down Weekend there were six or seven participants and four teachers including Saniel. Also, the teachers with him were not his assistants, but full teachers in their own right. Saniel taught the beginning session on Friday and the last session on Sunday, and the other teachers taught the rest of the time.

At the Saturday morning session there were three teachers in the room: Ted Strauss and Hillary Davis (a married couple) and a third woman teacher. They invited any questions or comments. It was difficult, but I felt that I had to be totally candid, so I said something like, "I'm here as open-minded as possible, but I have to be honest with you that there are some things that I don't agree with here. In particular, Saniel seems to imply that this form of realization has not happened until now and that this is something unique in the sacred traditions. I feel that this form of Awakening (as I read it in Saniel's books) has most likely already happened plenty of times in other schools in India and Asia and perhaps in other places we don't know of." I waited for the reply. I was thanked by the teachers for being so honest and taking the risk to speak my truth. I was then told that I was doing everyone present a service by speaking into the room feelings that others may have, but didn't feel safe enough to say themselves.

Then Ted said, "I understand your point and I can see why you'd feel that way, but I agree with Saniel and I don't think that this particular form of realization has appeared anywhere else that I know of." This was pretty much what I expected to hear, though I was impressed that he was so gracious. What his wife Hillary said next however was quite a surprise, "Actually, I agree with you, Krishna. I don't agree with Ted and Saniel on this one." She didn't seem to be joking. I was amazed. Then what the third teacher said put a smile on my lips, "Saniel teaches that?"

Here I was with three different teachers with their own very different comments on what I said. The strangest thing was that there was no interest in "getting it straight" or having the right answer and it all felt just fine. No one had a problem with any of it. There was room for disagreement. "Wow, " I thought, "This IS different!"

The second thing that caught my attention was seeing Hillary Davis work with one of the participants. Hillary, like me, has a background in Advaita Vedanta with Papaji. One of the central understandings of many in that school is that attachment to a person's personal story (how they see themselves, how they think of themselves and their past) is an obstacle to clear seeing and should not be taken too seriously. What I saw as Hillary listened to one person's story of suffering was subtle and difficult to convey: I could clearly see and feel that Hillary was seeing this person as Consciousness itself, free of all limiting definitions of mind, *and at the same time* Hillary was taking the person's story 100% seriously and seemed to be believing everything this person conveyed about their life experience. It was obvious that the person was being deeply seen as a person complete with limitations, but not held to them, because they were also seen as being free of them.

The actual seeing of this is really inexplicable, but when I saw it I immediately was reminded of a story about The Buddha. Someone asked him about the most important part of his Dharma: "Is it Emptiness? Is it no-self? Is it impermanence?" "No," he answered, "It is compassion. And anywhere that you find a teaching on compassion, go there." As I watched Hillary and other exchanges that weekend, I thought, "This is compassion. I need to learn this."

EMBODIED AWAKENING OF THE HEART: A SECOND BIRTH

I knew that the only way for me to test the claims of this work was in my own body, so I began working with Ted privately. After somewhere between six months and a year, Ted called me to let me know that he was going on a sabbatical and would not be working with any students for a while. I admit that while I liked Ted, I was actually relieved. Still having doubts about the claims made by the community, I was glad to simply read the material on my own for a while. I began to go to San Francisco every once in a while, visit Ted or attend one of Saniel's sittings, but life was uneventful until April of 2000.

A friend of mine moved to Hawaii and asked me to sweep her empty apartment before the owner took possession. While cleaning I found a brown paper bag filled with prescription drugs. She had several chronic conditions that made it difficult for her to function without the use of painkillers and sleeping pills, and this bag contained a variety. I called to ask if she needed them and she told me to throw them out. Now, in those days I was working the night shift. That means I would usually go to sleep at 5 a.m. and wake up at noon. If I wanted to get up early on the weekend it was very difficult to fall asleep early. So the way I saw it, this was my chance to see if this bag contained something that would put me to sleep without feeling groggy in the morning.

On the weekend I tested this out by taking one of the pills (a Percodan) and went to sleep. Now, I had been driving a bus for the city of Seattle (King County really) for about twelve years. They had a very strict drug policy, so I was really a very good boy for a long time. They do random drug testing, which means they can ask you to test anytime you're there. If you don't take the test, you can lose your job.

The next morning I woke up feeling pretty good, and without thinking anything of it I noted to myself that percodan is good if I need to go to sleep early on my weekend. That Sunday night I walk into work and there is this booklet on the counter that I had never seen before. It's a booklet that describes the drug policy of the bus company and lists the five drugs that urine is tested for. Of course, one of them is heroin. The fact that heroin was being tested for did not surprise me, but what did is that under heroin in smaller print the drug Percodan was mentioned because it's also an opiate. For some rather inexplicable reason it also told the reader how many days the drug is detectable by the test–five days. You can imagine I began doing some quick arithmetic in my head. "Great," I thought, "If I'm tested during work in the next couple of days I'll test positive for heroin, but what are the chances of that?"

Sure enough, on the fifth day my boss informed me that I had won the lottery and had to take a random drug test. The test results would take about two weeks. You can't imagine the depression I fell into after taking the test. I returned to driving the rest of the shift certain that the results would test positive for heroin and I would be fired. I began to feel a sense of grief, shame and inadequacy that I had not felt for a long time.

In fact, it felt worse than I could remember. I began to have thoughts of how shamed I would feel in explaining to my friends and family how I lost my job, or the shame I would feel in having to try to keep it from them.

Soon it became obvious to me that this feeling had more to do with my ultimate vulnerability to all of life's perils than anything specific. What started out as a simple fear of losing my job tapped into a huge pit of fear concerning just about everything. I was feeling just how unpredictable and uncertain life is, and I noticed it was an old, ancient feeling. At that point in my life my usual way of relating to strong feelings was to watch both emotions and the thoughts that stirred them until they disappeared. Or I would dissolve emotions by merging with them without thought. In either case I knew that the way to avoid suffering was to not become engaged with my thinking mind or pay attention to the story line it produced.

This time, though, I had a sense that avoiding suffering was itself the problem. This feeling was far deeper than anything to do with my present situation, and it was just an example of how exposed and helpless I really was as a human being–a human body. The feeling that ultimately I could not count on anything was devastating, yet it was not something I wanted to be relieved of–it was true.

I felt an urge to be authentic and honest about my real situation as this human body. This included thinking about it, worrying about it and anything else that my body needed to do to register this truth. I did not want to transcend it or even to feel it in order to dissolve it or "see through it" or go beyond it: I wanted to feel it to face its reality. When I began to notice that the feeling was fading, I returned my mind and attention to my vulnerability and thought about it, rather than allowing myself to forget. I made this feeling, that I had spent my life running from, my very object of feeling-contemplation and self-talk. I was driven to do this by an inner impulse, yet it was a very intentional and conscious endeavor.

As I allowed myself to go into the dread, I began to imagine my worst fears: I could end up homeless and helpless, incompetent. Even if not now, at some point I could lose my job. Exploring this fear further I began to think about the hundreds of handicapped people who ride the buses, and I realized that I really could be one of them at any time. The clarity of this was like coming out of a fantasy. I thought about a man who rode the bus with me who told me that he had had a car accident and was now brain damaged. Before, he was some kind of high-powered business type, driving his Porsche. After a car accident in which, he said, "The truck won the argument, " he became a quiet, gentle man who was very slow of speech.

Through this situation I began to recognize just how helpless I am in the face of possible outcomes and how naive the idea that I know what kind of life awaits me or what I can expect. I continued to nurse this bad feeling all night, reminding myself of the sad facts of life whenever I began to feel better. I did this with intention, though it was a totally organic impulse in being. This was no technique: this was real.

When I went home I sat in front of the altar that I keep for prayer and meditation. I called upon every form of divinity I could think of: my Master, Papaji; Sri Ramana Maharshi; and then "all the Masters and Enlightened Beings everywhere." Every god and goddess, Buddha, Bodhisattva, angel and saint. I called on Jesus, God the Father, Yahweh and Allah. I called on "all Beings that could help me that I was not aware of." I called on "God as You are, beyond what I can ever know." I even added the Waking Down teachers by name.

With this entirely sincere call to divinity in every form I could conceive of, I then imagined myself in the form of a wrathful Tibetan deity and invoked with a single prayer my fullest desire: "*I want to be here*!" I didn't want to be relieved of life, as ugly it can be. I wasn't asking to be freed of the worst-case scenarios. Something deep in me wanted to sign up for the full menu, whatever it may be, as horrible as it may be. Immediately after my single line prayer or invocation I went to sleep.

When I woke up the next day, I felt as if I were in the company of Papaji. I felt a tangible presence in which I was merged. My first thought was "I wonder how long this will last?" It was a very powerful and somewhat familiar feeling of intense being-force that usually happened in the physical presence of my Spiritual Master. Then I noticed something different. I sat down in front of my altar to meditate and I discovered a strange new sense that I had "no inside." This is hard to describe: the actual sense is that I am totally merged with everything in front of me and there is nothing of any special interest "behind me." This was part of some kind of "flashing forward" that happened in my sleep. Though the description of it sounds precisely like the experience of non-duality that I had enjoyed for years before, there was a real difference in its lived experience that cannot be conveyed in words. Not just formless Consciousness, but "Me-ness" or "I-am-ness" was merged with the entire objective world in a way it wasn't prior to this. There was a very gentle and very clear sense at my core that I was being all of my experience, both outer and inner, almost as though the "inside" was not any more "me" than the "outside."

After meditating I immediately had the urge to be outside walking in the spring weather. I was the entire walk: the sky, the breeze, the trees that I passed, the sidewalk itself. This was a psychedelic experience, except that my mind and usual sense of personality were safely and quietly intact (though greatly amazed) in the midst of this. Again, my thought was "I wonder how long this will last?" Thankfully, it never ended. I've simply gotten used to it. This became my "base line" everyday experience. At times I go into samadhis and states of bliss, and at times I can go into some pretty "down" states as well, but this basic Onlyness is my ever-present context. In fact, this was just the beginning of further changes in the personality and energetic bodies that were to come.

So after about two years using the Dharma and transmission of Waking Down in Mutuality, there was a shift in my experience of my body-mind such that there has been a fundamental difference in my own sense of what I am since April of 2000. I am, all at once: Consciousness, my body and all of its relationships (including everything and everyone that I perceive). "The one taste of emptiness and form" is obvious in a way that it never was. Saniel calls this kind of Awakening the Second Birth; I experience it as a deepening of my realization of Consciousness that I did not anticipate as possible. It is such an embrace of limits that the All of me is awakened: body, soul and (believe it or not) ego-personality. Previously, I had awakened in the midst of the dream. Now I am also awake as the dream itself.

This is not merely a belief or idea, but a bodily registered recognition. What is realized and lived is not the absence of duality, but the unity of duality and non-duality as Onlyness. As I began to reassess Saniel's claims for this Dharma, there developed a new appreciation of just how profound a teacher he is.

CONCLUSION

What I find particularly unique in this work is its understanding of both the evolution of humanity and the evolution of Awakening. While there is a great deal of overlap between this and other forms of Dharma (and in this sense it is in continuity with the ancient dharma), this is different in the sense that 21st Century individual human persons like us simply did not exist when those dharmas were developed. Even in the ancient Tantric schools which embrace all of life (including in some cases the personality itself) there are no teachings that take into account the 21st Century individual. The ancient teachings can only address what hasn't changed in the last thousand years. The way in which this work is different is the way in which we in the modern West are different. We are individuals–not tribal members, not caste members with a predetermined code of conduct and livelihood. In the culture and time that the ancient teachings were developed, everything about being a human was predetermined by society and tradition. Everything from what you did for a living to whom you married, even rules for how to live as a "holy man" were laid out. Figuring out what to do with our lives is a new dilemma. Up until a few hundred years ago, this business of deciding how to live our own lives simply did not exist.

So I found myself checking into the perspectives of Saniel Bonder not because they promised answers (they did not), but because they invited me to get in touch with my own honest questions. To awaken as Consciousness is an incredible blessing in itself, but I've found that the full validation of our entire experience catalyzes a transformation process that is at once natural and supernatural and our internal guidance system comes alive as never before. Today Consciousness is awakening in bodies and personalities that want to discover for themselves who they are. Fully honoring them to the point of actualizing their potential begins with confirmation of the finite individuated body/mind-ego alongside infinite impersonal Consciousness. This leads to a spontaneous and organic renovation of the entire human being. Eventually this renders one in transparent communion with and as the Uncreated Light of Existence simultaneous with being very passionately involved in life itself, determined to make your contribution to and as this glorious unfolding.

*"If I was asked to choose one word to define what my heart is flowing to,
that one word is God. And yet, I find that I am also God,
the object of my love."*

Cielle

Cielle Backstrom lived south of San Francisco with her mom, dad, four brothers and two sisters for the first eighteen years of her life. She went to College in Vermont and Europe and then lived in Michigan, New York, California, and Oregon and now makes her home in Iowa. She has three wonderful, creative children—Heather, Tommy and Collin. Being a mom is the biggest miracle of her life.Cielle was married in 2009. She and her husband, Jeffrey Backstrom, explore together the wonders of awakened life and devote their time to assisting others with energetic healing and spiritual awakening into the paradox of being divinely human. Her phone number is (641) 472-6562; *email:* cielle.cindy@gmail.com.

I AM ALSO YOU

Recently a friend asked me, "If you knew you had only five more days to live, what would you do?" The answer came quickly. I would take my three children to Hawaii to swim with dolphins, and in between swims I would write the story of my awakening hoping that my personal story would dispel their doubts that awakening is possible. Two weeks have passed. My children and I live in a small Midwestern town in southeastern Iowa far away from Hawaii. I realize that while waiting for the day that we travel to Hawaii, I can at least write my story.

I'm not an extraordinary person. I am a 52-year-old single mother living in a small town surrounded by miles and miles of cornfields. Fairfield, Iowa, is pretty much smack in the center of the United States. It is pretty much smack in the middle of nowhere. My three children range in age from eighteen to twenty-five. Two of them live at home with me. The third lives a mile away. I support myself by helping to run a furniture wholesale business. Most of my days look very ordinary: I go to work, grocery shop, prepare meals, do laundry, sweep floors. And yet in the midst of all this ordinary living some extraordinary things have happened to me. Some of them seem a little strange to me. Maybe they will seem a little strange to you, too. And maybe some part of you will overlook the strangeness and dare to grow and unfold in extraordinary ways yourself.

My grandmother was born in Ireland. She came to the United States as an adult, got married and had children and grandchildren. She brought with her from Ireland her Roman Catholic belief in saints and angels as well as her Celtic belief in fairies. She would tell me stories about angels and how many of the saints had been guided by them. She also told me stories of very ordinary people who were visited by angels. As a three to four-year-old I prayed to God every night. In my most ardent prayers, I asked God not to send any angelic messengers to me. I was especially insistent that I would receive no celestial visitors asking me to spread their messages. I didn't want to see them; I didn't want to hear them.

One night when I was about fourteen or fifteen years old I had a dream. I called it a dream because it happened when I was sleeping, but I knew that it was not a dream, rather a vision. In that vision I had a flash of perfect knowingness. It was as if the entire universe was suddenly illuminated and revealed to be an unending emptiness. Yet at the same time I knew that I and indeed all of mankind are divine, although that divinity needs to be remembered and unfolded. Somehow we will not reach the pinnacle of our divinity until, as one united force, we all stand together in the reality of our divinity and, as if joining hands in equality, become more than any one of us is individually. The more we are collectively living our divinity, the more we are one with God. I barely comprehended what was revealed. Along with this knowingness, a silent voice spoke to me without words, clearly directing me to share this vision, this message, with mankind.

I woke up in a sweat. I had no reference point for understanding this vision. No priests or nuns had ever spoken about such divine truths. At the time the very concept seemed blasphemous. Instead of being elated I became depressed. The request that I share this "message" with humanity was too enormous a responsibility for a kid. I had no words to describe this vision. My inability to articulate what I had been shown was coupled with the reality that there was absolutely nothing there except a perfection with no reference to any particular thing at all. Even so, this was a profound experience that was to change the direction of my life, and over the years words have come that point in the direction of what was revealed in this vision:

infinitely rich nothingness

perfect knowingness
the unbounded consciousness behind and supporting all truth
endless love of and for love
eternal, seamless
pure light without a source
supercharged, super still, pure potential
a thundering, vibrant silence
absolute emptiness that holds itself and all creation
unlimited perfection
an endless moment of Being in God

Lacking these words and feeling the enormous weight of responsibility, I became withdrawn. My vision of unlimited perfection collided with the harsh limits of being raised in an unhappy, alcoholic family. It seemed impossible to bridge the extreme limits of my home life and the supreme freedom of the unmanifest. My "dream" seemed as crazy as my family. I didn't know where to turn for consolation or guidance. For several years suicidal thoughts frequented my mind.

A few years later I was accepted at a college 3000 miles from home. During my first year of college I learned the Transcendental Meditation program. From the first few seconds of meditating I felt that I was coming home, truly home. I found myself experiencing the same Pure Consciousness that I had experienced in my "dream." I relaxed into knowing that such experiences were not crazy, that I could repeatedly experience this state of pure, creative intelligence. I knew instantly that I wanted to become a teacher of meditation and that maybe by doing so I could fulfill my obligation to teach about the divinity of mankind. Although my life did not change overnight, the suicidal thoughts quickly abated. Within a few years I was a full-time teacher of Transcendental Meditation and spent many years teaching this program.

Over the next twenty-five years I married, bore children, divorced, and entered a more standard career track in order to support myself. I continued with my daily meditation including advanced meditation practices. From time to time I was still bothered by the thought that I was really not sharing my vision with others. The closest I came to this was teaching meditation, but I still did not dare to speak of my own personal vision. I felt a restlessness, knowing that something was missing, that I wasn't really living my full potential and wasn't really moving forward in any significant way.

In my mid-forties while talking to a friend I mentioned that since a child I had a desire to swim with dolphins. He researched this idea and gathered information about programs with the focus of swimming with wild dolphins. Within days of receiving the pamphlets he gave me, I received an unexpected bonus at work. Soon after, someone gave me a gift of frequent-flier miles. I had the money and airline ticket to pursue this dream.

A few weeks later I was in the Miami airport waiting for a plane that would take me to Key West in search of dolphins. I called work to see how they were progressing on the creation of a new home furnishings catalog. As we spoke, my business partner printed out the press proofs for this catalog. Somehow in my mind I could see in a hazy sort of way the pages that he was looking at. I asked him if all the final edits and corrections had been made. He assured me that they had. I asked him to look again at the pages he held in his hand and told him of errors that I could see still existed. He viewed the pages and found this was true. I was able to see or sense errors on several pages. He verified that what I was seeing was true. Although he felt that the catalog was carefully proofed, somehow I was seeing errors that others had overlooked. I was getting a little freaked out and asked to change the subject. I didn't want to "do" that anymore. Seeing things that were not in front of me was just too much out of my normal experience of perception. I was way outside of my comfort range.

I got to Key West and linked up with a wonderful woman who led dolphin swim programs. For three days, with a small group of people, we traveled by boat out to sea in search of the dolphins. Each day we spotted them; sometimes they came close enough to swim behind the boat surfing in our wake. Generally, when we stopped the boat to enter the water, they would quickly leave. On the third day as we once again went out in search of dolphins, I sat on the boat becoming more and more confused and sad. I was struggling with the memory of the clairvoyant experiences I had in the airport. Even just the memory was outside my comfort range. I realized that this clairvoyance was part of who I am and that I needed to embrace and accept this part of myself. That acceptance was hard for me. I also somehow knew that the dolphins would not come to me until I accepted this. I took a deep breath, wiped away my tears, and stood up to scan the horizon. Within minutes I spotted dolphins as if to confirm my acceptance and understanding.

Soon after, while in the water, we were visited by a small pod of friendly bottlenose dolphins. They seemed like such ancient, wise beings. A very large, old, male dolphin swam up to me stopping just inches away and looked me square in the eye as if to say, "I came to you because you agreed to accept this gift of increased intuition. I hold you to this promise." Silently I agreed. Others stayed in the water some time longer with the dolphins. I swam back to the boat and climbed on board stunned by the agreement that I had just made. Over the next few months I continued to struggle with this agreement and what it meant in my life. Over time I found that trusting my intuition meant trusting my heart and following internal impulses that were leading me to more of who I am.

Since that time I have swum with wild dolphins in the Bahamas and Hawaii. Once while sitting on the shore on the island of Bimini I was awestruck with how immense the ocean is. Later that day in meditation I found my consciousness expand. As immense as the ocean is, I found that it was like a drop compared to my immensity. I knew that the totality of this immensity was nothing other than love, pure love. All that I am is love. All is contained in this ocean of love. Even my individual humanness is contained in this ocean. I am both the infinite ocean of love and the small confined individual with fears and foibles. It was a direct result of my interaction with dolphins that this realization came to me. I have spent many hours swimming with literally hundreds of dolphins. They have initiated in me the power of healing through sound and revealed to me many gifts of peace, expansion, love, spontaneity, trust, freedom, and more. These interactions played a huge role in my spiritual development.

Despite all of the wonderful changes in me, one very deep fear continued to stand in my way of deepening to my essential nature. In my meditation I would feel that I would get to a place where I was standing at the junction point of my individuality and the absolute. It felt that I stood in front of a door that would take me beyond experiencing the relative, ever-changing nature of life, into the nothingness of the Absolute. When I would reach that door I would halt, frozen in terror. I refused to open and step through that door. There is no doubt in my mind that this fear was the deepest fear that I could experience. It was a fear that there was no way that my limited nature and my unlimited nature could possibly co-exist. It was a fear of complete annihilation. I could not risk stepping through the door from my limited nature into the unbounded for fear that I would not return. Or worse yet that I would return insane. Investigating this fear with the help of a friend I decided that I was willing to pass through the door if I could do so with a guide that had traversed this path and returned as a sane individual. I would step through it if such a guide would stand near me to be a lifeline to drag me back to safety should I begin to disintegrate into nothingness or insanity.

Not long after I made this decision, Gangaji, an awakened disciple of Papaij, came to the town I live in. I didn't know very much about her, but I was drawn to attend one of her Satsangs. I raised my hand with a question, surprised that she called on me because there were about 400 people in the room, most of them her faithful devotees. She invited me to sit next to her. I looked into her eyes, She seemed to be the guide I was waiting for. I brought up my fear. She asked me if I would like to attend to that fear right then. I agreed to do so, intuiting that she would be my lifeline.

I imagined that I would be passing through a whirling fan composed of razor blades. All of my human identity was about to be shredded into a million pieces never to be reassembled again. I took a chance. The discomfort of waiting on the side of limitation had become greater than the fear of stepping beyond that threshold. Much to my relief I found that rather than passing through a fan of razor sharp blades, it was like walking through a sheet of water. On the other side of that sheet I was met by Myself, my True Self. The fear I had felt was replaced by liberation. That fear could no longer be found. I could remember it, but I could not find it anymore. The line that separated the unbounded from the bound no longer existed, and yet, paradoxically, there were still limits side by side the limitlessness.

Just as I had felt a shift in identity to be identified with Love as a result of the interactions I had with dolphins, I felt another significant shift in Self identity. Although I still experienced day-to-day existence with all of its ups and downs, I no longer felt at the mercy of those ups and downs. My greater identity was with that part of myself which is eternal, omniscience, omnipotent, full of light and love. Again, I likened this shift to the ocean. It was as if I was an ocean. I was able to appreciate that there are waves at the surface of the ocean, and sometimes those waves are huge and stormy. Yet the vast majority of the ocean lies in stillness. My identity shifted to be more with that vast, unmanifest stillness.

About five years after sitting with Gangaji and having that permanent shift in identity about who I was, I began to feel that still there was something more. My awareness, my sense of Self, was identified with the field of non-change. Although I noticed increased love for life itself and growing creativity, I didn't feel deeply connected to my body. It actually felt as if my sense of Self was located somehow just above my head. Life was rather like a movie that I viewed, projected outside of me. As when I watch a movie, I sometimes laughed, cried, was afraid, felt feelings of wonder. Similarly as I witnessed my own life, I felt the comfort and safety of knowing that the story unfolding is not real. What seemed real was my identity as somehow universal, beyond the roller coaster of my life. I felt detached.

A dear friend of mine introduced me to Saniel Bonder's teaching, Waking Down in Mutuality. That expression sounded odd, and yet I immediately knew that I needed to bring my awakening down into my body. I started working with his teachers and from the first meeting noticed an immediate enlivenment of the energy in my body in their presence, especially during the gazing meditation that they offered. I felt a powerful transmission of Consciousness and energy from them.

As I worked with these teachers both in person and by phone for six months, Consciousness continued to drop more and more into my body, and my experiences seemed to match what Saniel described as a Second Birth awakening, the birth of awakening to a new level of self awareness where Pure Consciousness or Witness Consciousness is body-centered. I asked for a Second Birth interview to check the progress of my deepening into this realization.

After talking for a few minutes, Sandra Glickman, the teacher that was interviewing me, asked, "Who are you?"

I thought for a moment in silence. "I am dual, both limitless and limited."

"Tell me more," she prodded.

To describe my unlimited nature was easy. I had been aware of it for many years. "I am unbounded, eternal, omnipresent. At the base of my existence is fundamental non-separateness, fundamental wellness, seamlessness. There is an "is-ness" or an "am-ness" that I am always identified with. It transcends, stands apart from all relative change and yet is the basis of all creation. I am that non-separate basis of all relative existence, all fields of change. I am That."

"Tell me about your limited nature," she commanded

That answer also seemed easy. My hands patted my thighs, "My limited nature is my body, my ego, my mind, intellect, emotions and feelings." Something whispered inside that there was more to my limited nature. I wasn't sure what that more was. I paused to see what would arise. My gaze was fixed on hers. I sank deep into her eyes. Words formed around a thought in a whisper. The thought was pure blasphemy, yet True. This Truth had to be spoken, and yet it seemed so unbelievable that I could only speak in a whisper.

"When speaking of my limited nature," I paused, tears welling in my eyes, choking back the words. Then I dared to speak the Truth so new and tender, "I am also you."

"Say that again," she insisted.

"I am also you."

The tears flowed now. My body shook with this recognition. The denial that had separated me from that Truth was like a thin pane of glass. I had dared to crack it.

Kali, the very thing I had feared the most in her, sprang into action. Sandra's words became like hammers (or maybe they were skulls) to shatter that pane of glass, already weakened, "That is the Second Birth! That is the Second Birth!" She showed no mercy. I was sobbing, hyperventilating, transfixed by her gaze. She continued to wield her hammers, "Nothing else you have spoken of up until this time is the Second Birth. This Is!"

As the shards of the glass that had separated me from this reality fell around me, I exploded like a supernova. Suddenly I found my limited nature simultaneously centered in all things. I was all things. It was awesome, unbelievable, yet True. Namaste took on a new meaning. My eternal nature bows to itself as found in you. I continued to shake, cry and hyperventilate. I grounded myself in her gaze.

"Yes, yes," her voice softened, "this is who you are."

I started to relax into this expanded state. I had often heard the expression "holding the space" for someone going through a "process." I needed someone as big and powerful as she to hold the space I was now experiencing while I integrated this new level of Reality. After a short time, I realized that my unmanifest, limitless ground of Being could hold this new realization for and with me.

I felt the exhaustion of both having just given birth and having just been born. I realized that the Second Birth was more than just an embodied feeling-witness consciousness. It was a true and awesome knowing that I was not just the unmanifest basis of all creation, but also that I was centered in all manifest creation, all things simultaneously. Non-separateness was experienced on the level of the unmanifest, but also on the level of manifest creation.

Shortly after the birth of this awakening into non-separateness, I noticed a lot of what I would call "activation" in my body. It was as if the cells were literally being transformed into a more celestial or refined material. This started in my heart. It felt as if light and energy were literally pouring from my heart. At times there was so much energy there I wondered if I was having real physical heart problems. There were no problems with my heart, just a lot of energy, healing and activation. A few weeks later the circle of energy spread from my heart and also reached my throat. Shortly after that it spread to my stomach.

This activation all seemed to be a result of and a part of the Second Birth awakening. In some ways it was confusing. For years when looking for my identity I had found myself to be vast Pure Consciousness that was somehow centered outside my physical body. Now I found my sense of Self, that field of pure awareness, centered in my heart. Sometimes I even feared that I had lost the pure awareness as it became nearly indistinguishable from my body.

The experiences that I had of expansion and oneness with all of creation were very intense. The intensity did not last as a day-to-day experience, but I was left with a knowingness and realization of who I am that does not fade. Sometimes I have other intense experiences that remind me who I am, but like all experiences, these come and go. I liken this to the concept of having never seen oneself in a mirror and then for the first time, with full recognition, seeing one's reflection. After that, even when not facing the mirror, one would have the unforgettable and ongoing realization of what one looks like. From time to time upon looking into the mirror again one's reflection would confirm what one already knows. Like that, further experiences have deepened the Second Life that I now live.

As my awakening continues to unfold, I find that my life is vastly more creative and many spiritual gifts have been given to me. My intuition continues to unfold and I grow to trust it more. When I feel that intuitive knowledge is somehow, mysteriously centered in my heart, I find that it later is confirmed to be true. If it is not "heart-centered," then most often it is not a true intuition but a random thought. I understood that I can trust my intuition in much the same way I trust other messages from my body. For example, when I am hungry, I trust the feelings of hunger that I have to be legitimate. I don't seek outside confirmation for this knowledge. Similarly, I've grown to trust the intuitions that my interior landscapes reveal. As I trust my intuition more and more, it reveals more and more.

The openness that accompanies increased intuition often leaves me feeling very porous so that I easily absorb the emotional pain of other people. It is not that the pain of others triggers memories of my own past pain, although this also sometimes happens, rather that I feel the pain of others inside of me. As I learn ways to ground myself to the energy of the earth, I am finding that I am able to be with this intuition about others without being so affected.

Also, as I deepen in my Second Birth I discover many defensive behaviors and rigid habitual patterns of reactions that I relied on over the years. These rigid patterns are like walls that propped me up and separated me from others. As they come up for review, the walls begin to crumble. The false support that I had so long relied upon is removed. Initially I might feel disoriented and as if sucked into the very patterns themselves. During this time I may feel confusion, disorientation, sadness, anger and pain even while I no longer questioned fundamentally who I am. I feel like old festering wounds are being cleaned and healed. The cleaning has been painful, and several times I've sought the help from professional therapists that are also awake. With amazing speed and grace these old patterns of limited thinking and suffering are being healed. Somehow even these broken and split off places and behaviors in me are being realized to be non-separate from Consciousness. This revisiting of old, disowned areas seems vital in reclaiming all of who I am.

The paradox of living the ever-deepening truth of non-separateness reveals itself in magnificent and surprising ways. For example, I find myself one with the Divine and yet at the same time madly in love with the divine, as if my love flows to something powerful, universal that is also paradoxically outside of myself. If I was asked to choose one word to define what my heart is flowing to, that one word is God. And yet, I find that I am also God, the object of my love. I am the lover, love itself and God, the object of my love. Love flows sublimely out of my limited self and back to unlimited Self, God. Life is so completely different and so completely the same. It is a paradox, one that I understand through living. I now am the paradox instead of just wondering about it. I unfold in confidence that I will be able to spread the message of the perfect divinity of mankind that was revealed to me in a "dream" nearly forty years ago.

One of the most exciting things that has happened to me since my Second Birth has been an acknowledgment of an unfolding and growing ability to access more subtle levels of creation. In fact, it was my involvement with Waking Down that gave me the courage to investigate along these lines.

About six months after my Second Birth, I attended a weekend workshop offered by two Waking Down teachers. The workshop included gazing meditation, the teachers spending a few minutes gazing into the eyes of each student. This meditation is a time of deep communion with self and other. Gazing with those who have been living an awakened life for many years catalyzes openings into who we are at deeper levels. On the second morning of the workshop a third teacher joined the gazing meditation, so we had the opportunity of gazing with three awakened teachers. Each student had a few minutes to gaze with each teacher, one at a time, interspersed with minutes of silence while the teachers were gazing with other students. This group gazing meditation went on for thirty or forty minutes.

By the time all three teachers had gazed with me, there were still another ten minutes remaining while the teachers gazed with other students. I took this time to sit with my eyes closed in silent meditation. During this time I found my sense of self shifting in surprising ways. For some unknown reason the thought of the ocean came to mind. Simultaneously with this thought I experienced myself become one with the ocean. I became the waves crashing against the shore, the great expanse of salty water covering most of the earth's surface, and deep dark cold depths devoid of life and more. All the while that this was happening, I still had an awareness that I was also Cielle, sitting in a chair in Iowa. I was curious: What would happen if I shifted my attention to the wind? With this shift, I became the wind. In some parts of the world a gentle breeze, in other parts a storm Once again I shifted my attention, this time to fire. I became fire. I shifted my attention to a waterfall. I became waterfall. I shifted my attention to the stars. I became a star. Throughout this ten minutes of silence I continued to shift my attention to physical realities, and with each shift I was united with, actually became, the object of my perception. As I became each object, even though my attention was there for only a short period of time, I knew that object so intimately that the shortness of time was irrelevant. I knew what it was to completely be that object. The experience was thrilling and also disconcerting.

When the period at gazing meditation was complete, Sandra

Glickman rang a bell. I shifted my attention to come back more fully into my physical body, still feeling some disorientation. Sandra asked if anyone had any comments or questions that they felt to speak into the room. I raised my hand and relayed the experiences that I just had. Sandra asked me how I felt. I replied that I felt disoriented, scared and a little shaky. I had no reference point in my life for understanding what had just happened.

In a calm, centered voice Sandra matter-of-factly stated, "Oh, you had a shamanic experience, a shamanic trance in which you became one with the elements. Life is rich and deep and full of mystery, and you are opening up to directly experience some of that mystery."

She gave me a reference point that did not deny my experience or make it wrong. She went on to ask me if there was anything I needed. I sat for a moment and realized I needed to feel more grounded. I mention this and said that I felt I needed to go outside for a few minutes and really ground myself to earth itself. Sandra invited me to do this.

So Waking Down seemed to activate or catalyze in me a shamanic opening that was otherwise dormant and, more than that, gave me a reference point for understanding it was natural and some people may be inclined to develop along those lines. After this opening and as a result of Sandra's reassurance that nothing was wrong, I started looking for ways to further develop this capacity. This has led me to outer exploration that has brought me to Peru twice in the last few years to spend time with Peruvian shamans and learn from them. I have also studied energy healing in the United States, and I am learning powerful techniques for healing the Luminous Energy Field that surrounds each person. At subsequent times when I may spontaneously or with guidance find myself taking Shamanic journeys, I am more relaxed, not so confused that they might be a sign of mental impairment.

Through my work with Waking Down I've grown to respect the glory and the mystery of the diversity of the more subtle realms of life that we as humans are able to appreciate. This is not to say that each person involved with Waking Down will become a shaman or an energy healer, but I do believe that each of us will unveil gifts of greater potential than we had previously been in touch with.

*"Now I can be yang, a full and united creative expression of Being,
Then Yin again, as I become the flute God's Breath blows through,
But Yang again, as I AM God's Breath blowing through it."*

Eduardo

Eduardo Sierra is a 63-year-old Chicano, a UC Berkeley grad who directed non-profits for over twenty years, helping start the "fair trade" movement. He became a hippie during the psychedelic revelations of the Sixties. He married and raised his family on The Farm, a spiritual community in Tennessee, then practiced Vajrayana Buddhism with two lamas for over six years before moving back to California in 2001. Eduardo is happily semi-retired and works at home on his Mac. In the wee hours between 2 A.M. *and dawn, he breathes in the silence and breathes out his poems.One of the fruits of this creative engine is* "Mutuality Matters," *his beautiful and inspiring little magazine which is available at:* www.mutuality.net *The love and clarity emerging in his life often reveals unending beauty and makes him one helluva grateful guy!*

AWAKENING INTO ONE TASTE

The story of how a Chicano/Buddhist guy,
A Berkeley Hippie from the Sixties,
Came to Awaken to his True Nature

It was October 2005, a clear, sunlit, beautiful fall morning in the Sierra foothills. That wasn't unusual. What was unusual was that I woke up to find that I no longer had a head ... talk about mind blown!

I mean, no head? It just wasn't there! This reminds me of the late Douglas Harding who wrote "On Having No Head." My view of every thing had radically changed. Where there used to be my head, the usual center of perceptual input and thinking, there was nothing: no duplicity, no duality, no self/other, no separate self identity. Instead there was a pervasive and peaceful sense of Oneness: vast, complete and perfect.

My everyday sense of self was obliterated. At the same time, there was nothing that I was not. I want to tell you a little bit about this experience; perhaps it will help me to further understand it or better yet, I hoped it would bring a benefit to my fellow travelers along the path. Pues ojala!

First, I must declare that what I'm trying to describe here in words is actually impossible. Which reminds me of one of the vows I took years ago: "The truth is impossible to expound, I vow to expound it." The eyes can behold vast views and big truths, but the mouth can express very little of it. So where does that leave me as I sincerely try to share my piece of the immeasurable? That's why I'm compelled to sprinkle my poems liberally in this piece. For me, poetry feels like a more honest means of expression in the face of the Absolute.

In any event, on my fateful morning of awakening, I felt enthralled and very curious, so I went outside to see what what was going on:

One Taste, Part I

I am swept by Being into the Heart of the Moment;
When the Light of Absolute Reality dawns, leaving nothing to shadow,
The appearances of a separate this & that, you & me, self & other, simply vanish.

I had an intuition to go outside amongst the cedars and the soft green grass.
As I did so, I literally swooned, for Great Beauty lives there.
So I go liquid-kneed in a sea of green, falling on the grass.

Here, amidst the birdies, the trees and the fresh gentle breeze,
I lay myself down onto the entire living earth and embrace Her completely.
Face down on the cool grass, warming in bright sunshine, I die in Her arms.

Now, listen closely. You hear all those birds chirping away;
Guess what? That's me—I AM singing.
It catches my breath and what's left of my mind is blown away.

In essence it's emptiness; it's a Great Sea of Silence,
With fluff and froth that comes and goes, but if you
Taste the here-now moment—it is all One Taste.

Yeah, d'ju notice that Great Silence that's all around,
Filled with profundity, depth and an abiding peace?
Yup, THAT's ME!

Soon after my awakening I wrote this note to my friend Hillary:

My Yang is Back

You are sweet, caring for the happiness of others as you do.
When I said my yang is coming back,
Well, what is yang for me?

It is being forthright even radically honest when needed,
Free to express wrath or love even as I speak my truth.
And stand up for it, and uphold it.

Yang is creative, yang is masculine without being macho,
Yang sans the hyper-masculine can shoulder great loads
Yet walk without trampling fragile flowers.

Now I can be yang, a full and united creative expression of Being,
Then Yin again, as I become the flute God's Breath blows through,
But Yang again, as I AM God's Breath blowing through it.

That fall, I found mystic poetry pouring out of my heart. I was writing poems inspired by the "Beauty Eye See." They were a celebration. Like Hafiz said: "*When I discovered God hiding again in my heart, I could not cease to celebrate...*" Dig it! It seemed I was experiencing reality directly for the first time in my life: "*... with nothing in between.*"

No Rumi Tonight!

There will be no Rumi tonight,
for I have drunk from the very lip,
Of the wine bottle itself,
  Nothing in between.

I will never be the same.

Once your cup is truly empty, and
Your lips are open as Wine comes 'round,
You meet Spirit, face-to-face, nothing in between.

So what, El Ed?

So, there is no right or wrong, nor good or bad,
No unworthiness, nor shame, nor anyone to blame.
There is Only Being being Being, in every being;

  Yearning to be held,
    Waiting to be seen.

One day, several years ago, I fell from a misplaced ladder, got a couple of cracks in my cranium, a big black-eye and a whopper concussion.

Busted, the universe had gotten my attention: I was on a self-occupied speed trip, spiritually heading the wrong way fast. I seriously needed to chill out and come up with a better plan.

My old spiritual beliefs, views and cosmologies had somehow begun to rot on the vine! Little did I suspect this rotting was a final phase before awakening. But I was heavy in my duhkha daze and that meant unending tears and dismal stretches of unhappiness. At that time two people from Waking Down in Mutuality (WDM), Hillary Davis & Ted Strauss, showed up in my life. They had moved to the foothills of the Sierra Nevada, near my little rancho. In the end, they did a magnificent job of watering my spiritual garden with that very nurturing mothering love. I think it's what Carl Rogers called "unconditional positive regard." This obviously quickened my awakening process. The rest was activated by the loving hands of two goddess friends.

Truly, my awakening took a quantum leap when tender and healing touch entered, stage left, through the lovely vehicles of two Enneagram Fours! These raucous roommates, Pia and Bernadette ("The Butterfly") jump-started my recognizing the divine within me! One was a divine masseuse, the other was a divine lover. Relating with them during this time was a spiritual and erotic celebration.

In fact, it was soon after our interactions grew deep and more intimate, that my poems started to pour out, as did the tears and the laughter! It was purification by fire: The heat of our bonfires brightened shadows and released ancient knots to my love and creative expression. It's been said somewhere: "Gold can only be made pure only when introduced to fire." What a beautiful fire! What shiny gold!

My kind and loving consorts were spirit's undercover agents for me to feel a "hand behind the hand," and eventually, to behold the Golden Buddha, Prajnaparamita, and her Perfect Wisdom. Before I knew it, a dam had broken wide open, irreparably busted. Through that gap have surged my poems.

> *[A Respectful Footnote on Prajnaparamita: She is the buddha related to the Heart Sutra, a pivotal Mahayana sutra that helped Buddhism to evolve beyond a monastic orientation to include householders. And, even though I had previously received her initiation and done her mantra, I could never fathom what it meant: "The Mother of all the Buddhas." Suddenly it was clear. She embodies emptiness which gives rise to all phenomena. It felt to me as though she took over my spiritual unfoldment, as my yidam*

or guide to awakening; I don't remember making a choice here, but it didn't matter!]

It was always easy for me to see the Divine in others, like seeing the goddess in women, for example. I just couldn't see the divine in my self. I guess the great equalizer came when I realized that neither "self" nor "other" actually exist!

I believe that touch, yes, warm, human, loving touch, triggered the final stage of my going beyond. For example, in session with Pia Maria during my lateRot, in a deep massage she visualized me as Shiva, the Godhead. It was easy to see her as the Goddess because she radiates it from the "deep feminine." But her invocation of Shiva opened a door in me to see myself that way.

This sort of sacred ceremony, holy touch and loving kindness, evoked a deepening trust within my body. It would relax, trust more deeply and create less separation out of fear. As trust grew, resistance melted. It wasn't long before I could see the Divine in me! This is a poem inspired by Pia.

Healing Touch

She's a devotee of Shiva-Shakti,
A recognizer and visualizer of the Divine.

One day, in sacred ceremony,
She uncorked my heart with
A simple, but impersonal kiss.
It brought on deep sobbing in me
For suddenly, I became aware
Of The Kiss behind the kiss.

That Kiss is Mother's unconditional love!
I AM LOVED BY THE MOTHER!
Her caring takes away fears and petty woes,
And heals the body, top to bottom.

It is a Blessed Kiss of SPIRIT,
Reminding me of who I AM,
And reminding me how very much
I am Loved by Her—I AM THAT LOVE!

For the remainder of the day, I was not the same;
I was way-open, too vulnerable, even to suit up for work.
I saw the pain, anguish, and loneliness of "me,"
Which makes me want "to fight or flight," but I stayed still.

Who has wounded this gently pulsing heart of mine?
Who has failed to notice this mystic poet as he enters the room,
Eyes blissed out, mind clear sky, flaming heart spilling over.
No one sees, everyone's bizy, self-occupied, or just ignoring!

And all that he wants is to be seen,
In his Love, In his Truth.

For some reason, a beautiful woman latched onto me around this time: The Butterfly. This became a simple yet exquisitely cosmic love affair—a blaze that kindles another blaze!

Butterfly was in the middle of her own blaze of awakening. She is a model-quality beauty, lithe figured with graceful moves and big expressive eyes. As a person she is a deeply loving, appreciative, engaging and bravely erotic. I looked deeply into her blazing eyes and saw her eternal soul.

At the time she came to me, Butterfly was full of spirit, new-found freedom, and a love and passion to blow the lids off corks left too long in their bottles. Like mine! There are some relationships that are only meant to be fulfilled in the short-term. So it was with Butterfly. She swept into my life and with her blazing passion, catapulted me into higher levels of self-realization and creative energy than ever before, and then she left! Such must be the way of the butterflies.

So, at the personal level, there was a lovely and passionate affair, but at the transpersonal level there was a union with the cosmic mother, the deeply abiding divine feminine. There also was an empowering of the divine masculine, if you will, in me. During this time of opening and self-discovery, synchronicity played in heavily with signs, coincidences and improbable displays.

For example, one evening Butterfly was due to arrive. I had cleared my space with sage and offered mantras to invoke a sacred space. When she arrived, she quickly sensed the space and got comfortable in it. She whisked off the music and replaced it with some tunes she'd brought for the occasion.

As our rapture and pleasure rose, so did my level of seeing. It started out I was admiring and touching her gorgeous worldly form, but soon, deep in her eyes I was seeing her eternal aspect, the goddess flowering and radiating within her! As I plunged into her depth, I sensed a presence of Being that was powerful, graceful and beautiful at once. So maybe I am seeing her soul, I thought. The music was playing loudly as we made love on the carpet, taking our time, drinking our wine. And as the eternal aspect of Butterfly manifested before my eyes, the music came into this song:

[*Listen Closely* by Steven Walters]

Friend, I know that you can hear this song, I see the melody in your eyes.
I needn't know your name, the song it is the same.

Sing the mountain, sing the raising sun,
Sing the flowing river and the valley just beyond.

The mystery has no ending, it just goes on and on,
Sing until the singer hears the song.

GATE, GATE, PARAGATE, PARASAMGATE, BODHISUAHA.

What?!?! Wow, that's Prajnaparamita's Mantra! It means something like: "*Beyond, beyond, gone beyond, gone beyond beyond, so be it.*" Numerous incidents like that made me feel that the "Mother of All the Buddhas" was sneaking into my consciousness from five directions. As our physical bodies peaked into a divine ecstasy, our energy bodies also surged into a blissful union and our transpersonal selves saw directly the "eyes behind our eyes." Coming, on three levels, at once, I'm sensing angels and celestial buddhas dancing in the air. My sense of self is blown elsewhere.

A month later, my Second Birth was confirmed by Sandra Glickman and I was still blazing. I was also becoming aware that my conditioning, my various habits and shadow sides, had not simply disappeared, but were now more clearly evident. The difference was I had this bright light of Consciousness to bring into the shadows, to observe, to notice their real nature and eventually to see them go.

The Roof Beam's Broken

"I see you now, oh builder of the house,
and ye shall build no more ...
For the roof beam has been broken..." ~ Lord Buddha

Ha! I've just caught a local thief,
One that steals my power and gives it away,
The one that defers to outside authority,
Then later complains, and rankles and rebels.

It is about me assuming my own AUTHOR-ity,

not habitually deferring to others.
About daring to allow my own expression
rather that using wisdom quotes to hide behind.

The fear lurking behind my lack of confidence
No longer compels; fear's fever is broken!
Ah so! We broke a roof beam together!
God bless the roof beam breakers!

As I write this, it is three years since my Second Birth. I've had time to reflect. How has it changed or influenced my state of happiness and well being? What has it meant in my ordinary life? At times I see the hand behind the hand, everywhere. How has it changed or influenced my state of happiness and well being? What's the diff?

One thing is this constant seeing into people deeply enough to appreciate the divine in them. Kind of like playing hide-n-seek with God. "Let's see what disguise God has put on this time?" It could be a little nerd, a gorgeous goddess, a poor kid, an old lady who hums as she ambles past my seat in the theater!

Seeing God, sometimes it is a matter of active mindful engagement (and not buying anyone's doubt); other times it's a matter of penetrating insight and patience (one who stalks darting light amidst shifting shadows). It seems to be easier as I go along.

Whereas the flash and blaze of the Absolute seemed to result from dissolving as a "separate self," now there isn't all the drama and distinction; relative blends into Absolute and reveals it was never separate. Now I find myself able to relax into no-mind states where, again, there's a feeling of having no head. It's a blending into the field of consciousness as I loose the grip of a willful and domineering mind.

And there is this delightful little dance with reflections and veils, allowing sacred glimpses of the face of Being. Light plays off of a quiet pond; its mirror-like reflections shimmer with ripples, then quiet again, a return to clarity and pure reflection.

Let that LOVE you are, reach far, reach all!
Reach everywhere and every One,
Let us shine and recognize
The radiant reflections we are for one another.
See it in the ripples of the divine,
Spreading out in perfect rings among us.

Often I feel like a little boy out in the world, full of awe and curiosity and plenty of wonder. Anything can be utterly fascinating, because in every bit of "ordinary" one can flash on the "extraordinary." In my wandering I am the cool observer, but I'm also the hot and passionate co-participant in this dance with the phenomenal world.

Even though I'm still finding plenty to observe in my subconscious mind, none of it surprises me much anymore. It's familiar territory with not much spook factor left in it. My own shadow side is part of the phenomena I study, as I continue to take the powerful light of Consciousness into darkness wherever I may find it. It's an ongoing thing. Maybe that's what they meant that the journey itself is the goal?

Finally, I want to express my deepest gratitude to the teachers, friends and buddhas-of-the-moment who have appeared, blessed me and resonated awakened mind to me in a way that touched, no, cooked me until, like an over-exposed radiation badge, it was all red, "goose-is-cooked!" I felt the paradox of being awake as the divine and concurrently existing as a foible and error-prone humanoid.

As I look back on my life, it is clear that I have been blessed in very many ways. I encountered spiritual travelers and teachers along the path in my early twenties, lived in spiritual community and raised my family of four there. I've also related with a number of genuine teachers. Some were more realized than others, but no matter, as it is said, "Pure teachings can come through impure vessels."

I can't attribute the fruit of my awakening only to the people and skillful means of Waking Down in Mutuality. They are the final chapter before my awakening, but each chapter, each blessing, each spiritual mentor along my way, played an important role. It's as though each one stood on the shoulders of the other until I was high enough to see clearly and finally wake up to my true nature. No, it's not a done deal—unfolding isn't over, it's ongoing. But it does seem that there is less and less of me, and more and more of what to be grateful for. Unending thanks to all!

"This was not at all about being blissed out and feeling high; it was about literally opening up my gut and landing in myself instead of endlessly escaping."

Shanti

Shanti Spierenburg was born in the Netherlands as Katinka Spierenburg. At nineteen she moved to Amsterdam to become an RN. She lives now, after many travels and adventures, in Lafayette, Colorado, with husband, Ed , a software engineer, and four-year-old son, Alexander. Besides being a mom, which has been one of the most humbling experiences in her life, she works as an RN at the local hospital.

I AM MYSELF

I was born the second child in a family with four children. My birth being unplanned put a lot of stress on this young family—my brother and I are only eleven and a half months apart. According to my mom I cried for three weeks straight, and they put me aside in a stable at night until I stopped crying because nobody was getting any sleep. I was born at home in a small castle in Holland where my parents rented a few rooms. The place was called Hemelryk, which means heaven in Dutch. I always thought that was a good start.

For whatever reason I always felt like a stranger within my family. I knew as a little child that "those" people were not my real parents and that I was here on a "mission." I did feel very alone most of the time. Also as a young child I had weird experiences where I would leave my body and hang as a big blob on the ceiling, being very big. That stopped when I was about seven years old.

After high school I moved to Amsterdam to become a student RN, not really out of choice but more out of necessity—since between my mother and me, there was something like a cold war going on. I had felt increasingly depressed and disconnected with everything during my teenage years, and my future seemed dark and gloomy. I fell into black holes of despair and sometimes wondered if I was going insane. I was plagued by horrible dreams where I was this young Jewish girl chased and finally found by the Nazis. The dreams lasted for most of my teenage years until I found a way to change the dream I was in by either making myself invisible or breaking out into a totally new dream. The deep holes of despair kept coming up though, and I was lucky that when I moved to Amsterdam I got in touch with a totally new life.

It was great to be away in Amsterdam on my own, especially when a friend brought me to The Kosmos, a meditation center where you could do anything from Zazen , yoga, Vipassana, dance, sauna and great vegetarian food. For the first time I felt at home. I started to meditate and make friends with people like me who were a little odd and looking for something different in life.

Not much later I met a man at a retreat who was dressed in orange and wore a mala (a necklace with 108 beads and the guru's picture) around his neck. Although he looked very strange, he seemed peaceful and connected to himself, more "real." I was very intrigued by him. We became friends. He was a disciple of Bhagwan Shree Rajneesh (Osho) and had been to Poona, India.

I started doing Osho's active meditations and listening to his discourses. Not long after we met, my friend Rudra went back to India, and although I loved the meditations and everything, I was afraid to become part of the neo-sannyas world–afraid of being "brainwashed." I decided to go to Poona, but only as a spectator.

About two weeks after my boyfriend left, I decided to write to Osho to ask him about groups. I remember sitting down late at night and starting my letter. Halfway through the letter I started to have this amazing experience where everything in the room began to change. A bright light filled the room and my being. I began to feel very joyous and peaceful. I was awestruck. I felt touched by Bhagwan.

That moment all my reservations went out the window. I decided to take sannyas and become a disciple when I arrived in Poona. The next day I dyed all my clothes orange, and what I couldn't dye I gave away. I bought a ticket, quit my job and said goodbye to my friends and family who were very supportive. Although when I took the train back to Amsterdam dressed in orange, my dad was a little worried and suggested I put a coat over all those bright clothes.

I took sannyas (became a disciple) in the old Poona, where Osho gave me my new name, Shunyo, and a mala. I don't remember much of what he said. I just remember that for the first time in my life I was really *being seen* and that I was OK. I also had the experience where for the first time in my life somebody reached into what I call my inner desert, a place of desolation and despair. It was my first big relief.

I didn't realize how shut down I was until I got to Poona. I did a few groups and many meditation retreats, even went to Goa for the necessary breaks. Every evening I would sit down at a quiet spot at the beach and watch the sun disappear. It was there that I started to experience what Saniel Bonder calls "the blazing forth of consciousness." It's an experience of a very alive silence that is so pervasive that no sound can disturb it. It was incredible. I remember thinking that the vastness of the sky and myself are One. One field of Consciousness. I never talked with anybody about that. I certainly didn't ask Bhagwan, because, although I felt very close to Osho at that time, he was like a god to me—infallible, pure and not human. I worshiped him with all my heart and soul. He was truly my Savior and showed me my first glimpse of the Divine.

To me Poona was my home, my paradise. I did everything to be able to stay. I lived in somebody's garage, sold everything to make money. I lived there for a year and a half and was a sannyasin for about twelve years. I lived in and out of communes—like Sadhana, a big international commune in an old jail in the middle of Amsterdam, and different communal houses in Boston. I was devastated when the Ranch, the commune in Oregon where I lived, fell apart. To be out in the world was the last thing I wanted to do.

My second experience with a spiritual group was a few years later. I had gotten married to an American sannyasin and moved to Colorado. I went to a dance-meditation evening with a woman who channeled a beautiful being called Oceana. Osho was gone, I still felt that my work wasn't done, so I kept checking things out. Again I had an experience that blew me away. This experience would get me ready to work with the Waking Down group in a way that was totally unexpected and definitely not a path I would have chosen "myself."

While dancing I swallowed a big ball of energy and I exploded into light. I was terrified, but also knew I wanted to work more with this entity. It was one of those teachings that had some really beautiful things to offer like meditation, breath work, community, great retreats in Hawaii and India. Initially a lot of the teachings were based on Osho's work.

Things changed when another teacher became involved. To me Osho's teaching was Tantric, meaning that you don't repress anything but go into feelings, traumas, and sexuality with awareness. Through that awareness things transform. Looking back, I see that with the new teacher the focus changed more to conquering/controlling one's fear, human weaknesses, and sexual feelings. It was more the classic oriental orientation toward "Enlightenment": to dissociate from your human traits and focus more on the "spiritual" part of your being.

To make a long story short, there was a split between the two teachers, and the one that I followed ended up creating a big mess. He had an affair with and later married a much younger disciple while covering up and lying about it. At first I was shocked; I didn't know what to do. I wanted to believe the "great" explanations he gave for his behavior. But, in the end, I realized I felt betrayed, used and stupid. I had seen red flags, especially financial ones, and I acted on some of those. But because it was such a mixed bag of great meditations, retreats and community, I had a hard time initially coming to terms with it.

Looking back I see I had definitely "given my power away." That meant in my mind that he was the "Awakened One," and because I was not "awake," he automatically was right. I had stopped trusting my own gut feeling. If things happened that seemed weird to me, I would immediately try to find excuses for that behavior. Even when I did confront the teacher, it was never acknowledged. There was a time when I thought I was going crazy. Of course, I was busy looking to see what was wrong with myself, and I ended up more and more angry and distrustful. I blamed something in myself that wasn't "pure."

It was such an eye-opener when I read in Saniel Bonder's book about disciples carrying their teacher's shadows: their teacher's unresolved stuff, their woundedness and fears (hidden, of course, behind a veil of "utter divinity"). I've learned that carrying their shadow material keeps you from doing your own inner work. You are always busy "protecting" your teacher's image.

Once I left, I saw it was truly a blessing in disguise. For me it was a necessary experience, and I decided to never worship an authority outside myself again. I see now how many "gurus" are trying to come only from their "divine" nature. There were quite a few stories surfacing at that time about the dark side of teachers coming into the light. All of this was very painful for me, but it made me ready for my next step. I was ready to live a "normal" life.

I had remarried and my husband and I moved out of the community and decided within a year that we wanted to adopt a child. Alexander came to us when he was almost six month old. I call him my good "karma." Being a mom sped up a lot of things for me. First, it was and still is a very humbling experience. You get to see yourself twenty-four hours a day.

I fell in love with this beautiful boy, and for a while my life was totally complete. I had never felt so full and alive and exhausted, too. There was a door that opened in me that was truly about unconditional love.

After two years things began to shift. Here I was with a great husband, a beautiful child, a fulfilling job, and more and more I felt lost. After all those years with teachers, I still felt that something fundamentally had not changed. I had lost my "great sky consciousness" experience, and I felt more fake and disconnected from myself than ever. I started to feel this quiet despair that did not go away. I felt I had failed at everything in life. Definitely I hadn't gotten anywhere spiritually, and because I had been so busy with that, I was a failure in the world, too. No big career, and because "the world" was never important to me, I had a very "fragile" bank account. Money was always the last thing on my mind, but now having a child changed all that. I felt I had made all the wrong choices.

Having a family saved me. My life wasn't all about me anymore and that helped me to keep going. I remember thinking I can do this if I just do it one day at a time, and then eventually I will die. I have always been so very good at projecting this upbeat persona that I even fooled myself at times. But in my dark moments I saw the truth. I felt something in me was giving up and I was terrified.

One night an old friend, Bob, came to visit and I could see in his eyes that something had changed. He wasn't acting nicer or more vulnerable; his eyes, his beingness, had changed. I was intrigued and hungry. He told me about his Second Birth and the work he had done with Saniel Bonder and the Waking Down community. I was shocked. Here was somebody like me, not a saint, not somebody who had incredible revelations while still in diapers. No, someone like me who had searched for a long time, had been a sanyassin, been with my other teacher, had given up just like I felt I was doing and through Waking Down had his Second Birth. He was awake!

I was very excited. I started reading Saniel's book *Waking Down* and I inhaled it. It was water for my soul. I recognized a lot of things and realized that Saniel had a knowledge that I hadn't met in a teacher before. Also, the book itself was pure transmission for me. I could hardly sleep at night after reading it. So many things fell into place: my "sky consciousness experience," searching out of pain, carrying my teachers' shadows, starting to wake down in my teenage years–so many things.

The next week I went to my first Waking Down sitting with Bob. Though I came in smiling and seemingly feeling great, I totally broke down crying within minutes of the gazing/transmission with CC and Toresa. It felt as though I'd had a broken heart all of my life, and I was finally in a setting where I allowed myself to feel it. It finally felt truly safe to let go. In the beginning this is what I would do at sittings. I would cry my heart out, and after that I would feel this profound relief–as if parts of me had been crying out for a long time, but I had decided not to hear them because those parts were wrong.

Especially after that first sitting, I connected with an inner power that I had never felt before. The gazing/sittings put me into a high transformational gear. This was not at all about being blissed out and feeling high; it was about literally opening up my gut and landing in myself instead of endlessly escaping. One escape was, of course, trying to "wake up" so I would never have to feel again. I was going in very rapid tempo through many layers I never even knew existed in me—as if my Beingness took over and started moving me through. There was a lot of abandonment stuff. Ordinary events triggered huge reactions. I remember not being asked to a friend's birthday party, and I cried for two weeks straight. Through all this the sittings were a life saver. My husband, who after his last experience with a teacher is totally allergic to anything that has to do with spirituality, was totally there for me. I felt devastated and held all at the same time. It was an incredible experience.

The sittings were mind blowing–so much true intimacy and incredible holding and acceptance by the teachers, mostly CC and Toresa. Not having a super guru-type around but real teachers who were in touch with their humanness and divinity all at the same time gave me the permission to truly be myself. So I went through several layers in incredible speed. I started the sittings in the middle of August 2002 and did my first Waking Down Weekend in December.

The retreat had seven awakened Second Birth teachers and about twenty-six participants. One amazing thing that I experienced was this incredible sense of greenlighting–not only spiritually and emotionally but also very strongly physically. My body knew that whatever I felt was perfectly OK. It was a field of Love, Respect and Acceptance that I never have experienced anywhere else this way. I was perfectly OK being there with all my neuroses, fears, anger and any other human emotions that I carried in my body. That was an incredible experience. And to be held with all that stuff in unconditional love without having to change! Because it was OK to be the way I was without any of my masks on, that triggered my willingness to let go into the deepest dungeon inside of me, my darkest secrets that I even had kept from myself. Also, the gazing was powerful for me. I remember gazing with Sandra, and I felt she took me on a tour through the universe.

Of course, something happened that triggered my final breakdown. As part of the Waking Down Weekend everybody got to choose three teachers that they wanted to work with. One of those would then be leading your small personal group. I didn't get any of the teachers I had written down. I was a little disappointed, but being a "good student" I didn't complain.

The next day after the morning meditation someone said that everybody got at least one of the choices on their list. I felt very shook up and told CC that I didn't get anybody on my list. She then said, "But, Shanti, the other teachers really *wanted* you in their group!" That word "wanted" just broke me down totally. I had never felt wanted. *I never felt wanted*, ever. I sank into the feeling that I shouldn't be alive. I had no right to live. I was a big mistake. I cried for hours. I couldn't stop. I had tried so hard all my life to be a good girl, a good disciple, to gain the right to be alive. I was exhausted.

In my small group with Ben Hursh and Tony Konopka I went even deeper into that feeling while totally being held by everybody in the group. I then ended up being reborn symbolically and welcomed with love and excitement. By the end of the day I felt totally empty. Nothing to say, nothing to do, just be there. I guess I had landed in my version of what Saniel calls "the Core Wound." For me it's the pain of not being accepted or wanted in this world and the sense of being very unimportant and disposable—unseen.

The next morning we did this really long gazing meditation. Afterwards I closed my eyes. At a certain point I started to expand and expand. Everything and everybody became me and was in me. The sounds of the airplane. People coughing, crying. The sounds of birds. It was all me. There was no division . No separateness. I sensed this fluid Beingness that was me and everything else. One Being.

After I opened my eyes things looked different, brighter. As if a veil had lifted. I had this kind of expansiveness before in Hawaii where I became the clouds and the thunder while sitting on the beach, but it didn't last more than a week and never had this physical component to it.

The next few months I was in this state that I only had heard about: my mind quiet, an incredibly deep relaxation and feeling of sensuality in the body. Everything was so bright and direct, and I was feeling very raw because of it. Also, there was bliss and peace, the perfection of everything. I felt that the birds flying over, the trees I walked under, everything was a part of my body. The frantic urge to seek was gone. Just being here was it. There was a pressure on top of my head as if a valve had opened up. And sometimes the psychedelic experience of sitting and hearing others talk and experiencing that I was everyone talking. Also, I so wished I could just be in nature. I would have loved to be able to go to Hawaii and sit at the beach. Sitting there, nothing else. Instead I had to go to work, and on my days off I had a two-year-old. Anyway, it was a great honeymoon. I was lucky it lasted so long.

Saniel does talk in his book about the Wakedown Shakedown, the process where you start to integrate the shadows, the dissociated parts of yourself that you split off because they are too painful to handle. The first year after my Second Birth was a big change. Initially I would feel very raw. Many times, very painfully, I was extremely sensitive to people's emotions, their reactions or non-reactions. The world seemed so much brighter and more intense. My buffer was gone. For the first time I felt *here*, very sensually in my body in a new way. I was actually *in* my body... and enjoying it immensely. Soooo sensual. I felt authentic, real. But by all means *not perfect*.

I had a period where synchronicity was happening. It was like living in never-ending magic. Objects would appear that I really wanted, like a Buzz Lightyear from *Toy Story* for my son when it wasn't made anymore. On the other hand, I would get triggered by a seemingly harmless event that would throw me deep into my inner dungeon. Very dark, very hopeless, definitely an inner hell that would sometimes last for a few weeks. Then suddenly I would wake up in the morning and it was gone. Afterward, I would feel more integrated and here and connected. One time I had a symbolic past-life dream that left me waking up in total horror. It was all about being abused, raped, victimized, killed as a woman. It stayed with me for a long time. Also, I went through a period where I would ooze negativity, powerlessness, jealousy and resentment. I felt it coming out of my pores and in my breath. It lasted for months until, for now, it is gone.

Since my last episode of Wakedown Shakedown I feel again a deepening sense that I am being held at all times. I had some very deep plunges in my first two years of Wakedown Shakedown, and I know I am not done. What is strengthening me is the feeling of being truly seated in Me. My gut has opened up, and I feel an inner power that is coming in, that wants to manifest itself. I am struggling to find a way to express this new life in a different way, like finding a different work where I can express more of the new me.

Sometimes it is very frustrating. It feels like a crucifixion of my unlimited spirit/power within this limited body/world. I can't stop working as an RN just because I'm ready for something else, since I'm a big part of supporting our family right now. It's very painful at times.

I am living my life, seeing how it's unfolding. For a while it was very helpful to go to sittings where I was seen and received. Now I am going through a period where I just want to be on my own. Meeting old spiritual friends and sharing with them your Second Birth experience is something Saniel warns you to do only if you really have to. I really had to. I was so excited to tell them this was a possibility for them, too. But I don't fit their dissociated picture of awakening. I am not always "lovely, vulnerable and compassionate." *I Am Myself*, Human and Divine all at the same time.

There are moments that I feel like I am truly the divine in form, and there are times that I feel truly pissed off. Living the paradox is getting clearer to me now. Feeling my divinity and my very intense human emotions all at the same time is quite a trip. The act of holding it all without acting out or repressing any of it is becoming easier. I am more and more in a state of wonder and awe of *every moment*. Every "ordinary" moment is becoming more and more divine. I feel more and more I am sinking into and becoming *that*. At times it just moves me to tears *being here*. After oozing what felt like a never ending human negativity, I do see that every step on the way was a necessary one. Even the teacher that I felt used by–that was a necessary step on the way. I am grateful to all and everyone of my teachers.

Right now I am living my life. I see how it unfolds, and I have no idea how it is going to look. As Saniel says, it is only a new beginning. It has been a great ride. I do feel reborn with unimaginable new possibilities and, at the same time, a never-ending beginner. I wish this deep inner healing for everybody and am eternally grateful to this incredibly ordinary giant, Saniel Bonder, and the great Waking Down community.

"I realized deeply, profoundly, that even though I was established in this pristine stability of Consciousness, I still didn't know who I was."

Adam

Born in March 1950 in New York City, New York, Adam Ladd was raised in New England, attended University of Wisconsin (Madison) and University of California (Berkeley), married and moved to Oregon, became a Naturopathic Physician and Acupuncturist, helped raise two children, traded commodities, studied addiction and addiction counseling. He recognizes and is grateful to many spiritual influences and teachers.

WONDER FALLS LIKE RAIN

I had a dramatic and tumultuous transition into my Second Birth. It was characterized by catharsis and rapidity. In some ways it was not unlike my first birth fifty-four years ago, which was a premature one, and also rapid. I first met Saniel on March 18, 2004. I fully "dropped" into my Second Birth on April 9, 2004. The time spent between these two dates was, to say the least, both perplexing and wondrous. I had no fundamental understanding of what was going on at the time.

I had not anticipated such an event at all initially. But to say that I was not ready for such an opening in my life is not correct. Truly, my time had come, and only later did I happily acknowledge that my goose had been fully cooked. What I needed, apparently, was exposure to this "awakening Siddhi" from an adept (in my case, Saniel Bonder), and the gentle, affirming grasp of my birther (Linda Groves).

You see, in the background and prior to all of this, I had been going through a lengthy mid-life crisis, which had been brought on initially by the death of my sole parent a number of years before, followed by a transition to a new career which wasn't going well, and subsequently deepened by the difficulties I was having with one of my adolescent children and his use of drugs while living on the streets of Portland. All of the circumstances of my life seemed to have fallen apart.

Truly, I was in a profound state of despair when I met Saniel. Spirituality held no promise for me anymore. My whole being felt exhausted. The interior life of thinking, reading, philosophizing couldn't inspire me. Everything I had tried, even antidepressant medicines, had failed to lift me enduringly out of this emotional and psychological deadness.

I found out later that this period of time is referred to as "the Rot," and in my "Rot" I felt like all the external events in my life had pounded me to a pulp. Clearly I had been living for a long time (maybe even years) in a limbo in which there was a chasm separating me from the world that I wanted to love and be a part of. I was unable to feel any love or hope at this point in time, and I had no goals, either long term or short term, anymore in my life. Quite a state! I had stopped seeking for an answer to my incompleteness, to my suffering, in largely every way.

This brings us to spring of 2004. I had never heard of Waking Down in Mutuality. I just happened to see a flyer in a local food store announcing a Waking Down event with Saniel Bonder. I was familiar with Saniel (by name and face only) because of my spiritual quests in the 1970s when I had been a devotee of Adi Da. So, I was curious. Saniel and I had shared a guru.

But was this Waking Down event going to be more guru-worship? I had long ago left Adi Da behind after three separate attempts over the last thirty years to mold myself into the life and image of a spiritual aspirant in his challenging community of practitioners on the West Coast. Even though this larger-than-life teacher had never let me down, I had been unable to live his sadhana perfectly and had failed to muster up the requisite effort and tenacity. As a worn-out guy in my early 50's, I had given up on the dream of spiritual awakening altogether. I considered myself a spiritual failure in this lifetime.

So, when I attended the Waking Down event and met and sat with Saniel, I was not expecting any real or lasting effect. I had even prepared myself beforehand against a letdown by saying, "Whatever happens, happens. I'm not expecting anything. Let's just see what he's up to."

Imagine, if you will, sitting down in this gathering place, amongst a lot of strangers, in front of a spiritual teacher whom you do not really know. And then imagine that while exchanging glances with that teacher you are touched so deeply in those few minutes that a tangible current now courses down your frontal line, forcefully and literally filling your belly with benign energy and "presence," somehow altering you permanently physically, emotionally, mentally, all without you making any conscious decisions about the event.

This was the beginning of a period of time in which I was in a state of powerful enlivenment. It was unrelenting and all consuming for me. From that initial moment my internal sense of myself, as well as my perceptions of the external world, were enhanced, augmented by a powerful new presence. Fullness and energies coursed through me. I wept uncontrollably throughout the days and nights. I was caught up in transcendental swoons which were blissful and new. Sometimes I felt as if it would be difficult to sit still any longer and had to take long walks to generate physical movement. Sometimes it was difficult to hold on to a fork and extremely challenging to hold a conversation with anyone.

I found out later that this period of time could be identified by the term, "Initiation of Being" or "Initiation of Spirit." I found myself over the course of the next fourteen days in a continuous uproar, a whirling onslaught of transitional experiences. These phases I went through were altogether delightful, divine, and intense, maddening, and, as I said before, full of joy and tears, wonder and sorrow.

Then, very abruptly, I found myself one morning in a complete state of calmness, characterized by a clear sense of watching or "witnessing" everything that I did and everything that was going on. My internal storm had abated.

These are some of the things that I remember. There was a marvelous detachment and peacefulness. A simple act, such as washing dishes or sweeping the floor, would seem to begin spontaneously, and then it was as if the steps of the action carried themselves out all by themselves. All of life flowed and moved without a "Do-er." The body moved, and it wasn't even really "mine." The action was performed, and I was acutely observing everything about it, unconcerned and calm. Pristine and vast. I kept thinking, "This is great. Is this the Second Birth? How long will this last?"

It wasn't until later that I found out that I had entered a state of consciousness which could be identified by the term "embodied feeling-witness consciousness." One of the odd things I wrote down during this time was the fact that no one noticed my pristine and calm state of consciousness. I thought everyone would notice how extraordinary I felt. Unrecognized, I continued in my daily events: make dinner, do the laundry, host an out-of-town visitor, have consultations with my CPA, meet and socialize with new friends and associates—all while in this witness state of Consciousness, and no one had the faintest clue about who I was or what I was perceiving. There was just this absolute spaciousness.

One evening I was watching television with my fourteen-year-old daughter. We were watching a sitcom, "Will and Grace," and I was just fully present in my Witness Consciousness. But in the corner of my mind, as the laugh track came and went, I noticed a powerful uneasiness and a sense of anguish. I realized deeply, profoundly, that even though I was established in this pristine stability of Consciousness, I still didn't know who I was. I still had a much deeper need to know, "Who am I?"

All of my spiritual searching in my life had been centered around and propelled by this central question of "Who am I?" This was a question that had arisen spontaneously at the age of twenty while I was in college, and I had been obsessed and perplexed by it for all these years with no solution found.

I got on the phone the following day with Linda Groves, and I told her of my agonizing split in Consciousness, even though I was established in this peaceful and vast witness state. It was then, through her guidance, over the course of a few minutes, I was led through a consideration which spontaneously culminated in my being able to experience Consciousness and my suffering at the same time, together. All my energy suddenly descended (at least my experience of it was one of descent) into the Realization of Beingness as Myself! I coalesced into this integrity which is unparalleled. I had entered into full and irreversible awakening as both a divine and mortal individual (my Second Birth).

How can I account for this pivotal event in my life? What incredible grace led me to the exposure and moment of ripeness which bore fruit soon after? Maybe it was fortuitous to have entered this process, as I did, as a curious bystander, unprepared and available. This is obviously true for me, yet I feel that, in some ways, to be unprepared for such a transformation made things worse. I really didn't know what was going on. I was in no way prepared. I feared for my sanity at times.

Since my initiation into Being and Second Birth, now six months, I have studied Saniel's books intensely, and participated avidly in a Human Sun Seminar and one-half of a Waking Down Weekend. I am on a journey. It appears that the teaching seems to corroborate my own personal experience and that of many other awakened people as well. It appears that each and everybody goes through this in a similar pattern, no matter how "prepared" or not!

Whatever the case, in my Second Life I have sighed many sighs and cried many tears. There seems to be an unraveling of all that structure of repression and non-allowance. I am deeply conscious of my patterns of psychological and emotional suffering, and I feel immense gratitude, thankfulness and relief.

It is a blessing. It is a divinely human awakening.

My thanks to all the adepts who have served me!

"I realized the Ground and Totality of Being that I had so desperately desired."

Linda

Linda Groves-Bonder is Saniel Bonder's wife and primary spiritual partner and a Senior Teacher of Waking Down in Mutuality. She and Saniel now offer their services through their own company, Extraordinary Empowerments. Linda is a charter member of the Waking Down Teachers Association and, with Saniel, a founding member of Integral Institute and the Integral Spiritual Center. Ken Wilber calls Linda "a brilliant teacher in her own right." She cherishes her ongoing transformational work with clients, individually and in groups. Linda is also a professional jazz singer-songwriter.

I WANT MY AWAKENING AND I WANT IT NOW!

My spiritual journey started when I was a little girl in a big mid-Western family in the late 50s. I considered myself a good Catholic. I attended Mass every Sunday and holy days with my mother and brothers and sisters. With my then-agnostic father's agreement, my mother had all us kids attend Catholic parochial school through sixth grade. So I absorbed the teachings of the church from an early age.

When I was eight or nine, however, the doctrines I was hearing made me start questioning. How could the same God who loves each and every one of us eternally also damn us to hell forever if we happened to break His rules? I asked the nuns, the priests, and my mom real questions—and it was hard, because I was extremely shy. They'd say things like, "Have faith—God works in mysterious ways." I was open to the mystery of God, but what they were saying just didn't ring true for me. None of them were able to give me satisfactory answers.

At twenty-one I graduated college in Indiana and moved to California, where I started an eclectic spiritual search. For years I explored New Age expressions, kundalini yoga, channeled teachings on Consciousness and energy, and various readings and lectures. These investigations all yielded some good insights.

However, at the core of my being something was always missing.

I felt that "something-missing" as a literal void deep in my solar plexus. Not "the Void" as a positive, ultimate experience, but something missing at my very core. None of the meditations, affirmations, and other practices I tried ever filled that emptiness.

That changed when I met Saniel in October 1994. A friend had insisted: "You must sit with this man. He's amazing!" After a few Sunday sittings, I started to feel something being stirred up in my body, especially my solar plexus.

In the beginning Saniel's teaching on Consciousness and a lot of the other concepts just went right past me. What anchored me in the work instead was my feeling of his transmission, especially through gazing. Soon I felt my existence unfolding below and deeper than the mind. And then, gradually, the concepts started making sense, like light bulbs going on with a deep "Aha!" in my being.

In the first year I had a few kundalini experiences, including wonderful visionary dreams. One day I felt energy bouncing around inside my body, hitting the insides of my skin. I shook and vibrated uncontrollably for at least a half hour. Finally Saniel really focused on me and put his hand on my heart for awhile, and the experience ended. And once, in my apartment one night, I was lying on my bed saying affirmations before sleep. Suddenly a pinpoint of white light shot from the ceiling down onto me, so that I felt consumed by it. Then, in an instant, it retreated upward with another ring of white light around it—and then I was completely gone. I had no sense of form or of being in my room or any other perception. It was absorption into Nothingness. When I came back into my body, in a split second the white light shot back down from above with the halo around it; and I was here again. I couldn't move my body for awhile, but I felt no fear. I had no idea how much time had passed. I was at peace, just complete peace.

All those experiences were moving for me, but they came and went. I knew they were glimpses into something that was coming to stay, and that's what I wanted. But the work Saniel offered was not about trying to get more altered states and hope they'd become permanent. So the teaching that most reached me in the beginning was Saniel's description of the Core Wound. When he talked about the fundamental split in our being, where we intuit our limitless nature and yet we still feel separate, limited, and confused about who we are, I felt a deep recognition of the truth of that teaching in my solar plexus, right where I had been experiencing the void.

That was how I began to pass through "the Rot." It wasn't a devastating collapse of my entire life. Many things were wonderfully in place for me. I loved my work and made good money as an independent photo-stylist. I had great friends, a supportive family that I loved dearly, a beautiful little apartment on the bay. And, after many months of caring and careful mutual consideration, Saniel and I became intimate partners.

So what could be wrong? Well, this emptiness. It couldn't be filled by any of the things of life or even meditation. My life was good, but I couldn't escape a fundamental agitation in my core. Months went by where I lived with a kind of flatness, until I just had to face a fundamental fact: I was separate and very confused about who I was. More and more, though I didn't altogether understand it, I was feeling the bite of that Core Wound at the center of my being. Nothing could make it go away or even buffer me from it any more.

One day I showed up at Saniel's apartment devastated by this knowledge. The moment he welcomed me in the door I pleaded for him to help me. I collapsed to the floor in the middle of the living room; my body just couldn't even hold me up anymore. I'd been praying for clarity every night, but now I was desperate.

Sobbing, I told Saniel how horrible I felt: "I just feel so separate! And there's nothing I can do about it anymore!"

Part of me wanted him to scoop me up and save me from that despair. Instead he stood over me for a moment, looking at me, not saying a word. And then he walked into his office and closed the door!

Only later did I realize that was the perfect thing for him to do in that moment: to leave me there to fully *feel*. Eventually I sat up. I thought, "This is it! I am just this separateness. And there's nowhere else to go." That gave me a deeper connection to my Core Wound. And soon afterward I started to feel huge shifts in my awareness, not only intellectually but deep in my body. These eventually led to a major awakening.

During a meditation with Saniel and a few other people at his apartment, I had a clear vision of me, Linda, sitting in lotus position, floating in an empty background. All of a sudden that form of "Linda" exploded in all directions to infinity. I wasn't just viewing this; I myself exploded completely. For some unknowable time I was totally gone. Then suddenly my form recongealed into millions of little bright white, vibrating hearts. I realized that the hearts were every cell of my body being Consciousness itself, and that in that initial explosion the hearts had touched all creation.

I knew this was a major event. Gradually it became clear that from that explosion forward I was effortlessly established in what we call the "embodied feeling-witness consciousness."

Through the next nine months I lived easily in that witnessing condition. Yet my essential realization of Being was incomplete. I felt the Conscious nature in my body, but I also intuitively sensed it hovering just behind me, above my left shoulder. This may sound somewhat disembodied, the way the witness is described in certain spiritual traditions. But it didn't feel dissociated. I just felt there was still a missing link I had to find. During those months Saniel, Van Nguyen, and others in our work helped me do that.

As time wore on I started to feel a dull complacency. It made me question what I needed to do to get on with my realization. The frustration became extreme, a flatness I couldn't shake. One day, as Saniel and I were driving home from Santa Cruz, out of nowhere I opened my hands wide, smashed my palms onto his dashboard, and screamed at the top of my lungs, "I want my awakening and I want it now!!!" Tears were streaming down my face. Saniel was so startled that he swerved into the next lane; luckily there wasn't any traffic! But he loved it. He immediately assured me that this was not just "ego" talking, as some might think; it was a "divine insistence" coming from the deeper Truth of my being, struggling to be born.

That led to an animated conversation. We stopped at a restaurant by the beach in Half Moon Bay. It was a beautiful evening. For awhile we stood and enjoyed the glorious sunset over the ocean. Then, over dinner, Saniel and I continued our discussion.

I told him I sensed a need to connect more with the love that I often felt opening my heart wide and including all beings, and to find a way to make that open-heartedness permanent. Saniel thought about that. Then he said he could appreciate what I was saying, but he didn't think that was the next step. Instead, I needed to do something that might feel counter intuitive—a deeper investigation of Consciousness itself. He felt the flatness was because the witnessing nature of Consciousness was already well established in me. There wasn't anything else for me to learn about that. But even though I wanted my heart to open wider to all things and beings, he said that the actual "direction" to go was not outward or inward exactly, but just into feeling the intrinsic mystery of Consciousness.

With his help, that's what I did. I primarily used the verbal or mental enquiry, "What is this Consciousness that I am embodying?" Another one was, "Where is Consciousness now in this moment?" I didn't try to inquire all the time. It just became a natural part of my daily rhythm.

About a month later, one afternoon I was again sitting in meditation with Saniel and a small group of our friends. As I drifted into sweet, peaceful absorption in the All, suddenly there was the sensation of Consciousness itself moving from behind me, where I'd felt it so much for nine months. It streaked around my left side and appeared right in front of me—and then in a split second it merged right into me. The experience literally knocked me backward. I found myself sitting there with my eyes closed, a huge smile on my face. I knew in that moment that Consciousness had realized Itself to be *that* and me simultaneously. I also now understood what friends of mine meant when they spoke of "Consciousness recognizing itself to be Consciousness."

I know some of this sounds energetic, and not just "pure Consciousness." Yes, the event had an intense energetic aspect. But more and more, over time, it became obvious: I had realized Consciousness bodily in a whole new way. That feeling of "something missing" fundamentally left me during that meditation and never reappeared.

It was such a profound awakening that even my personality shifted—on the spot! In all the previous sittings, still very shy, I had rarely opened my mouth. But that day, when we resumed conversation, Saniel said he'd seen me sitting there with that huge grin and laughingly demanded, "So, what's up?" I exuberantly and loudly told him and the others what had happened. They were all a little startled by how strong and forceful I was—this was not the typical demure Linda! But there was no holding back now. I had a new voice.

I had realized the Ground and Totality of Being that I had so desperately desired. Saniel asked me to continue investigating it, to see if anything was missing. But I couldn't find anything missing anymore. I couldn't even ask enquiry questions. And we soon concluded that this was indeed my Second Birth.

As it happened, the next morning after that awakening, Saniel and I sat in meditation again with a few friends. This time I clearly felt in my body and my awareness that I had fully landed as Consciousness. But while I was enjoying sweet sensations of being here so alive and awake, I suddenly had a vision of hundreds of different faces of suffering souls from all races and cultures coming at me in rapid succession. They connected me so deeply with the pain of the world that I burst into uncontrollable sobs. I don't think I had ever cried so hard in my entire life. After we came out of meditation, I knew I had truly connected with the suffering of humanity and of all living beings. My heart was broken open with compassion for creation itself. It was all I could do to get through the next few days without being plunged into that depth of pain again. Eventually I moved out of that raw exposure into a more balanced holding of the pain and bliss of life simultaneously.

Looking back, I feel that compassionate initiation into the depths of suffering fulfilled my desire to open my heart to all life, which I had told Saniel about the month before—the same day my Being also shouted aloud its desire to awaken.

As the months progressed, I found a strong impulse and need to teach this same process of embodied awakening to others. With Saniel's approval, I started holding weekly sittings and working with people individually. After about a year and a half, I lost interest in my photo-styling work, and concentrated on teaching the Waking Down process on my own and with Saniel and others. This has been such a rich, fulfilling exploration, not only with my clients but also in my own journey.

My awakening took place on August 26, 1996. Now, nine years later, I continue to grow, integrate, and balance the many parts of my divinely human being. As I look back, it's obvious that my Second Birth catalyzed the most challenging, wonderful process of transformation in my whole life.

For this book, I've only told you the story of that awakening. But that's who I was and what I experienced such a long time ago. So many changes have happened since. Among other things, I've resumed my professional career as a singer and songwriter alongside my teaching work. Living this "Second Life" in mutuality has deepened my appreciation for the brokenness and the wholeness of human beings in ways I could never have imagined. I am so grateful.

One of my greatest blessings is intimate marriage and partnership with my beloved Saniel. As this book is published, we are celebrating over ten years together. I count my blessings every day that I can be with this amazing man.

And then there is the blessing of this extraordinary community of our friends, students, colleagues, and clients in the Waking Down in Mutuality work. I am so deeply grateful to be among these people, embarked together on this journey of the Heart.

"CC and I; quietly, day after day, abide frequently in: just this."

CC and Michael

Michael Radford was born and has lived most of his life in Northern California and now resides in the Denver area with his wife, CC Leigh. He majored in psychology as an undergraduate, later earned an MBA, and currently develops wind energy projects in the Western United States. Michael credits the Waking Down teachers and community with catalyzing the self-realization he'd sought for 30+ years. The result has been an ever-deepening peace and joy, right in the midst of the messy, mysterious paradox of divine human life.

CC Leigh grew up in Massachusetts but found her true home in the West, both in California and in Colorado where she currently resides with her husband Michael, their two cats, Gracie and Bodhi and their mini-Australian Shepherd Tucker. Her first spiritual teachers were her many dogs, who taught her to be present in her body, to seize the moment, and most of all, to keep her heart open. She credits her years spent as a dog breeder/trainer/animal behaviorist with honing her ability to observe well, listen deeply, and understand beyond words, skills she now uses in her work as a senior teacher of Waking Down in Mutuality. In addition to providing guidance and support to individuals and groups, she has rekindled her love of gardening and hiking in the Rockies, while continuing to explore the unique qualities of awakened human life.

A WAKING DOWN LOVE STORY

(CC's story is in regular type; Michael's is in italics.)

"Dancing in the fire" pretty well describes our journey together. It all started in 2004 at the Transfiguration Retreat in Estes Park. Michael was a participant in a small group I led, one of those uniquely synergistic groups where everyone seems to really serve one another's process and the heart connections quickly deepen. I could not help noticing Michael: a beautiful but very broken-hearted man, who came to each group meeting resolved to reveal yet another of his (in his opinion) most shameful aspects. Every day he arrived tense and hurting, and by the end of group left more relaxed, growing ever-more radiant as the week progressed.

By the time I arrived at Estes Park in May, 2004, I was falling helplessly, at an ever-accelerating pace, into the depths and heart of my flaws and brokenness. I'd been participating in the Waking Down work for about eight months. The deep holding and greenlighting of the WD teachers and community had gradually produced a profound relaxation in me around all of the traits and qualities of my personality that I had previously spent my entire adult life striving mightily to fix, change, improve, or even annihilate. The man (me) that CC sat with in our small group somehow knew, with quiet certainty, that when he'd spoken every last terrible truth about what was in his mind and heart, he would be free.

As a single-woman Waking Down teacher, doing an intensive event like this had its own special "burn," since I longed to be met by a worthy partner but was constrained by our ethical policies from acting on any impulses I might feel toward any of the participants. But Michael got my attention. His daily confession of his "sins" wasn't your typical courtship behavior, but it was like catnip to a kitten as far as I was concerned. I could not help but admire his great courage in so freely revealing so much about himself.

At the end of the week, Michael approached me and asked if I might be interested in spending some time together after the retreat, to see what potential there might be for us romantically. My heart leapt at the idea, but I had to be very cautious about moving forward. Since we were both single and unencumbered, my main concern was that Michael be well-supported and not under undue influence from any power differential between us. We consulted with our support teams, including Michael's teacher, my teacher-peers, and Saniel, and found that there was a consensus that Michael was strong in himself and ready to enter into relationship if that was his wish.

The event that precipitated dropping into my "rot" to a most profound and irrevocable degree was the break-up of my marriage in May, 2002. For the first time since my teens, I spent the next two years alone, without a hint of a romantic relationship in my life. The first year or so was the most lonely and painful I'd ever experienced. But there came a moment, sitting in the desert one evening, where I somehow embraced solitude and became, myself, the only companion I needed. So, when I met CC, while there was some subtle interest in her as a woman, the old, familiar feelings of being smitten and totally absorbed in her as the be-all and end-all of my existence were strangely absent.

We spent a magical week together driving and exploring the Colorado Rockies in the springtime. Only later would we establish that Michael had had his Second Birth during that pivotal retreat, gaining a reprieve from his habitual way of being and opening his heart to himself, to life, and to another human being. I suppose our relationship got a boost from that, with the temporary ego-displacement that often accompanies the Second Birth leaving Michael susceptible to an infatuation that might not have a basis in reality. But given where we are today, I can safely say we had what it takes to build a real and lasting relationship.

It was, indeed, magical. In retrospect, I recognized that, during this time, I was literally being the peace and bliss which I had sought for over thirty years. My mind was quiet, my heart so open and full that it often ached in the most deliciously painful way. Brief encounters with a waiter or check-out clerk were profoundly moving. There was no fear, no pain, no future… just this, in this moment. The glorious Rockies and the lovely, enlightened lady I was sharing them with were an ongoing delight. I was moved to tender, joyful tears often.

Yet the road from there to here has not been an easy one.

By the end of that week we decided to take a bold step: Michael would leave California and we would get a place together in Colorado. Before I knew it, we were setting up house in a sweet apartment at the western edge of Ft. Collins, looking out to the foothills of the Rockies. At the age of fifty, after being divorced for sixteen years, I was in love with a man I truly admired and respected, to whom I wanted to be committed for the rest of my life.

Within weeks Michael's conditioned self began showing up as it got triggered by any number of things I did or said. And (to be fair) I, too, was triggered by Michael at fairly regular intervals. We did our best to ride those upheavals, stay in communication, and keep finding one another. Through it all I was aware of a deep bodily "yes" toward Michael that persisted no matter what was happening on the more obvious levels of our interacting. I simply felt better with him than without him. I'm not so sure what Michael was feeling: I think he found me frustrating and disappointing and wished I would just get over those things that made me sad or unhappy, so he didn't have to experience those feelings himself.

The transcendent "vacation" in the wake of my Second Birth gradually drew to a close. My mind became more and more active (although, in the interests of accuracy, it's never reclaimed its dominant role in my awareness). Living with a woman again launched me expeditiously and deeply into my version of the infamous "Wakedown Shakedown." One powerfully conditioned element that came up within a couple of months was my profound fear of losing love. CC traveled to Seattle to teach a workshop, and I went through several days of personal hell filled with jealousy and fear. That passage lasted 4-5 days and totally sucked, but it then vanished and hasn't reappeared since. Less powerfully felt, but more intractable, were the feelings CC triggered in me of being thwarted in my attempts to please her, to make her happy. I also responded to what I perceived to be her perfectionism by often interpreting it as invalidating my fundamental competence.

Although I was basically delighted with our new relationship, and welcoming of the opportunity to learn and grow together, I continued to feel unhappy at times, or sad, or dissatisfied with some aspect of my life—including Michael sometimes. I didn't mind these feelings, particularly, having learned that they are just some of the ways I experience my life. But I felt Michael's frustration with my discomfort and felt increasingly pressured to "take control of my life" as if I ought to be able to be more positive or happy. On one hand, I figured he was trying to be supportive of my well-being, but it felt more to me like I was being told to not feel what I was feeling. It was as if the more he pushed me to "be happy," the more some aspect of me insisted on being the opposite. I didn't want to be controlled or made to deny any part of myself. In truth, I didn't really expect Michael, or anyone, to "make me happy."

My mom gave birth to me when she was only nineteen and had four children by the time she was twenty-four. She had oh, so much to handle, and her frustrations came out as controlling anger, which was really scary to the sensitive kid I was. My survival strategy was to do whatever it took to make her happy. I became incredibly attentive to her emotional state, and at the first hint that she was displeased, I'd launch into my repertoire of "make Mommy happy" behaviors. This way of being and operating carried over into my adult life and every one of my romantic relationships. "Who I was" was the man who could make any woman happy if I set my mind to it. When CC and I met, that deeply-conditioned self-identity was still present, and my inability to produce that result consistently with CC caused me considerable pain and was the source of recurring upsets for me in our relationship.

I tried to convey to Michael that I didn't hold him responsible for how I was feeling and that I was fundamentally okay no matter what the current mood state was, but that didn't seem to be sufficient. As our romantic relationship failed to bring the fabled happiness we both subconsciously wished for, it felt to me as if Michael entered a slow-motion sulk that wouldn't quit. He became unavailable in every way, uninterested in being helped by anyone, no energy for trying any techniques or anti-depressants, and unavailable to process anything that turned up in our relationship. Weeks turned into months. I felt totally helpless.

This period that CC speaks of occurred concurrently with my giving up my lifelong smoking. Nicotine had always served as a buffer from feeling, and with that gone, I dropped rather precipitously into a deeply gray, sometimes black place. Nothing mattered. Life held no attraction, including, sadly, my relationship with CC. I was clear, in the midst of this, that my state of being had nothing whatsoever to do with her or our relationship. It was, I recognized even then, simply a stark, inescapable encounter with the part of myself that I had most feared—and always stridently resisted—the simple recognition that life has no intrinsic meaning or purpose. As I dropped ever further into that encounter, I became, in my own experience, pretty much unavailable on most every level. I increasingly saw myself as unfit to be in an intimate relationship.

The teacher in me did her best to simply hold Michael with patience and understanding. But the woman in me had other ideas, and she grew restless and dissatisfied and about ready to bite his head off (if you know what I mean). She (I) felt impelled to call him out, challenge him, get a response of some kind. She wanted a partner who would engage with her and be real with her, who was in his body, not languishing in a spiritual malaise. Michael and I had agreed when we started our relationship that we would be equal partners, not teacher/student. He said he wasn't looking for a teacher but for a real woman and mate. So the woman in me had to speak her truth, as risky as it was because there was no way to know what would happen, how Michael would respond. To my horror, my request for Michael to show up more in relationship precipitated his decision to leave the relationship and return to California.

Leaving CC was difficult in the sense that it violated the deeply conditioned part of me that believed I should always put the needs of others ahead of my own, and that I should avoid causing pain at all costs. But I was clear that my presence, given my condition, was a constant and growing source of pain for CC. I really could foresee no end to my profound malaise, and although I knew CC wasn't ready to give up on us, I just wanted to be alone.

I couldn't believe it. I knew we had problems, but I was convinced we could make our way through the Core Wound of our relationship to the other side, to the birth of something real, deep, profound. Still in touch with the "yes" I felt toward Michael, my heart had so enfolded him that now I felt ripped asunder, kicked by a mule, mortally wounded. Within less than a week, he had packed his things and left, and I walked around for days, then weeks, in a fog of pain. Christmas season, everywhere I turned there were sentimental touches that sent shards of hurt through me. I was in danger of bursting into tears whenever I passed a rack of greeting cards in a store. I was a wreck.

He seemed to do it so easily, saying "no" to what we had and walking away. From California he phoned every few days to check in on the poor wounded one, as if he was totally fine (the smug bastard!) and I was the only one with problems. That confused me: If he was done with this relationship, why did he keep calling? I double-checked with him: Is it over? Do you not love me anymore? He said, no, he didn't love me.

I said we had to stop talking, because it was causing me even more pain. So we took a break, but I found that I couldn't put it down. I had too much backed up anger which finally came to the surface, demanding to be heard. He said he wanted us to remain "friends," but in my book friends take responsibility for the pain they've caused, and I hadn't heard any of that from Michael. If he wanted my friendship, he was going to have to hear me and feel me and get me, even if it was only to bring a full and final end to our romance. So we got on the phone again, and I told him what it was like to be abandoned and betrayed, to have the one person I most trusted to be in mutuality with me bail out and leave me hanging, alone and unmet. His leaving also brought on a re-experiencing of my father's betrayal when he abandoned our family early in my childhood, compounding the devastation of Michael's present-time walkout. I let him see how shattered I was and spared him no feelings.

Something happened then. As if the dry, dead husk of the old conditioned Michael finally tore open and began to bleed. All the uncried tears began to seep out of the cracks, and Michael "got" the real, raw pain of his betrayal, letting it in where it could touch his shriveled soul and begin the healing process. At least that's how it seemed to me. I felt how truly sorry he was for the way he'd hurt me, and I got how his apparent smugness was his way of trying to defend himself from crushing guilt at not being able to be there for me.

I can't really say when or how things began to shift after my return to California. Although free of the ever present reminder of my failure to meet

CC and show up in our relationship that her physical presence was, I couldn't bring myself to totally cut off communication. The occasional phone calls were the best I could muster, and as down and dead as I still felt, I wanted to make myself available in that small way for there to still be some relationship. When she was finally able to fully express her anger and sadness and pain at my leaving, it somehow cut through the cloud of indifference that had surrounded me for many months. It landed, and perhaps that was the beginning of the end of that dark passage in my Second Life.

In that moment, I became willing to consider trusting him again. It's not that I trusted him, I didn't. In fact, I now knew beyond a doubt that he was capable of hurting me in the most devastating way a man can hurt a woman. But if I was really honest, I knew that any man at any point could do something similar. Sure, some would stick it out longer than Michael did, but the betrayal wasn't only about Michael leaving me, it was about the betrayal of trust and honesty and intimacy, a betrayal that we are all capable of, and that we all do whenever we aren't able to face what we don't want to see about ourselves. While I could not admire him for leaving me, I could respect that he had to honor the imperative of his soul to allow himself to be stripped down to essence, a process he could not compromise on to shield me from excruciating pain and loss.

Michael's willingness to really let in my experience paved the way for me to let in his: the impossible situation he had faced as he found himself unable to show up in relationship. He could continue living with me in Colorado, where I would continue to feel rejected by him because he couldn't pony up any juice for relating, or he could leave in the hopes that a clean break would be less painful in the long run. A real no-win situation.

I grieved deeply the loss of the early sweetness and the naïve trust I had extended to Michael at the beginning of our relationship that I would never be able to feel again. I was sobered by how bloody difficult it is to simply love another, even when both are in their Second Life and supposedly conscious and awake. I felt wounded, weary, and afraid to open up again.

By the time CC and I met, I had already confronted my ugliest, most powerful broken zones. I had been them, acted on them, ruined my marriage, destroyed trust and any vestiges of self-respect or self-worth I had. I had met the dark beast, and he was me. I'd recognized, on the other side of my profound self-disillusionment, that I was incapable of being other than I was being. So, I didn't stay with CC because, fundamentally, I didn't want to. And I didn't begin to rekindle our relationship, for my part, because of anything CC wanted or didn't want. I did a damn fine job of being utterly self-attentive and self-centered. I was literally incapable of doing otherwise.

The reawakening of our relationship, this time on a sobered, realistic—and sustainable—basis, remains a mystery to me. We just kept communicating, speaking our respective truths. Neither I, nor, I think, CC, were trying to "get back together." We were simply honoring our human selves and the "other." Somehow, affinity and affection deepened, and our connection strengthened in a most natural, if, at times, improbable way. Friendship and emotional intimacy developed organically, often in the midst of raw candor.

There was something else this time that was different from past breakups. I had no illusions that I could replace Michael with a "better someone." I didn't see our problems as personal so much as due to the human predicament and how all the garbage of a lifetime comes up and gets in the way of being intimate. I couldn't wipe away my conditioning no matter how much I wanted to, and I knew Michael couldn't either. I couldn't guarantee I wouldn't cause him pain. And that sucks.

What we could do, we did. We kept talking, kept revealing to each other what it was like in our reality. We both acknowledged that when all was said and done, there was still this inner "yes" based on nothing much—even though it didn't, perhaps, make sense to anyone looking from outside at the wreckage of our relationship. Nevertheless, it felt like enough. Michael seemed more available and willing to show up and participate in the dance of relating, and in response I rekindled my willingness to take on the risk of loving, knowing full well that I could get hurt again. The alternative was to stay safely out of relationship where I would not be challenged, would not have my faults exposed, and where I would only have half a life. That's a trade-off I'm not willing to make.

I don't know much about man-woman relationship. I have a few insights about what makes women tick and what might facilitate a nurturing relationship, but whether I act on that seems largely not under my control. In the end, as in virtually every other area of my life these days, I just try to navigate down the river of Michael's life with some candor and compassion, and a little bit of grace. On one level, I truly don't need a relationship with a woman (or maybe even want one). But I seem to keep choosing CC as my partner and the center of my life. If she were gone, I'm convinced I'd retreat to a stone hut deep in the desert ... alone, in solitude...

Have I said I love this man? God, how I love him with every fiber of my Being! He is my true and worthy partner, and I am forever grateful that I found someone who can and does meet me in the places that count—in being real, authentic, honest, and available—and in profound, passionate intimacy.

We spent a year in a long-distance relationship, commuting between Colorado and California, rediscovering our ability to play together and our comfort in one another's presence. Michael found work in California, and began suggesting I might want to join him there, but I confess I was reluctant to leave Colorado and the wonderful mountains I love. While not quite back together, living-wise, we were quite "together" in our hearts. I was looking forward to some happy-ever-after time, time I felt was well-earned after weathering the difficulties we had gone through.

Fate had a different plan, however. On March 1st, 2007, Michael phoned me from his doctor's office barely able to speak as he told me through fearful tears that he had just been informed that he had cancer, that his liver was "riddled with tumors." In a flash, my happy-ever-after dreams were wiped off the slate.

Moving faster than I had ever moved before, I booked the next flight out to California and got there by evening, to hold my beloved in my arms while the tears streamed from our eyes. How could this be happening? Hadn't we already paid enough dues? This time it felt like a betrayal by God, by Being, by life maybe. Who knows? It just hurt like hell. Every bit of him was precious to me: his voice, his hands, his strong muscles, and those eyes, those beautiful eyes. How they would bore into my soul so deeply, so brightly, so tenderly! How could I ever see them again without this horrible refrain that says no matter how long he lives, he's going to leave me too soon, and I'm going to be cursed to live without the one person whose very existence is life to me. How can I walk this next phase with him? And, Oh God, how will I ever walk through life without him? It's too soon to be facing this end game. I want my happy ever after!

The preliminary diagnosis was adenocarcinoma—the "bad," usual kind of pancreatic cancer. The prognosis was that I had 90 days to live. Within hours of the news I was graced with a profound serenity and acceptance—no fear of dying, no regret, and no sadness for myself. Life became incredibly simple and focused. What I was solely focused on was the grief and fear of all the people who loved me. It was going to be easy for me. Once the pain cranked in, so would the opiates, and I'd make it through to the other side without too much discomfort, I hoped. But I'd be leaving CC behind, and my parents and sisters and extended family and many friends and Waking Down brothers and sisters. My heart opened profoundly, and embraced and held those who courageously brought their pain and grief to share with me.

Through some strange twists of fate, Michael's cancer turned out to be a fairly slow-growing kind. Because it has already metastasized, it can't be "cured," but there are things the doctors can do to slow it down, keep it at bay as long as possible. Together Michael and I entered the strange world of being cancer patient and partner, learning everything we could about cancer and how to treat it. I grieved long and hard for lost potentials—carefree days I would never know again, things we would never do, for the forced shift in priorities, the rude way we had to confront our mortality, stripped of the comforting illusion of having plenty of time yet.

Still, this disease is also an ally. It forces me to stay in the present far more than I would otherwise, because I have no refuge in the future. My life is here, now, today, with my lover who is here now today. I do not know when I will hear the dread words, "It's growing again" or "Michael doesn't have long now," but I know they're out there waiting for me to catch up with them, on some sunny day when life is doing its thing and I've maybe forgotten to be afraid for a moment.

So that's the paradox. Death stalks us and we know it. Right now we're alive, and in the strange way of life, we have to do all the many mundane things one does in order to live as if life were going to continue for a long time. Part of me wants to grab Michael and run away to fulfill our wildest imaginings, now, before we can't. Then I yield to the fact that we need to be "responsible" because, hey, he might live many years yet, and after all, we need a place to live and food and gas in the gas tank. Living this way is different than anything I have encountered before or expected to be facing. I don't know how to do this.

But death is stalking all of us anyway, so is it really all that different now? It's easier not to think about it, but none of us know when we're going to check out of this life. That's the gift here: Michael and I have to think about it and make our peace with it, because it isn't going away.

It's still easier for me than those who love me and want me in their lives. CC took many months to begin to make some peace with the prospect of my "premature" death. For much of that time, I'm a bit ashamed to admit that I often wasn't very understanding. Having been told that I'd be dead in three months, and then learning that I might live for years, life became a gift. Not in the classic I'm-so-grateful-for-each-moment-of-life way, but simply that I've gotten a much better deal than the one I thought I'd paid for back then. Coupled with my long, profound encounter, and ultimately, relaxation into "life is empty and meaningless," the mysterious passage that ensued in the wake of being told I would be dead very soon has left me simply... here.

Right after I came to California that fateful March, Michael asked me to marry him and I said yes. We kid about it now: At that point he was given to think he might only have weeks to live, so it wasn't too much of a commitment on his part. Over the following months, we occasionally revisited the topic. It took me a long time to get to where I felt I might be able to hold both the thought of a happy wedding and the grief I felt about Michael's cancer without coming completely undone. Then I found it somehow, the resolve and the ability to be happy in spite of cancer, in spite of the new limits of our life together.

Again and again, I marvel that this can be so. That the terror of losing my beloved can recede and the appreciation for each day can rise to the foreground of my awareness. Little bursts of spontaneous appreciation crop up without warning. Delicious lovemaking leaves me sated and happy. My work engages me and my life feels meaningful, and lo and behold, Michael reports something similar for himself. Somehow his long slide into "empty and meaningless" sufficiently released that pattern, allowing him now to explore what matters to him, and what he wants to do with the time he has.

On June 22, 2008, Michael and I had a delightful outdoor wedding in the Sierra foothills, surrounded by family and friends whose eyes were brimming a bit with tears of appreciation that they could share our joy and hold us close a little bit longer. There's nothing like a death scare to make life, Oh, so fervent and precious. Don't you think?

Many years ago, I recall reading Don Juan's admonishment to Carlos (Castaneda) to be aware of Death, floating behind and slightly off to one side, always. I've been blessed with that awareness. CC and I, quietly, day after day, abide frequently in: just this. She is my treasure, my partner, my lover, my friend. Frankly, I work at staying alive in large part because she wants me around. It seems a small thing to do for the one you love.

"The next morning I discovered I was passionately in love with women, all women, everything about them–their bodies, the way they moved or were still, the sound of their voices, their feet, hands, eyes, hair, everything, and, most of all, the mystery."

Bob

Bob Valine lives in the mythical State of Jefferson, near Ashland, Oregon, where he teaches writing and math part-time at a local community college, writes poetry and stage plays, takes long walks, and enjoys family and friends. He has compiled and edited this book as a labor of love, hoping readers will meet themselves within these pages.

DOWN THE RABBIT HOLE

The first time I saw Saniel Bonder was in front of the Yoga Center in Corte Madera, Marin County. I'd been invited by my old sannyasin friend, Gayatri, to come meet someone she could "finally sit with." At the time I was living and teaching in the great agricultural heartland of Central California. I loved my students and my work, but I was starved, perhaps more desperately than I realized, for a gathering of kindred souls. Thus, the trip to Marin and the beginning of my journey down the rabbit hole into the world of Waking Down in Mutuality.

I say that because during that afternoon in Marin my spiritual world began to be turned upside down. My spiritual quest began with Osho. I never had a close encounter with him, a conversation, a cup of tea. He was this amazing God-Being driving by in a Rolls-Royce with a twinkling smile and wave or the eloquent, charismatic speaker above me on a stage, in a book or video. I couldn't imagine myself being anything like him, even though he said we all were. He was enlightened, incredibly rare and special, and I was equally ordinary, flawed, and in the dark. He was the guru. The Divine One. The Miracle.

After Osho died, I found other beautiful teachers. Again I put them on a pedestal. They were enlightened, and, frankly, though I was drawn to them, loved them, followed them, obeyed them (most of the time and not always unquestioningly), I felt I always failed them. I never ever, ever, ever thought of myself as someone who could be awakened.

Then I met Saniel. There he was, the guru, in oldish jeans and colorful shirt, pulling up in his non-Rolls Royce, all by himself with no one offering to help him unload the few boxes from his trunk. I couldn't believe it. I looked around to see what his students were doing. They were doing what they were doing before he drove up: talking to each other, laughing, coming and going.

Maybe you're thinking, "So what?" Well, where I went to Spirituality School, the teacher, the guru, whatever he or she was called, was given the Sacred Treatment. I'm not criticizing. I loved being in the role of disciple, devotee, student. That was the only way I could be with Them. My choice, not theirs.

What did I do with Saniel? I rushed over and helped him unload his boxes of books and tapes into the Yoga Center. Of course.

There were about thirty people gathered for a Sunday afternoon sitting. Saniel and Linda sat on pillows in front of a semi-circle of chairs. Once people finally stopped wandering around and chatting and Saniel got their attention by saying something like, "Well, I guess it's time we got started," I felt a little more in familiar territory. My friend, Gayatri, had pointed out a number of other awakened people in the audience, so I was trying to figure out how they were different from any of the other people in the group. Some of them looked really together and in a good mood and others looked distracted and on edge, and then there was the one lying on the floor looking like he was getting ready to take a nap.

I don't remember a lot about this first sitting over five years ago–except for two things. They started out by doing something called "gazing," which I didn't do because it kind of freaked me out. I figure, now, that I was one of those guys used to hiding in the crowd. In fact, I know that's the way I always was in a group. Don't call on me, please, please, please. Gazing was optional and it's just looking into Saniel and/or Linda's eyes for a minute or two, but it wasn't something I was ready for. (It's turned out to be something I love.) The other thing, right after the gazing, a tall, attractive woman stood up and burst into tears.

I've seen many tears shed at satsangs, and I've spilled my share (usually in joy). What followed, though, was something I don't remember ever experiencing with an awakened teacher, and I'm not sure I can explain it. The woman became the center of the room, not Saniel. Her anguish, her anger, her experience were received by Saniel and everyone–not just welcomed, but embraced with gratitude and a sense of awe and mystery. No one tried to solve her problem or explain it or anything like that. She was received and held by Saniel and the group, and that was that.

The sitting in a very organic, relaxed way continued. I don't remember much, except being surprised at how disorganized it felt. At the end Saniel asked the group who would like to join Linda and him for lunch. My hand shot right up. I figured it would be a mob scene, but what the hell. It was fun to be with these people. I looked around the room. I didn't see any other hands in the air.

At a restaurant in Mill Valley I had lunch with Saniel, Linda, Van, and my friend, Gayatri. It was casual, friendly. No great discussions. Mostly small talk. As bizarre as it may sound, what I remember most about that lunch is watching Saniel eat a hamburger. He did it with great gusto. He felt incredibly "real" to me–ordinary, very human, down to earth and something more. After lunch we wished each other well. Said goodbye. And that was that.

The next day, back in the Central Valley, a funny thing happened. I was totally zapped. I didn't want to open my eyes. I didn't want to get out of my big old chair. It was like I had melted. That went on for about twenty-four hours. I had no idea what was happening. What if anything it meant. The following day I was back to my old self. By the way, though I had enjoyed meeting Saniel, Linda, Van and the others, I wanted nothing to do with spiritual groups or teachers anymore, thank you very much.

Ten months later I was really bored and lonely again. I kept in touch with Gayatri from time to time. She mentioned that the Waking Down group was having a retreat on the Northern California Coast: hot tubs and gourmet food, a relaxing good time to be had by all. I thought, Why not? I'll volunteer. Seems there was one slot open because somebody had cancelled at the last minute.

I had to go to something called the Human Sun Seminar a week before the retreat. A requirement. It was in Marin, so I thought, what the hell, at least it's scenic. I also had to read Saniel's book, *Waking Down*, and have a couple of phone conversations with someone named Ted. (He turned out to be the guy I thought was taking a nap at the sitting.)

The Human Sun Seminar was a lot of words. For two days. I'm not good at listening to words. Reading, yes. Lectures, no. Again, Saniel came across as very natural, human, and not the pedestal type. Then the most amazing thing happened during a question/answer period. Saniel got angry. Really angry. A very beautiful, gentle soul in the back row asked something nondescript about something. The tone was polite and hesitant. Saniel exploded into a beautiful rage. I froze. I'm sure my eyes could have held tea cups.

Saniel was forcefully saying he'd had it with something the fellow in the last row had been saying when a small man stood up and quietly said, "Saniel, you're wrong." There was total silence. Then another person said, "Yes, you're off-base here, Saniel."

More silence. I could see Saniel struggling. I don't know what he was thinking or feeling, but it looked to me like a mighty tug of war was taking place inside him. After a few moments he took a deep breath, looked around the room at various faces, then back to the man in the last row, and apologized to him. He said he was wrong. He was sorry. And he said it again. Then he continued with the questions and answers.

I don't know that I heard much for a while after that. For starters, I couldn't believe what I had just seen. Nothing in my past experience prepared me for it. To begin with, you didn't correct the teacher or guru in that way. You asked questions, and if you didn't agree, you figured there was something lacking in your understanding. The teacher was always right in a very basic way. They are the ones who are enlightened. They see things in a way you can't know until you're also enlightened. The pedestal syndrome. Oh, I've been scorched with the ridicule and anger of an awakened teacher, and I have felt humiliated, frustrated, confused, furious, impotent and, worst of all, remained silent. I had just experienced something totally different. I had no idea at the time how important it was for me. It would turn out later to be a key to my Second Birth.

The weekend passed by. I heard one phrase, "greenlighting," which I really liked. It seemed to mean that whatever I was feeling or thinking in the moment was OK. Go with it. That's you. It's real. It's not something to try to change or avoid. I figured it gave me permission to step off my own pedestal.

A week later I drove to Irish Beach on the Northern California Coast for the first Transfiguration Retreat. Irish Beach is a beautiful coastal community with green hills, white sand and the long blue blaze of the sea. I stayed in a large home with several other participants, the sun shone throughout the week with one brief exception, the food was wonderful, and I slept in the front room with a hot tub outside on the back porch.

But a funny thing had happened on the way to a laid-back vacation. Talking on the phone with Ted and reading Saniel's *Waking Down* and *The Conscious Principle* had stirred me up. Two years earlier, while standing with a beloved teacher in the mountains above Boulder,

Colorado, I had experienced everything as love, including myself. At that moment I saw the perfection of everything, all of creation, and the love, the unconditional love, that is the source. From that moment on, a huge relief and relaxation swept through me. I accepted myself. I was OK in a way I had never been before, and my relationship with my teacher was transformed. The fear was gone. The self-doubt. The embarrassment at being me. I was still the same bumbler and stumbler, but I was OK. Me and the leaf falling from the tree, we were love. Yet something wasn't right. I wasn't "connected" somehow. I saw the beauty and the perfection of creation, and I knew it was all Me, but there was a distance, a disconnect. I was "free" and I was still searching for something.

Now I had gone down the rabbit hole of Waking Down, and I didn't understand what was happening. I was confused, emotional, dissatisfied, swinging high and low, so when Saniel gathered us all together the first evening at the retreat and asked us what we wanted from the week together, I wasn't thinking about hot tubs and a beach. I told him, not really knowing what I was saying, "A Second Birth sounds OK to me."

During the week we met in the morning as a large group with all the participants and teachers and in the afternoon in small groups headed by a teacher. I asked to be in Ted's group. There were seven of us and Ted. I figured after the retreat that I'd really lucked out because, along with Ted, three others in the group were awakened (what that meant at the time was a mystery to me). What happened was that these "awakened ones" were really vulnerable, honest and going through some heavy stuff (some of it in the group with each other). They set a wonderful example for me who had always hidden in groups. Again, there was an incredible "holding" of each other, a feeling of safety that I hadn't felt before in a group setting, large or small.

We followed the format in our group of giving each person about twenty minutes to share or explore whatever was up for them. When my turn came I decided to share my precious story of how I now experienced everything as an expression of love. The group listened politely. When I finished, there was a pause. Then a woman said, "It doesn't sound very real to me." Someone else agreed. A few heads nodded.

I was stunned. Hell, I had just poured out my heart as honestly as I knew how, and they weren't buying it. In that moment I knew I had a choice. I could pull back, defend myself, argue, or smile meekly and feel misunderstood and so forth. I saw, also, the other choice: let go of everything I knew, my beautiful, wonderful experiences of love, my beliefs, hopes, dreams–all my good ideas. I felt like I was standing on the edge of a cliff, and in front of me was a black, bottomless chasm. At that moment I decided to step over the edge of the cliff. I had no idea why I was doing this. Somehow, deep inside, I knew it was right. I leaned forward and gestured with my hands that I wanted to hear more.

I don't remember now much of what they said. They were gentle, questioning, interested. No one had any answers. What I took in was that something was missing for them in what I had said, in the way I had said it, a passion, a grounded force. Something. I didn't have a clue.

After the small group ended I began to realize that I was angry. Not at anyone. Certainly not at my small group. Nor at myself. I felt a sorrow and terrible anger because I had lost what I cherished most: I had lost my world of love.

I went to bed that night curled up in my anger. I woke up in the middle of the night and looked out the large picture windows. A heavy fog blocked the sky and sea, everything beyond the porch railing. I felt the silence. In the morning I got up and went to the window. Everything was blue and green and light. A roommate was sitting in a chair reading the newspaper. I said to him, "It's all a damn painting." He gave a half-smile–I don't know if he really heard me–and went on reading the newspaper. I looked out over the tops of the houses, the trees, at the sea and the blue sky, and it was flat and empty. It had no meaning. No words. There was no purpose. Everything was a flat, meaningless painting, and I was really pissed off.

I simmered through the morning until, at the large group meeting, Saniel pretended to be angry. Someone said something, and Saniel replied to the effect, "Would you rather I be angry?" The fiery make-believe anger flashed forward for a brief moment. Unlike when he had really been angry a week or so before, when I was shocked and fascinated, this time the make-believe anger touched me deeply. I wasn't upset. I was amazed at how much passion Saniel felt, how he shared it, how honest he was with it, how much he cared, how serious he was. At that moment I realized how important, how serious everything is. This is a California fun-in-the-sun guy talking. Serious? Only if it's serious fun. May sound strange, but from then on I was serious, very serious about everything. I don't mean I went around with a serious face, anything like that. I mean from then on I really cared about what I was doing and what was happening with me, through me, for me.

That afternoon in my small group, as I was trying to share how angry

I had been feeling, a passion rose from deep inside and I began to sob. A huge sorrow filled me with blackness and despair. Someone asked what I was feeling, and I didn't know. All I knew was that my heart overflowed with a hopeless sorrow. Someone else asked me if I had any past lives' memories. I thought, What a ridiculous question! Then the memories came, memories that I had touched on in work I had done exploring myself years earlier–memories of bitter, horrible deaths, dying for noble ideals, for God or the gods, archetypal memories of distant times and places, and always the same terrible feelings of despair and betrayal, either my own innocent death or the self-righteous, holy death I administered to another. With these memories, whatever they were, I knew the dark passion I was lost in—distrust. I didn't trust anyone, anything. I never had. I'd sensed it during my life. I'd lived my life as one who doesn't really trust. I didn't trust myself, my teachers, God, life—no one, nothing.

I shared with the group what I was feeling, what I saw now. I don't remember what was said, if much of anything. I felt received and held by the group. It was as though I had given them a wonderful gift.

I went to bed that night in another black mood. But along with the anger and sorrow was a clear sense that I was aware of everything, and that I was fundamentally OK. I'd done a lot of work over the years with Consciousness, the Watcher—that limitless, unchanging whatever that we try to describe in words. Now I noticed that awareness was clear and strong in the midst of my emotional storm. I didn't think of it until later, but through all this unfolding of darkness and pain I continued to know myself as that and trusted that. Even when experiencing total distrust. And this is how the term "greenlighting" had helped me. For the past two days I had given myself permission to fully experience and be whatever was happening for me.

Again I awoke in the middle of the night. The dark sky was clear and sprinkled with stars. I felt a deep calm. The waters of the sea inside me gently rocked me back to sleep.

The next morning I discovered I was passionately in love with women, all women, everything about them–their bodies, the way they moved or were still, the sound of their voices, their feet, hands, eyes, hair, everything, and, most of all, the mystery. I'd always been a great romantic about love and women. You know, across a crowded room I'd discover the love of my life. I did look across crowded rooms a number of times and meet someone, but the romantic lyrics in my head never matched reality. This was different. It's hard to describe. For the first time in my life I really appreciated the beauty and mystery of a woman. There was nothing intellectual or romantic about it. It's like when you go to a beach and feel the sand squishing up between your toes, and then the first slap of the cold water on your legs. The incredible beauty of experiencing through the body. Somehow a shift had happened. My body was like a sensitive receiver, and it really liked women. For me this was new and wonderful. You could say I now "experienced" the goddess in women, and I was on my knees in gratitude and awe.

That afternoon in my small group I shared again my vision of love. Again I tried to put into words what can't be said. This time when I finished I looked over at Ted. He was in tears. This time they felt my passion. I was more real. All I knew is that I felt more alive, present, in my body. Yet, at the same time that I felt this surge of joy and delight of being in a body, I also experienced the painful limitations of flesh, blood, and bone. The image that came to mind was a crucifixion. I was limitless, free, all of creation and beyond, and I was a fragile, imperfect, limited human being. For a few months after the retreat I wore a small, gold crucifix around my neck as a reminder of who I am—that wonderful and painful mystery.

The rest of the retreat flew by in a glow of wholeness and well-being. At a mid-week party I danced with a woman in a way I never had before. We didn't touch, and yet our energies moved in a magical rhythm that was sensually passionate and wonderfully free. It was more than sexual. I felt like I had made love to a woman for the first time in my life.

On the drive home my body went crazy with energy. I had the radio on, and the only thing I wanted to listen to was hard rock and Beethoven. Loud. Very loud. I thought at the time, "This music feels incredibly gentle and soothing—like 'Mary had a little lamb.'" I stopped at a restaurant for lunch. I could feel what people in the restaurant were feeling. I felt a love for them like the music on the radio–loud, strong, powerful. I saw them as perfect just as they were. I wanted to laugh and cry at the same time. I loved them so much, and we were all perfect expressions of the mystery, the one heart, the love that pulses through the veins of all creation. Also, on that drive home I said goodbye to my old self. No more selfish, self-indulgent California boy. I didn't know what it meant or what would happen, but that guy was history.

When I got home I collapsed for a few days. I could hardly move. I didn't want to open my eyes. I felt great, but it was like my body needed a timeout. Maybe it was an energy burnout. Maybe I needed a little time to adjust to the new energy force running through my body. Anyway I was soon back teaching, back living my ordinary life. I noticed changes. I had a confidence, a certain fearlessness, an instinctive need to act in the moment, to do what was right. For example, my old fear of groups was gone. At our first teachers' meeting I asked every question I needed to ask. I was the only one asking questions. I was present, engaged. I was myself. Also, if I suspected I had hurt someone's feelings or there may have been a misunderstanding, I was right on it talking to that person, finding out, apologizing if appropriate. On the other hand, if someone said or did something that hurt me, I let them know. I didn't attack them. I just made sure they knew how I felt.

I'd like to say that my life was filled with joy and zest and confidence from then on. Didn't happen that way. Rather quickly after my Second Birth I became extremely sensitive to the pain and anger and suffering all around me. Women, those beautiful goddesses, for over a year they became a fiery darkness for me. I saw no hope, no light, no joy there. And a few years later distrust struck again with an even greater force, and I was in a deep depression for a month before the shadows lifted.

Now, almost five years after my Second Birth, I experience both the savage darkness and the precious beauty in all creation. The journeys into my inner darkness, into the night of my soul, still happen, often when I least expect them, usually triggered by events that appear insignificant. Yet, each time I travel into those painful, confused, hopeless places in myself, each time I've been reborn into a deeper, fuller day living more and more the amazing mystery that I am.

"Stay on the air mattress. Energy will take you to the right place."

Maria

Maria Stoecker was born and raised in a small town in Northern Germany. She left her hometown to become a teacher and lived and taught for more than thirty years in Berlin. She raised two children and began to explore the question, "Who am I?" Her spiritual quest brought her to Ashland, Oregon, where she would like to settle down to live close to her daughter, son-in-law, grandchild, and, of course, the Waking Down community.

HOW TO LOSE A FALSE TOOTH— A RESIDENTIAL RETREAT WITH SANIEL AND LINDA IN PETALUMA

Have you ever thought about doing a Residential Retreat with Saniel and Linda? Decide after you read my report, but–see a dentist before going there.

As I prepared for this visit, my unconscious had already created an exciting horror picture show in my dreams. I dreamt about my own death three times during the two weeks before. So, was this visit about death? And what was ready to die?

Saniel picked me up at Fairground Station and here we were–in Linda and Saniel's inviting, quiet, beautiful, radiant home. For a short moment well-known feelings and thoughts arose: me, with the founder of WDM and his wife? Am I worthwhile? Am I intelligent enough? Am I spiritual enough? Am I really a candidate for Waking Down in Mutuality? Did I bring the right questions? Did I read enough? Is my past the "right" one?

Being in their home I pushed those questions away, not yet knowing that I had brought my most important issue with me. We chatted a bit like normal people on a visit. Linda showed me the house, and then I went to bed, being very tired and happy to be just by myself in my comfortable room. This first night I slept deep and quiet.

Next morning, after a delicious breakfast, we had our first session. Sitting on the sofa (which became my spiritual home during the next two days), I told Linda and Saniel the story of my life. Nothing special. I had told it a thousand times in my thousand therapies: nearly having died in the first moments of my life, or should I say "been murdered" by having been fed cow's milk, which a newborn baby can't digest? Life on earth received me vomiting, dehydrating, being hectically fed with a metal spoon and water. I cried desperately through my nights. Nobody cared–a child has to learn discipline from the first moment. Then I had to learn the strong rules of a Catholic Northern German village.

When I was three years old, another big chapter of my life started: I was sent away by my parents again and again. I lived with aunts, friends, cousins, in holiday camps (as a three-year-old!), was threatened with foster care (because I was difficult to educate! Ha!), was sent into a boarding school, and sent away, sent away, sent away, just escaped death again in car accidents, during a surgery, and swimming in the ocean. My father abused me emotionally. When I became a young girl discovering boys and falling in love, they stopped sending me away; instead my home became a prison. I wasn't allowed to go out anymore. My relationships didn't work; my beloved boyfriend died when I was twenty-one. I raised my children without love, just continuing my own story, not knowing better, and so on and so on.

A "normal" life story. Saniel and Linda listened. I felt their compassion. After one and a half hours we finished our session with gazing. I felt Linda's compassionate love for my life story, I felt Saniel's brilliant mind–mother and father, female and male, took care of my wounded heart.

Then something strange happened–I became dizzy. So I spent the rest of the afternoon on my sofa, being dizzy, thinking and writing about having been sent away, not being wanted, and death.

A wonderful dinner, talking to Saniel and Linda again and reading to them what I had written: *Today during our session I found out something very important: My deepest wound is the fear of death. I came into the world being confronted with death. I experienced being close to death during my childhood several times: I was sent away, threatened with a foster home, I was told that I was totally unworthy, that nobody wanted me.*

And I remember having been led into a past life a year earlier where I was a teacher, teaching against the church and its practices, being tortured for that and surrounded by a ring of energy by my torturers. My daughter Hannah said, "They didn't do it for your actual life, because they knew that you would soon be dead. They paralyzed you for all your following lives." Is that some kind of death energy inside myself? Do I still fear death when I'm teaching?

So I have to go back to the fear of dying and experience that my death is the birth into a Second Life, because this time I'm wanted. Will this knowledge help me to confront death, step through the portal of death, trusting that there will be a completely different, new life? And how will I get there? Being with Saniel and Linda is being with my new spiritual parents, who want me, support me, and see me being special and worthy. I feel well and safe being with them. I hope they will lead me to the portal of death.

I'm also thinking about the relationship I want. Is there a man strong enough, a sensual man, a man on the path? Does he see and enjoy my beauty? Do I see his? Do we feel our hearts? Do we want to connect?

I also found out that in the past sexuality was the only possible way to connect deeply with a man, as my heart was shut so firmly. Saniel said that I might not have been addicted, and I think he is right–a great relief. Now I understand why it nearly killed me when Holger betrayed me. Now I understand why I must have been shocked to death when Klaus died. I felt it was the punishment for our "forbidden," deep, sensual connection. I never again have been so innocent in my sexuality.

My father and mother both carried the seeds of death inside them. My father had been a soldier in World War II and a prisoner in Russia for six years, where he nearly died from hunger. My mother had given birth to a dead child. What a horror–being pregnant means creating new life! She created death with her first pregnancy. Her fear of doing that again was my first experience in her womb.

So all my actions seemed to carry the seed of death inside them. Now it makes sense that I always started projects in my life, never finished them, and then let them die. "I'm not good enough" (I'm not GOD enough) was the bullet which killed them. This feeling arose from my death experiences. My body and mind system learned to dance on the surface of death, always afraid to fall. So welcome, Death. I want to embrace you so that you can become a powerful part of my life.

God, please help me come to my awakening. Please help me to face my fear of death with the help of the new parents you sent me. Please let me find my passion in dying. Please let me serve the earth in your name so that we might go on living. Amen

After reading the text to Saniel and Linda, a deeply compassionate and understanding love covered me like a warm coat sheltering the heart opening.

I went to bed. During the night I had a "wild" dream again, so I got up early in the morning and sat down in the garden. How beautiful to feel the fresh air, to smell Linda's flowers on the porch! I connected with Mother Earth, thanking her for all her beauty, caring, abundance–the exciting surprises she offers every day.

I heard Saniel preparing for his meditation group in a yoga center. "Please give me just two minutes," I called, and then I joined him. The next chapter of my visit started: When meditating I felt quiet, but somehow uncomfortable.

Back in Saniel's car, I felt a huge wave of feeling uncomfortable crush down on me. "Yes, now I can feel it–Saniel and Linda don't want me either. They don't want me to be here, they'd like me to leave, they just want my money. I'm stupid, nonspiritual, unworthy. Nobody wants me." I felt like throwing up, like in the first hours of my life: Nobody wanted me, nobody comforted me, life wanted to get rid of me–I felt like crying every night. It seemed that my whole body, every cell, had stored this ugly information and now told me to run away and be on my own.

"Saniel, I feel really bad. I feel that nobody wants me, even you and Linda don't want me to be here. It's terrible. I want to run away, to be alone, to go home. I don't want to disturb you any longer."

Instead of allowing me to follow my impulse, Saniel invited me to stay in the living room with him. Back on my sofa I shared how terrible I felt. My whole body was full of self-disgust. I felt like vomiting, everything felt tense, my heart was squeezed by an iron hand. I wanted to run far, far away.

"That's like being in the birth channel," Saniel said. "It's narrow like that, and it squeezes your whole body."

Listening to Saniel words, I felt some hope of getting out of this state. I have given birth to two children. Yes, that's how it feels. Linda joined us and her loving compassion comforted me. Finally, I felt better, released.

Sitting on my spiritual sofa again, I scanned my whole life using the body consciousness of not being wanted. Yes, there it was in each situation: meeting people, being on holiday, working, offering workshops and talks, being invited to parties, being on retreats–my body always offered me that well-known feeling from the beginning of my life: "Go back again. They don't want you!"

And what did this grown-up, intelligent, rational "me-mind" do? It played the role of the self-confident, gifted woman, dancing on the thin ice of feeling rejected with quivering knees and an anxious heart.

"Suppose they get to know me? Suppose they send me away because they don't want me either? Suppose they get to know how unworthy I really am?" That was the basis of my life? What an ugly, rotting, stinking feeling was that?

Only one day left. Is there enough time to recycle the amount of garbage I'm carrying inside me?

Today we will do the trip to Mount Tamalpais and Stinson Beach. We sat down in the car. It felt like going on holiday with mama and papa. Saniel and Linda were talking about the new home they were going to rent, about moving and everyday life. How relaxing–a normal family conversation. No spiritual highlights, no intellectual "salto mortales" (dangerous summer). Taking a deep breath, I enjoyed the beautiful landscape.

Mount Tamalpais offered her holy space. A tree on top of the mountain invites a climb of its ramified trunks and branches. Lots of fog covered the Bay Area. We walked around, hung out, and enjoyed the dancing mist. I took photos of Saniel and Linda kissing. Before leaving we gazed. Gazing in a sacred space was special.

Saniel said, "I feel there was some tribal healing, too. You are German. I am Jewish."

Another wave hit my body. Pictures arose: dead, skinny bodies heaped up in front of a concentration camp, a mother pressing her child against her breast, trying to protect it with her arms from being shot by a Nazi officer in the background. No chance–they were shot together. Human beings shoveling their own graves, knowing they would fall into them some minutes later. In deep desperation and sadness I started crying. A deep numb pain wanted to show its desperate, suffering grimace.

I cried as if wanting to resolve the pain of all tortured, killed human beings, the pain of all who had been killed in the name of God, terror or stealing resources. Can you ever heal the insanity of men killing men, humans killing humans? Homo sapiens killing Homo sapiens? Homo insapiens killing Homo insapiens? Homo insane! The pain is too deep. The only thing I can do is to express its desperate depths.

I was dizzy again. We returned, stopped at Stinson Beach. I lay down on a blanket with Linda and Saniel and listened to the humming sound of the ocean, heard children playing, people laughing and chatting. The wind blew some sand into my face. This is how peace sounds, I thought. Our trip ended in a little restaurant's garden, having lunch together.

After having returned "home," Linda and I sat down in the living room, talking about relationships. My relationships. Again I recognized that this feeling "nobody wants me" was the leading edge of my decisions to be with a man, was the ground zero for the failure of the connection. How to be in a relationship when you don't feel worthy, when you need a man to prove that you might be? What if you need a man to prove in every second of your being together that you are precious? A horror scenario! Being so needy can't work, and it didn't.

Tonight I don't want to have dinner, although Linda offers halibut (hmmmh!). But I'm not hungry. Lying in bed I'm thinking, "Is there enough time for my process? Is there enough time to go where I want to go?" But the process isn't developing by me wanting and thinking it. It's being in the flow. It's being led by some energy wanting "the best for me." Thinking about my process and the flow I remember a past adventure where I had to surrender to a river. I tell Saniel and Linda the story the next day.

Once upon a time, my son-in-law's friend Evan asked me to join him on a rafting trip. He invited me to raft on The Rogue River in Oregon on an air mattress. Yes, on an air mattress! At first I hesitated–it's too crazy. Then I agreed, asking for a life vest for this extraordinary trip.

We started in Ashland and stopped at a gas station in Shady Cove to rent a life vest. When the attendant got to know our plans, he became very anxious and warned, "Don't do that. Nobody's ever done it. I even don't know whether it is allowed at all. Many strong swimmers have drowned in the undercurrents of the river."

As I had already nearly drowned in the undercurrents of the Mediterranean Sea during a holiday, I decided not to do the trip. "No, thanks, Evan. Don't want to repeat that experience. You may do this trip alone; I will wait for you on the bank. Maybe you will arrive alive on your mattress."

Evan answered, "This energy here is too negative. Let's go somewhere else," and drove us to another place near the river. Here we ran into an old man living in a trailer. He got to know of Evan's plan and my refusal to join him. So he came towards me, "Please do the trip. It will be a great experience for you and your life. You will be safe. My spirit is with you." And as he not only offered me his spirit to guide me, but also his life vest, I finally agreed to join the adventure.

We sat down on the air mattress with some bottled water and a life belt made from a car tire and started our journey. Exactly two minutes later an accident occurred. Rowing the "boat" with some branches, trying to steer it, we collided with a bridge pillar and fell into the water. The current pulled me under water. I knew it could throw me against the concrete pillars a any moment. Suddenly, I felt Evan's hands grabbing me and helping climb back on the mattress. After Evan first took care of "saving" me, he returned to the rolling seat himself. I felt protected and safe. Without drinking water and "paddles" we continued our journey.

Now the most amazing river journey began. I experienced "the flow." You can do little to change the direction your "boat" takes. The river moves you and guides you every second. It leads you across rocks, around rocks. It washes you ashore and shows you the merry-go-rounds of the river's whirls and spins you under the branches of overhanging trees. It invites you to react. It's not about being passive; it's about being alert, about watching and making decisions on what will happen in the very next moment. It's about lying flat on the mattress when rocks are showing up. It's about using your arms to protect yourself from being wiped away by branches. It's about using your hands, paddling, finding your Self in the whirl. It's about being in the flow! It's about being okay with what's happening, knowing that you can't change the river, and it's about knowing that your energy helps to create your way with attentive Consciousness, using your body and your skills.

In the evening, sitting in a restaurant close to the river I looked at it, feeling and thinking, "The River and Me," knowing that we were friends now, thankful and proud having experienced the flow.

After telling Saniel and Linda my story, Saniel said, "Stay on the air mattress. Energy will take you to the right place." I love that sentence. And it's right. I still don't know what this energy is about and how these two teachers manage to transmit it so powerfully. But it happens. And maybe this energy wants to connect desperately with us, wants to find its loving way into our system to express its loving power through us. I went to bed–my last night in Petaluma. The next morning there would be a shamanic healing session with Saniel–my wish before leaving for Ashland.

At five o'clock in the morning I woke up. Something knocked at my heart's door. It opened. Outside was UMC (Universal Moving Company) waiting, asking politely to be allowed to move a new Consciousness in. "Yes, of course, come in," my heart answered. What a wonderful, never-before-known-feeling. Slowly and cautiously IT poured its energy into my heart, filling it with mutual consent and love. Then it radiated into my whole body. I was amazed, happy, content and calm. I had always wanted an explosion. Now there was a subtle power at work, conquering my whole body, invading every cell.

Did I open the space for the loving moving company cleaning my cells from past suffering, supported by compassionate loving beings? Did I prepare my Self by that big cleansing? Are compassionate beings holding loving space like a big vacuum cleaner helping to get rid of suffering or to transform it? I have to think about that.

Surprised, tender and happy, I stayed awake. Again I scanned my life. This time I was able to connect being in deep love with everyonething. What an amazing journey sending my heart to all those places where I had been afraid not to be wanted! I am the one who wants the loving connection. I am the one who attracts by radiating. Every body is the "I am" radiator. By radiating our love, being in matter, we attract and connect.

Suddenly I remembered that I already had experienced this divine loving feeling, but it was caused by chemistry. I always was seeking, yearning, to meet this experience, this feeling again, without taking a drug. And now I know–I was looking to receive it from the outside!

O, no! There is no outside. After Consciousness moved into my system I knew: I am exactly what I was looking for in the outside. Thank you, Consciousness, for the subtle tenderness of your cautious moving in. And thank you, Saniel and Linda, for guiding me there with Waking Down in Mutuality in Petaluma.

After the Shamanic session with Saniel the next morning, I had to leave. Going home, how does it feel now? Feels like taking all the love inside with me to pour it into my place and connect with all beings.

"What about your false tooth?" you may ask. After having surfed through my loving universe in the morning, I fell asleep again. When I woke up and decided to brush and floss my teeth–kliiiiiiiiiiiiiinnnn nnng–a crown jumped off my tooth directly into the sink. I unscrewed everything. It was gone. So good-bye, false stuff, good-bye to holding onto my fears, my feelings of not being wanted–all the pain that closed my heart. But in this case I will get a new crown, because I don't want to look like a pirate when smiling with my new-gained happiness.

Being back home, what has changed? First of all, I've got a new tooth. Second, life's themes go on showing up. Third, I received some compliments: "You look radiant." " I like to be in your stillness." "Now I really believe people can change."

Two months later, writing this report, I feel grounded and strong being myself and being okay with it–no acting anymore, no hiding. I would like to live in community with other people now, because we want and need each other. It's so relaxing! I can feel my heart now, and I love scanning other people with it. I love to feel my love for every being. I've got a much bigger picture about me and my life themes. I trust in being and laugh about life's teasing phenomena.

Also, I'm able to relax into matter, the fact that I'm finite. That means, for example: "Yes, body, you good old companion, you grow older and start to wrinkle. One day we will say good-bye to each other. By then those wrinkles will look like wrinkles on a gown grown too big that just wants to fall down. Till then, I want to enjoy every moment we are together, even sharing the pain you offer me and celebrating being on earth with other human beings, looking for connection with their open hearts, creating beauty, love and honesty in mutuality. And I know, one day, when We/You are ready to leave me, I will be afraid about the unknown waiting to embrace me. And that's okay, too.

Thank you to Paresh Rink, my wonderful language teacher.

Thank you to Ted Strauss and Hillary Davis who have been my first beloved Waking Down in Mutuality teachers, convincing me with your brilliance, humor and knowledge to join the new "club."

Questions of a Heart Just Opening

Are you ready
To touch your vulnerable heart?
To listen to its hoping beat?
To let it stay alive
In a time of hopelessness?
Do you caress its feelings
Even when you can't allow
YourSelf to express them?

Are you strong enough
Not again to reject
Its pounding desire?
Are you courageous enough
To keep its precious door open
Despite the hurt
That once extinguished
All light in your eyes?

Are you grown up enough
To allow it to stay open?
Because once it has been touched

It wants to look
At all delicate surrounding beauty
With its tender eyes.

Do you believe in your own truth
Not condemning the ones
Who have to protect themSelves
For survival?
Can you stand the loneliness
That sometimes follows honesty?
Can you be with the joy
Your body remembers
Once having been
In desiring, radiant, explosive
Connection?
Do you trust life
That it will happen again?
Can you take your heart
Into your own tender hands
Comforting it
For feeling it hasn't fulfilled
Its longing for love?

Are you ready
To embrace the world
Without having human hands
To hold you?
Do you trust yourSelf
To share your thoughts and feelings
Just by offering them?
Can you enjoy all the moments
Being with yourSelf and themSelves?
Can you offer your gifts
Being content
That they are taken
Just with thankfulness?
Can you bear that
Your heart's endless tender universe
is touched by everyonething?

You have arrived.
You are ready for love.

"I was free to be who I was, however that might look."

Ben

Ben Hursh was born in Hayward, California, in December of 1930. He graduated from Hayward Union High School in June of 1950 and enlisted in the Air Force. He received a hardship discharge after 21 months of service when his father had a stroke, and he came home to support the family. He went to work for Pacific Telephone Company in 1955. He became a serious spiritual seeker after an emotional breakdown in 1964. He had a profound realization of the unity of all things while experimenting with LSD in 1967. This led him to take up various spiritual paths until he discovered Waking Down, a path to a spiritual awakening taught by an old friend, Saniel Bonder. He awakened in May of 1998 and a year later started training to become a teacher of Waking Down.

RELEASING THE UGLY BEAST

I am presently seventy-three years old but have been a spiritual seeker since I was a small boy. I was born in 1930 in Hayward, California, right at the beginning of the Great Depression. I don't remember soup lines, but we frequently had people come to the door asking for food. The streets were always torn up because of public work projects. It was hard times, but we were lucky as my Dad made a good living selling coffee and spices door to door.

When I was about five years old, we moved to San Jose and I started having mystical experiences. No one could tell me their significance, and I was too young to understand what was happening. Even though they were very pleasant to feel, they frightened me because I felt like I was disappearing.

I remember on one occasion when I was about six. I was watching a sunset when I began to feel myself merging with the sky. I started to feel less solid, and it seemed my body was disappearing. I was becoming one with the sky. I went running to the house yelling for my mother. She asked me what was wrong, and I answered that the sky was trying to eat me. She tried to reassure me that the sky wasn't trying to eat me, but I knew better. I couldn't convince her I had been in real danger. This experience led me to believe that my mother wasn't going to be much help in explaining these phenomena to me. She had no clue as to what I was talking about. I had many more of those kinds of experiences, and after enough repetitions there was less fear and just the pleasant feeling of oneness. I never told anyone about this. I didn't think anyone would understand, and they seemed sacred and private occasions.

It was about this time in my life, I think I was about six or seven, when I began to be aware of the pain of loneliness and feeling completely separate from everyone and everything. A neighbor and schoolmate of mine invited me to go to church with him and his family. It was a fundamentalist church, but my mother and father gave their permission. So on Sunday I went to church and heard my first words about Jesus. I don't remember what they were, but I do remember I never went to church with the neighbors again. The reason was that my friend and his family had made a 3D cardboard model of what they thought Heaven looked like–a large walled city with large buildings with cathedral-like spires and painted gold. When it was finished they showed it to me and said if people lived their lives like the Bible said we should, that when we died we would go to Heaven where everything was gold and be with the Angels. We would spend all our time singing praises to God for all eternity. This sounded very boring to me so I stopped going to church. I wasn't much interested in the payoff.

During my school years, starting in the sixth grade, our school offered a Bible class. It was one period a week and I always looked forward to it. I would imagine I was living at the time Jesus lived and I would join his group of followers and become one of his disciples. This interest in Jesus continued into adulthood when I started an investigation of the different Christian denominations. These included the Presbyterian, Methodist, Baptist, Morman, Catholic, Congregational, Christian Science and probably more that I am not recalling. I belonged to each one, some as long as two years, and tried very hard to meet all the criteria of the denomination I belonged to. But I was never able to connect with any of them. I also read the Bible looking for some clue about God, some revelation that God even existed, some evidence that would remove my doubt. Christianity demanded a faith that I couldn't find. I wanted to have faith so I would know I was saved, but no matter how much I longed for assurance that God loved me I never could dispel the doubt.

I was always very disappointed that my choices were not more clear-cut. Which denomination was the right one? They all proclaimed that they were the truth. Which baptism was right? It all seemed very vague and the penalty for a wrong choice was eternal damnation. That was a heavy price, and I was very angry with God for creating a system that put me in such jeopardy.

I discovered Alan Watts in 1957. Here was a person who addressed my deepest feelings. I began to devour his books, and when I completed his books I expanded to the study of Zen Buddhism. I became aware of how much Western culture and geography had limited my search for wisdom. I never even considered any other options outside of something Biblical and associated in some way to Christianity. Buddhism made more sense to me than Christianity ever did, so I continued my reading on Buddhist precepts.

My life went on in an ordinary way. I had a job at the phone company. I was married and had three children. On the surface it seemed an ordinary conventional life. But I was very unhappy. Life seemed to just be a struggle, and I found no joy or happiness in anything I did. Old friends became a bother. I hated being around my children. My wife and I had a kind of a non-relationship. We lived together, but there was no intimacy. I didn't know what to do. I couldn't connect with Buddhism in a way that provided my life with purpose. My life became so heavy I couldn't carry it anymore, and at age thirty-four I gave up and fell into a catatonic condition that required my being committed to the mental ward of the county hospital in Martinez, California.

It was while I was in the hospital that I began to realize that I was living my life as I had assumed people, mostly my parents, wanted me to live it. In this way I thought I could get the love and approval I needed. However, no matter what I did or how hard I tried, it never got me the approval and feeling of being loved I wanted so desperately. To the contrary, it seemed my reward was disapproval and criticism.

When I was released from the hospital, I had been told that they had done all they could to help me and I should be fine. However, I was still feeling the threat of another collapse on the horizon. I was unhappy and frightened. I didn't know what to do or where to turn for help.

This was in the early sixties, and I had heard of the experimenting being done with LSD in the treatment of emotional problems. In addition, Alan Watts had written a book about his LSD experience called *The Joyous Cosmology*, so I was very curious about psychedelics. I started a search, and after several months I found a qualified guide and began experimenting with psychedelics as a path to emotional healing.

I had no idea I would find much more than that. What I found was a sacred world of unity and love. I felt the presence of God as my own being, and everything was only That. I had found the Truth of our condition, and I couldn't understand how I hadn't seen it before, as it was so obvious. Though the essence of that realization stayed with me, I also was left feeling that something was missing from my life, and I had a great longing to find what that was. Even though I knew I still had a lot of work to do, I no longer felt the threat of another breakdown. I had been healed.

I became a LSD Guru of sorts, guiding people on trips so that they might find their divine center. I worked with about fifteen people over a ten-year period. They all became friends and I still see some of them. Many made profound changes in their lives based on the work we did together.

While using LSD and mescaline I began doing a lot of serious exploring of my psyche. That is when I discovered that I was living my life based on mental suppositions of what I needed to be happy instead of any real feeling for what I truly wanted. I was a programmed robot with no idea of who I was or what I wanted. This discovery was very important to me, and I began experimenting to find out what kind of being I wanted to be and how I wanted to live my life. I became a serious spiritual seeker–a quest that took me down many spiritual paths. I read a legion of spiritual books and took up the practice of Zen at the Zen Center in San Francisco where the Zen Master Shunru Suzuki Roshi lived and taught. I became a minister in a church that was a spin off of Scientology. I also spent time with various spiritual teachers: Ken Keyes, Adi Da and Andrew Cohen.

I had left my wife of eighteen years and my three children and found companionship with a seventeen-year-old girl who lived across the street that I had often taken LSD with. After two years of living together we got married. We had the same spiritual interest, and in spite of the twenty-one year age difference we had a lot in common. We were together for five years and then we separated. A few months later in 1975 I met Janette Favro, and in 1977 we got married. In 1979 we moved to Washington where she had been born and lived most of her life before her move to California.

After forty years of spiritual exploration I began to experience a shift in my perception where there was no separation between me and what I was experiencing. I was experiencing everything directly, but the pass into total Awakening eluded me. I oscillated in and out of profound states of various kinds.

The years passed and by the time I was sixty-seven years old in 1998 I was in utter despair of finding any kind of permanent spiritual fulfillment. Then one day I was reading *What is Enlightenment?* magazine and I saw an ad for Waking Down, a path to awakening that had been founded by Saniel Bonder.

Saniel and I had known each other in the Adi Da community, and I was very curious as to what Saniel's teaching might be. I ordered his book *Waking Down*, and Saniel's teaching spoke to me in the depth of my being. His words leapt off the page and touched my heart. I recognized the Consciousness he was describing.

I phoned Saniel and told him of my experience and said I wanted to explore his teaching further and what should I do? He suggested I start working with a teacher, so I contacted Ted Strauss and we began working together on the phone. I also arranged to attend the next Waking Down Weekend.

The introduction to the event started on Friday night. The teachers that would be working with us that weekend were Saniel, Linda, Ted, Rene Hansen and a teacher by the name of John Dudley. John Dudley radiated a wild energy, and Saniel joked that they only let John out of his cage to teach at Waking Down Weekends. John was a wild character who described himself as a kind of daredevil motorcycle guy who had broken most of the bones in his body while taking dangerous risks with his motorcycle. John scared me to the bone, and I went to bed that night worried about how I was going to be able to spend an entire weekend with such a wild man.

I lay in bed unable to sleep wondering what it was about John that scared me so much. He seemed like a nice enough guy, but he possessed some wild quality that terrified me to the point that I was tempted to go home and not do the weekend. I continued to lay wide-awake in bed considering what I was going to do when I saw a vision of my own wild nature–a great ugly hairy beast that I had locked in a cage in a deep cave where no one would ever see it. I realized it wasn't John's wildness I was afraid of—it was my own. It was the part of me my mother and father never wanted to see. It was forbidden and I learned to keep it hidden.

I felt the enormous amount of energy it took to keep that monster locked up. Suddenly I was very tired and I realized I had to let it run free. I didn't have the energy to keep it hidden anymore. So in my vision I let the hairy monster out of his cage, and he was set loose on the world. I felt such a feeling of freedom and happiness that I was ecstatic. A great energy was released in my body. I felt wonderful.

On Saturday morning I happily went to the event and reported what had happened to me that night. Everyone was amused that I had been so afraid of John's wild nature.

I spent all day Saturday in a very ecstatic state. When I went back to my room that night, I only slept a few hours when I awakened to the feeling of a powerful energy descending through the top of my head and filling my body with great pleasure. Then there was an increase in intensity and the force of the energy became uncomfortable. My body went rigid and I started to have muscle cramps in my calves that were very painful. After about fifteen minutes the energy level decreased and my body began to relax. It was then that I realized myself as Consciousness. There was no separation; there was only the seamless unity of Consciousness and Matter. I was the witness and the event. I psychically saw a small blue flame with a white tip burning in my Heart on the right side. I had fallen into the Heart, the source of Being.

Then another remarkable thing happened. I felt a great shame. I was ashamed of existing. It seemed as if I recognized myself as every terrible thing I had always been afraid I was and tried to hide from everyone. I was all those things. The entire human race felt as I did. I felt great compassion for everyone, and I cried for several hours while Ted held me. When the pain of recognition subsided, I knew I was transformed. I was free to be who I was, however that might look. I had no choice but to be that. There was nothing hidden. I was totally vulnerable to life. There was nothing I could do to protect myself or try to look good. Everything was sacred, filled with a divine energy that came from the center of my Being.

It was a remarkable time. As I drove home to Washington I traveled through a garden of flowers blooming alongside the road and in the fields. It was spring and the world seemed to be celebrating my awakening by bursting forth with its amazing show of renewed life. It seemed to be pointing to a cycle of existence we all share. My personal spring and blooming coincided exactly with the Earth's season of emerging color and new life.

As time passed I discovered there were more emotional obstructions that needed to be revealed and assimilated into the conscious totality of who I am. All of these discoveries opened the door to liberation and freedom, and I looked forward to finding them. Each discovery unlocked another door of the prison so a great bliss became possible. For the next weeks I walked through a transformed world in wonder. Totally vulnerable, open and free.

I was now able to live from an awakened point of view and enjoy a tremendous sense of freedom and happiness, but there still seemed to be a flatness in my life that persisted. Something seemed wrong and I couldn't discover what it was.

In 2000 there was an event organized called a Transfiguration Retreat at Irish Beach, California. My wife Janette, who had taken up the study of Waking Down, and I attended. In one of the large group meetings Saniel gave a talk on how none of us seemed to take this work seriously and we were not appreciating the profound nature of what we were involved in.

I felt like he was describing my attitude exactly. I realized that even though I been awake for fifteen months, I had never publicly proclaimed my awakening. I had only confided in a few close friends because I was afraid of having to meet the demand of living my life as an Awakened Being after having publicly proclaimed my awakening. I felt the fear of people thinking I was a pretender and not awake, and I realized that I had found what I was feeling that was wrong, I found what I felt was missing. I needed to proclaim my awakening.

I stood up in the room of some thirty-five people and proclaimed myself awake as Consciousness. I felt a physical dropping in my body as if a huge weight had fallen from my chest into my stomach. I had taken possession of my awakening and for me that was as important as the awakening itself. Even then I felt reluctant to move into teacher training, but a most remarkable thing happened.

Most of the current teachers were at the retreat, and over the next few days every one of them approached me and told me that when I began teaching not to hesitate to call on them for help and support. My response was thinking to myself, "I never said I wanted to teach, where is this coming from?" Finally, it became obvious to me that I was being called to teach.

I talked to Saniel and Ted and entered an internship that culminated in formal training sessions and working with students as a mentor until I was finally invited into the Teachers' Circle as an interning teacher.

After some time had passed I was granted full teacher status. This has been a great gift, a chance to share what I have received.

So much has been changed for me since my Second Birth. My heart has been broken in love. Love for every living thing, for the world, for the universe and the Mystery of Being. The door opened and infinity was revealed, all hope of knowing anything vanished. The only option was to surrender to not knowing. We are infinity appearing as the finite. There were no sign posts, no maps to tell me which way to go. Everything was a Mystery, a wonderful freedom was possible. I was released into uncertainty. I was terrified, I was filled with joy. It was as if my death had already happened, but I kept on living.

The greatest change I observed was the realization that I was not separate from anything. It was obvious that life was not about millions of separate beings trying to survive, but was about one Energy or Consciousness sharing this planet appearing as apparently separate beings, but lived by the same Life Force. The whole of existence is one thing, one event always becoming itself in infinite possibilities.

This realization didn't provide me with any new knowledge. I found a great peace; my mind is quiet. There are no thoughts or confusion about who I am. There is no need for seeking because there is nothing to be found. There is only Consciousness. There is only me.

This is my true self revealed. I am all that there is. I am the single life force that appears as everything. I am the paradox of creation and destruction. This is not all I am. Ultimately I am an Unknowable Mystery.

I have come to the understanding that all human beings share the error of feeling separate. They look for some way to relieve their fear and loneliness. This opened my Heart to feel the shared pain of all human existence. I was filled with love for people and a great compassion for the condition we find ourselves in as humans.

Does the Second Birth provide the relief we seek? My experience is that there is relief. It is only by embracing our worst nightmare that we can feel free. To not avoid what we fear, but accept it as our condition, is our freedom realized. Our hearts open in love for our fellow beings, and the fear is transformed to strength of Being. We stop exploiting the planet and the animals and people that live on it. We see that there is no us and them. The sacredness of existence is obvious as the condition of all that IS. We can see that the Universe, Galaxy, Solar System and the Earth are part of a Living System that extends infinitely.

If we can Awaken to a Second Birth, we truly Dance in the Fire. There is relief. There is the conscious recognition that there is no problem to solve—just our lives as they appear. There is only the present moment. That is the Dance we learn—beauty and the ugliness embracing as one thing—Dancing in the Fire.

THE AWAKENING

I'm really not polite.
Oh, I say please
and thank you,
and oftentimes I do.
I can open doors
for people
and say excuse me, too.

But one night four years ago
while sleeping in my room
the Goddess came and got me
and took me to a tomb.

Deep inside this damp, dark hole
someone dug a pit,
the Goddess shined a light
and that's when I saw IT!

A great hairy, ugly beast
howling out in rage.
I cowered out of fear
as it banged against Its cage.

The Goddess handed me a key
and bid I ope' the door.
I opened up the lock
and dropped down on the floor.

The beast was now let loose
and It was running free.
Then It turned around
and made a lunge at me!

It put Its arms around me

and hugged me to Its chest.
It squeezed my ribs so hard
I nearly lost my breath.

Then I saw a sight
that gave me a surprise:
It was trying to embrace me;
I could see it in Its eyes.

I knew I must embrace It
if I wanted to get free,
so I put my arms around It,
And It was part of me.

So now we are one,
that angry beast and me,
and both of us as one
are running wild and free.

So that is why I warn you
Its rage became my light,
and I can be quite dangerous,
and I'm really not polite.

"I saw myself as a participant in a great cosmic dance…"

Janette

Born in 1949 and raised in Seattle, Janette Hursh spent the first six years of her life in a multi-generational, Italian-Catholic household. This might explain why even though she appreciates a crowded, boisterous atmosphere, she's learned to relish solitude. As a child she spent a lot of time alone exploring hidden places in neighboring woods, swamps and fields, delighting in these wild brambles as her secret hideaways. She never spent serious time on any spiritual quest; rather, she followed where her heart led which was eventually and happily to a life of embodied awakening. Janette and her husband Ben live along Pacific Coast of the Olympic Peninsula where their modest cabin is nestled in a moss- and fern-blanketed rain forest. Here, in the deep woods and on the sandy beach is where she re-discovered her joy in the natural world with a fresh sense of belonging and kinship to the ever changing seasons. Her email: chinnassword@yahoo.com.

TANTRIC DANCE OF THE DIVINE FEMININE

Beloved, you are the one you seek to
embrace, glorify and worship.
The human body is a pulsing, breathing,
exquisite manifestation of the Divine Heart
that lives and breathes all things.
We are the high priests and priestesses of
these living temples, tenderly attending to
the sacred fires of our own true hearts.

Ben would be coming home soon. It was May 1999 and over the past few months I'd been a cautious rather than willing participant in his latest spiritual quest called Waking Down. He'd just completed a weekend workshop in Marin, California, and I was feeling both anxious and curious to hear about this event. When Ben finally arrived, he jumped out of the car and swept me into his arms, holding me tightly against his body, kissing me and ardently telling me over and over how much he loved me. *Who are you and what have you done with my husband?* If we had a basement I would've checked for pods. In our twenty-three years together we'd always been loving and close, but this was something else entirely. His energy was intensely passionate with a grounded fierceness I barely recognized. And I liked it!

We talked late into the evening and throughout the following days. Ben explained to me that he'd transitioned into his "Second Birth." This awakening was something he'd yearned for all his life. The changes in him were palpable, deep and real. I began to rethink my aversion to anything that hinted of organized religion and decided that Waking Down might merit further investigation.

That June I began to study Saniel Bonder's books. I worked earnestly with a Waking Down teacher and poured over every available Waking Down text, kept a faithful journal and studied as though my life depended on it. Something always seemed to pull me forward yet felt teasingly just out of reach, like grasping fog, reachable yet elusive. It was an invigorating, maddening and enlivening process. I felt totally at the helm of my own destiny for whatever it held. I attended my first Waking Down Weekend in Larkspur, California, that summer and was moved by the ease of the event: no formalities, simply the welcoming from everyone I met.

In August of 2000 the first Transfiguration Retreat was held at Irish Beach in Mendocino, California. It was a fabulous time. It was also during this time that I experienced my first Tantric opening, even though it was not yet part of my vocabulary. I was falling in love with so many men--deeply, passionately in love. There was one man in particular. We didn't have much personal contact, but the *Shakti* that flowed between us felt like a connecting cord of energy and light. I continued to enjoy all of this delightful newness, and thought perhaps I too had had my Second Birth. When we returned home from Irish Beach, I phoned my teacher for clarification and validation. My descriptions sounded good, but no cigar. Actually, I would have been disappointed if that had been a Second Birth since I knew in my heart I didn't feel complete and that there must be something more. But what that might be I didn't have a clue.

That September the Human Sun Seminars were being offered as a precursor to attending Waking Down Weekends. Ben wanted to be able to teach the Human Sun Seminar, and so we made plans to attend one in Boulder, Colorado, followed a week later by a Waking Down Weekend. During that week in Boulder I began to experience what the traditions call *Sahaj Samadhi* (the natural state). This altered state of being had spontaneously occurred for me once before in 1978 while studying the works of (then) Bubba Free John. At that time in my life I was relatively new to the spiritual circuit and had little or no knowledge of Eastern mystical experiences. I've experimented with a lot of psychedelic drugs, but wasn't prepared for a sudden shift in consciousness and became completely disoriented, certain that I had a brain tumor or some other terrifying malady. For the next twenty-two years my fear and ignorance pushed this extraordinary phenomenon far into the safety recesses of my unconsciousness. I made myself forget it ever happened.

After my initiation into Waking Down I was better prepared to welcome *Sahaj Samadhi* with more confidence. This confidence didn't come from conventional knowledge but with a pristine certainty and a new reality altogether. It was as though all that I perceived in the phenomenal universe was a projection of me reflected back to me. I was the object, the mirror and the reflection. There was no difference from what was visible or not visible, and it all began and ended with me.

In our hotel room late in the evenings after bedtime I would touch my eyelids to see if my eyes were closed or open since I couldn't tell the difference. There existed a vibrational signature to everything in the room. The walls and furniture seemed to resonate with a subtle living light-energy. This wasn't visible light, but I could see with illuminated awareness everything manifesting as the activity of consciousness. I remember looking at the floor tiles in the bathroom and laughing because I felt no sense of separation from tacky linoleum. I couldn't even be certain if I was awake, dreaming or sleeping; it seemed dream-like but at the same time solidly real. I'd wake Ben to ask if there was a TV or lamp in the room, and he'd assure me that indeed there was. Even though, I still needed and was almost afraid to touch objects to be certain I wasn't imagining my surroundings. They were solid enough, but at the same time I could see and feel the dimensional shifts of these objects. It was as if all my life I'd been looking though crystal clear glass. Now the glass was gone, the veil lifted. Sitting comfortably on the sidelines and watching life from a safe distance was no longer an option. Suddenly I'm in the game and a full participant in my own life and all without a play book. Looking back I now believe I was shifting through my own multi-dimensionality. The "doors of perception" were opening, and it was an extraordinary, new and exciting experience.

This *Sahaj Samadhi* continued during that Human Sun Seminar, and my heart began to open to others in ways I'd never experienced. I became more empathic and unusually more vocal than I generally am in large group settings. I began to see the hearts of others, their joys and pains not separate from my own. The man from Irish Beach was also there, and we spent a lot of time together and I became more deeply in love. I confided this to Ben, and he acknowledged that he too had similar experiences of falling in love with many women.

Late one evening I couldn't sleep so was writing a card to a friend—just a travel note, nothing special. I began to think lovingly of what I now considered to be my Tantric partner. Suddenly I lost all sense of time and space. My body stiffened and I felt a blast of energy in my tailbone that rose rapidly up my spine toward my head. My first jolt of *Kundalini*, the serpent power. I felt the opening of my crown chakra with a beam of the brightest white light streaming into infinity. I then literally saw that blinding beam of light return from the infinite through my open crown and crash land into my heart with a resounding thud, grounding me to the earth. My heart began to explode with wave after wave of such unspeakable bliss in what I can only describe as an orgasm of the heart. That bliss may have lasted a nanosecond or hours; I was free of the bondages of time and space. If this was anything like *Nirvakulpaka Samadhi* (formless ecstasy) I wanted it all the time! This extraordinary state was a jolt—a sudden and brief, glimmering recognition of the heart's true nature: to live in the absolute bliss of being.

The week following the Human Sun Seminar Ben and I maintained a busy schedule meeting with many people in and around Boulder. We even convinced a couple of friends to attend the upcoming Waking Down Weekend. Then, one morning in our hotel room I woke in such abject misery I didn't even want to pull the covers away from my head. We'd made plans for the day, but I told Ben to go on without me. I turned off all the lights, closed the shades and put out the "Do Not Disturb" sign. In the darkest corner of that room I curled myself into the smallest space I could fit and, with my heart broken, sobbed and wailed for six hours. I wasn't just experiencing shame and sorrow, I was shame and sorrow. This was the agonizing truth of my existence. I felt undeserving of the space I was taking up on earth and shamed by my need for sunlight and air. I dared take only shallow breaths, so convinced that my being alive was an insult to life itself. This was the "dark night" of my entire being. The bitter certainty of all the shame, sorrow and pain I'd ever inflicted on self and others in the past or may inflict in the future were compressed within those wretched hours.

The aching of my troubled heart eventually subsided, and by the next day it became only a lingering memory, but one I can recall with crystal clarity. I've never given birth but have noted how women can describe in great detail their most painful birthing labors. I realized my labor pains had begun. I felt frightened and ignorant. I knew there'd be pain, yet it all seemed to blend seamlessly with a curious expectation.

Everything accelerated for me in Boulder during that Waking Down Weekend of September 2000. In my small group on the second day I was almost jumping out of my skin. It wasn't my turn to talk, but I said I really, really had something I needed to say–now! I could feel the *Shakti* weave a current of energy and light from the base of my spine to my heart, infusing the sacred tabernacle in my womb with an intensity I'd never before experienced. I placed my hands over my womb and said, "This is where my power and my love emanate from. Everything I am, say or do comes though here." I placed one hand over my vagina and one hand over my heart. Reaching out to the group from my womb, I asked again, "So what do I do with this energy? How do I live this power in the world? In my spiritual work?" No one had anything to say, but our group leader, a trusted friend, was nodding her head with a mischievous all-knowing, Cheshire Cat grin. I was reeling with the delight of this profound sexual mystery. To my dismay it seemed completely baffling to the other group participants and especially to me.

This incredible sexual energy continued to build, not with the immediacy of sexual tension that needs relieving, but with a powerful intensity that heightened the awareness of everything in and around me. On our drive home from Boulder I was seeing everything through new eyes. I saw it all as a reflection of the play of consciousness. Every blade of grass caressed by the wind almost sent me into orgasms. I marveled at the trees yearning to penetrate the sky, the softly rolling hills sighing to meet the clouds. Valley clefts swollen with rivers and streams seemed to flow in and though me. I was being sexually penetrated by life itself. The living and dying of everything sent me swooning. It was cosmic foreplay, the perpetual coitus of phenomenon, all contained in unspeakable sublime mystery.

I saw myself as a participant in a great cosmic dance and exclaimed to Ben, "It's so cool to be part of all this!" That proclamation stopped me mid-speech. With an unwavering certainty I altered my statement: "I'm not a participant in this dance, I AM the Dance!" That should e been a shocking revelation, but it was more of, "Of course. How could it be otherwise?" I am alive in and as all things. No separation from any event; I'm not even experiencing an event. I am the Event. I am Consciousness; the mystery of all that arises and dissolves is me. All the love songs and sonnets have been written for me. *I am the Beloved of my own Heart.*

I made a joking comparison that all my life I've been chugging along in a comfy old Rambler, and then suddenly I'm screaming down the highway behind the wheel of a hot, new Ferrari, and I can't even remember if I know how to drive! All my familiar sign posts were obliterated in that instant. Everything was new, but also everything was exactly how it's always been. I was adjusting to the paradox of awakened bodily existence. Ben delighted in my exuberance and said I was like a little kid on Christmas morning with lots of shiny new toys.

My awakening was a precious gift of the Goddess, and I strongly feel that others should hear the story of how this sacred trust continues to emerge. I intuited—knew in my body—that sacred sex is a doorway to the Divine. I was both bewildered and delighted to consider this path wherever it took me. I confided with a few trusted friends and soon found myself devouring books: *Passionate Enlightenment: Women in Tantric Buddhism*, *The Art of Tantra*, *Chinnamasta: The Awful Buddhist and Hindu Tantric Goddess*, *The Sacred Prostitute: Eternal Aspect of the Feminine*, *The New Sexual Healers: Women of the Light*, *Kali: The Feminine Force*, *The Cosmic Yoni* and many more. These texts opened a brilliant window into the journey of the sacred sensual that mirrored my emerging spiritual expression. Reading them was like coming home.

In retrospect I see how the event of my Second Birth awakening coincided with my evolving sexuality. First appears the wild child, exploring with delight and abandon, no shame, only wonder at this amazing energy, completely enamored with life and love of everything and everyone, including oneself. Next, the bewildering demands of adolescence—all the "I want it now!" with little consideration of others or consequences, just full speed ahead regardless of the outcome. Following, is the rebellious teen impatiently testing and throwing all caution to the wind, cocky and over-assured this phase will last forever, and if it doesn't there's always some Great Parent (God?) to blame. At last stands the mature, sexually responsible adult, reasonable and open to the counsel of others, gracefully owning this powerful Tantric sexual expression as the creative and transformative force of the Divine Feminine tempered and balanced with the steady heart of the Divine Masculine. This adventure of the heart has been seasoned by life-experience with the willingness to change and make amends with love, always with love.

As my journey deepened I saw the richness of these sensual Tantric mysteries begin to manifest as my own. I yearned to completely unleash the Goddess's wild unpredictability and the freedom to embrace this most esoteric and erotic aspect of the Divine Feminine in whatever form it appeared. I felt a strong inclination to take Tantric lovers and to explore, with my beloved Ben's unfathomable understanding, the path of the sacred sexual.

I began to live the heart of the Divine Feminine edged with the joys and sorrows of the Tantric Goddess. Sacred sexual healing is amazing and beautiful work of the heart. It's also daring and transforming work that empowers both partners with a seductive new freedom. I welcomed and encouraged my lovers in their explorations as truly animal-sexual beings. These are not shameful excesses; they are the creative and joyful expressions of the erotic body. I shared with these men my dearest heart-mystery: that I could literally feel my hands reaching from my heart and out through my vagina to embrace and draw them into me, into my sex so they might touch my heart and find a healing. I surrendered my body and heart to my lovers in the sexual sacrament of love and mutual worship. Such passion becomes true prayer when we behold the Divine light mirrored in our lover's eyes.

During this time I was a Waking Down mentor with hopes of eventually becoming a teacher. I hoped to help others understand that there exists an ancient history of Tantric sexual healing and joyful, loving non-monogamous partnerships. I realized this was a dangerous line I was walking. Even so, I dared hope that a brave few would want to hear something of what my heart longed to express: that indulging the body with sexual love can initiate a healing balm for the wounded heart, the broken spirit and the lost soul. However, I opened this dialogue once with a small group of specially invited Waking Down friends and confided how my life as a Tantric sexual healer had enriched mine and my lover's spiritual lives. This tender confession was met with misunderstandings ranging from angry disbelief to complete outrage. Their offended outbursts cut my heart like a knife.

Sexuality is a tenuously harnessed power; lusty, wildly unpredictable, a bit threatening and even dangerous; much like the Goddess herself. These sacred sexual mysteries are outside the comfort zone of society's demands for morality. They're also outside many traditional spiritual teachings. My chosen path might have been easier if I had a circle of friends with whom I could share my heart's deep longings and tender sorrows. My motives for wanting to live and speak openly as a Tantric sexual healer became suspect and viewed as insincere. In 2003 I made the painful and difficult decision to part with Waking Down.

All too soon, living this Tantric path of the sacred-sexual became more difficult than I'd originally reckoned. My lovers would realize their healings and begin to celebrate their role as sexually confident, sensual males. This generally meant it was time for them to leave me and find new heart-mates of their own. These leavings became more difficult and heartbreaking for me to endure. It left a sorrowful, yearning ache in my heart and in my womb. I began to realize that perhaps I wasn't strong enough to love so deeply, so completely, knowing that the time of loving this way, though glorious and wonderful, was temporary. While I pondered my role as a sexual healer and whether or not I could continue, I became focused on a journey of personal healing.

Since that time my spiritual/sexual Tantric expression has continued to unfold in unimaginably captivating ways and is a process that will forever astound me. This delightful expansiveness began to slowly shift over the years and eventually morphed into an altogether spectacular new initiation in the spring of 2006. I've always loved the earth and have long known her as a living, breathing, dynamic, *sentient* being. Within her great core beats the heart of a mother's love. This great heart hears every heartbeat and feels every footfall; every breath and sound is carried on the wind without bias. She experiences everything: our shared jubilations and our quiet pains, our pride of stewardship and our hateful wars. For all her blessed abundance she asks only our love in return. To me Medicine Mother Earth is the epitome of the Goddess incarnate. Fiercely protective and wildly unpredictable, she soothes us with lazy warm days then terrifies us with raging violent storms. This might seem frightening and destructive, but maybe it's just Kali teasing and flaunting in her wild Goddess dance.

One day that spring I was drenched in the lushness of the Olympic National Forest gazing in wonder at the myriad life bursting about me. It was an exquisite moment when I realized that not only did I love the earth but was deeply, passionately *in love*! In one juicy instant I recognized that my gift to the earth would be the role of husband. I delighted in this sacred partnership with the same relish that I shared with my Tantric lovers. Now the Earth was to be my lover and I hers. What a wonder! Upon my return home I prepared a solemn betrothal to the Earth as my promised consort. In the moss-carpeted, fern-clustered wonderland of my beloved woods, she and I consummated this sacred partnership in joyful ceremony. Tall trees gallantly witnessed our vows and plump huckleberries offered the wedding feast. I am in awe and revel in this marriage of our hearts.

Since that time I've done many healing ceremonies with and for the Earth. I've always felt a special kinship with the Earth's elemental tribes of the plant, animal and mineral kingdoms. Now, with a passionate sense of belonging, I see stories in the grains of sand and hear my star-sisters sing. I gossip with the trees and share secrets with the clouds. There are telltale weavings in the wind. The moon is my friend and I marvel as galaxies spin in their own miraculous sagas. I feel welcomed, held in love, and at home in the universe.

For me Tantra is the fluidity of the receptive Divine Feminine in sacred orgasmic embrace with the penetrating heart of the Divine Masculine. Eternally entwined, forever separate. It's *Siva* and *Shakti*, lingham and yoni; the harmonious and creative life force dance of the Heart-Divine.

"Somehow, Realization was supposed to be much grander, more expansive, more something."

Bill

Bill Trout was born in Philadelphia, Pennsylvania, and following graduation from high school, moved to Virginia to continue his education. He lived in Richmond since 1975, where he worked as the in-house art department for a Fortune 500 corporation. He met his wife, Mary, also a graphic designer, in 1982. Their son, Alex, was born on Christmas Eve in 1992—a circumstance that has elicited much sympathy and not a few jokes. Alex was home-schooled by his mother. Bill was a teacher of Waking Down in Mutuality loved by many students. He passed away in 2008. We honor his contribution to our work.

UNBELIEVABLY ORDINARY

At the time I first encountered the Waking Down work via the Web, I'd been on the Spiritual Path (what I usually call "the Dharma Circuit") for about twenty-five years.

Even as a child, I'd had something of a religious/spiritual bent. This was sustained in part by the fact that my prep school had chapel every morning, and I was in church on Sunday—making six days in a religious service of some sort out of every seven (at least during the school year) from the time I was nine years old until I graduated high school. I'd considered entering the ministry or at least attending divinity school in an effort to find out what it was that was really going on in an Ultimate sense. What did it mean to truly be a human being? Or, at the very least, what was the right and ethical way to live?

Like many people in the late 60s and early 70s, I got interested in the spirituality of the times thanks to the Beatles, the Maharishi, et al. While in college I began reading some books on these topics. Despite differing cultures, language, and emphases, there were many similarities between the ideas I read. How could this be? It seemed that there was some Universal Truth or Mind operating way beyond reality as most people defined it. Moreover, this Truth/Mind was apparently accessible directly. I didn't need a school, church, or someone in a pulpit to tell me about God. I could find out for myself in an immediate, experiential way. The search was on. I started reading in earnest and began doing hatha yoga postures, breathing exercises, and meditation.

By the time I graduated from college (the first time), I'd been initiated into TM, taken a home study course for an Advaitic school in California (in which I considered a career as a monastic), taken a course or two in Buddhist philosophy and modern Hinduism, done a huge amount of reading, and attended lectures by Ram Dass, among others. And I was doing my best to keep a regular spiritual practice together despite the fact that I did not have a teacher or real community.

I moved from Williamsburg, Virginia, to Richmond and practiced kundalini yoga and Nichiren Shoshu Buddhist liturgy with my two roommates and ate a lot of sprouts. But by 1985 my practice had largely evaporated. I still read a lot, but without much enthusiasm. When a friend got me interested in the Gurdjieff group here in Richmond, I jumped on it as though it were my last opportunity for salvation—which I guess is how I viewed it. There was a very remarkable woman teacher, a community, and a practice. What more could I ask?

I involved myself with the Gurdjieff Work for fifteen years. The teacher was a truly gifted and insightful woman. The community was an interesting group though I didn't get to know many of them really well. The Gurdjieff Work emphasizes (among other things) seeing one's automatic or habitual ways of being—what Gurdjieff referred to as a person's mechanical nature. In the course of doing the assigned tasks and exercises, I certainly experienced that in myself. In so doing I learned a great deal, but I never really came close to overcoming my mechanicality. In addition, my teacher had a strong interest in meditation, which I'm told is uncommon in teachers of the Gurdjieff Work. Our group practiced sitting meditation quite often, with some sessions as long as twelve hours. We also incorporated some Buddhist practices in mindfulness. I got a sense of what Consciousness was or what expanded awareness might be, but these were glimpses at best. I tended very strongly toward disorganization and a lack of focus in my life, so I think that having a regular, disciplined practice for which I would be held publicly accountable on a weekly basis was probably helpful.

But try as I might, I never really felt that I belonged. I always felt that I was the poster child for "No Efforts." I saw myself as a failure—deeply flawed and unavailable to the means for my own Awakening. I just didn't work hard enough, and if I wasn't making it, well whose fault was that? This dovetailed neatly into my own deep-seated feelings of worthlessness. I began to feel that I'd never achieve anything in this life, and wondered whether or not there was really anything to achieve period. Was there even a God? Maybe all this was, if not a gigantic con game, at least a monumental exercise in self-deception.

By 1996 the handwriting was on the wall. While I continued to attend the meetings, and very much enjoyed the discussions led by the teacher, I began to look elsewhere for a practice. Why I did this I don't know. All I can say is that when you've been "seeking" for all your so-called adult life, it's a hard habit to break (more of my mechanical nature, I suppose). I read U.G. Krishnamurti. I meditated using CD's that induced delta waves in my brain. I attended retreats at the Himalayan Institute in Honesdale, Pennsylvania. I went to the Zen Mountain Monastery in Mt. Tremper, New York, where I learned to play the shakuhachi (sort of). And I read some books by, and participated in an introductory course about, Adi Da. I felt Da's writing to be very powerful, though I found His idiosyncratic Use of Capitalization to BE Very Annoying. Other stuff left me cold. People would gush ecstatically about the transmission and powerful energy they saw pouring forth from his videotaped talks, but I never felt anything. I thought the whole Worship ME part of the practice was suspect. When I read about some of the abuses that this had engendered, I was convinced that Da wasn't for me.

In July of 2000 I was doing some web searching on Da's name. The search turned up Saniel Bonder. It wasn't a name I was familiar with, so I went to his site. It frankly wasn't that great a site at the time, and the marketing flavor of the home page and its text didn't sit well. But the rest of the material was fascinating. I'd never read anything like it, and I read it all. In addition, there was going to be a weekend workshop about two hours from my home at the beginning of August. I decided to take it.

It's difficult, with what seems like several lifetimes between then and now, to fully remember the person who attended that workshop. I was shy, insecure, terminally self-conscious, and if I'd been any more introverted I'd have been inside out. I was completely convinced that I was hopelessly substandard issue. I had no talents or abilities that someone three days dead couldn't display better and in greater abundance. I didn't trust a soul, having had the experience that any time I opened myself up to someone, they stuck around long enough to find a weapon they could use on me. I figured that if I kept quiet, out of the way, under the radar and in the background, then I had half a chance of being safe. I was very much in "check this out, wait and see mode." I probably didn't say five words the entire weekend.

It was an unusual weekend by any standard, but the most significant event for me came at the very end of the workshop during one of the meditations. I looked at Sandra Glickman, one of the workshop leaders, and she became the living embodiment of the Hindu goddess, Kali. I'm not talking about the traditional iconographic representation of fangs, blood, necklace of skulls, etc. But she was absolutely the most fearsome, terrifying thing I'd ever seen. I knew I was looking at the face of my own death, the person/being that would surely kill me. Remember that spiritual work at this point still rested largely on the "Kill Bill" theory. One's ego had to be relentlessly assaulted until it either crumbled and/or dropped away. Now, here was that death looking me in the face. I'd never had an experience like it. I decided that anything or anyone who could produce that was worth my attention. I went up to her before I left and asked if she would mind working with me. Sandra graciously agreed. We've been working together ever since, something for which I am profoundly grateful. I also found that she was not that frightening, really.

February 3, 2002, fell on a Sunday–eighteen months, two Human Sun Seminars, one Waking Down Weekend and a Transfiguration Retreat after that first workshop. I was not having a particularly good day. I had gotten up relatively early, fixed breakfast for my family, followed that up with the dishes (I think) and by around 11:30 or so was collecting clothes for doing the laundry. Feeling somewhat abused and taken for granted, I plopped down on the edge of my bed and looked disconsolately down the stairs (the bedroom is located in what was the attic of the house and it looks rather like a loft—the stairs are clearly visible).

All at once, it was as if the tide ran out and left me, like a shell or piece of driftwood, just sitting on the sand. I was just there, utterly and completely there with no pretense, no personality, nothing. I couldn't have provided a social persona if you had offered me real money. Gurdjieff had said that man was a plurality, with many different personalities trying for dominance at any one given time. I'd had no trouble with that; I'd had zillions of different voices in my head telling me what to do for almost as long as I could remember. Suddenly, there on the bed, everyone shut up. There was just one person there, me. I still had thoughts, but they were just part of the scenery, like a car radio out in the street that was turned up loud enough for me to faintly hear. They were no more or less important than anything else. And the whole experience of myself as there was so unbelievably ordinary. I was literally the dust on the floor. Aldous Huxley in *Doors of Perception* quotes William James (I think) as saying that God is the hedgerow at the bottom of the garden. I related totally. Things just were. I just was. There was no distinction to be made between the two. I remember thinking, "Well, at least I'll have something interesting to talk to Sandra about." And I picked myself up off of the bed and went to do the laundry.

There's a Zen expression, "Before enlightenment, chop wood, carry water. After enlightenment, chop wood, carry water." I went through the rest of my day just as I normally would. What else was I going to do? I had assumed that what had happened that morning would evaporate as so many other experiences had done. It didn't. Things had such presence. I was really there, not lost in my head or anywhere else for that matter. Everything had that simple, clear, direct quality that I did associate with Zen. As time passed, it was obvious that something had happened, but I didn't know what.

Sandra did.

The minute I got on the phone that Wednesday and began describing my experiences, she started saying that I should arrange for a Second Birth confirmation interview. I appreciated the vote of confidence, but I wasn't at all sure that I was ready for that. I was willing to concede that I had, as the saying went in yogic circles, "pierced the veil," but my thought was that the veil hadn't come down entirely. I'd had a glimpse of what "Reality" might look like, but I was by no means ready to admit to seeing/experiencing It always and everywhere. Somehow, Realization was supposed to be much grander, more expansive, more something. There was no really clear defining moment. No balloon popped. No angels sang. No eruption of liquid light inside my skull. Nothing. Just dust on the floor. How enlightened was that? But after three weeks of discussing this, I came to realize that my thoughts on the subject were just that. Thoughts. They still sounded like that car radio out on the street—background noise to my world, but of no particular interest. Maybe something was going on, but I was still very much stuck in my preconceived ideas about what the experience of "Enlightenment" was supposed to be. This despite the number of times that I'd read and heard that it's never what you expect.

What came next wasn't anything that I expected either. I arranged for the interview, which took place some six weeks after the actual event. I passed and began looking forward to the blissful life that all the books I'd read said would surely come. Most people who have their Second Birth do experience some sort of "honeymoon" period during which they feel a greater expansiveness, openness, feelings of bliss, centeredness, etc. I did not. This is not to say that anything was bad or unpleasant. There just were no big changes other than what I've described, which was enough. No great highs or lows. Just pretty much life as it had always been, only more so. But I did start to notice that I had a hard time remembering what I had been like before my Second Birth. It had started to seem as if I'd always been this way, which is to say "Awake." I wasn't even sure that anything had really happened. Then what we in this work call the "Wakedown Shakedown" hit.

Many people seem to believe that true spiritual growth and evolution are characterized by easeful, blissful, graceful transitions from one sunny upland to the next. I don't agree. From where I'm sitting, that's a New Age myth—charming but completely without merit. St. John of the Cross did not write *The Dark Night of the Soul* about his Bermuda vacation. I don't discount the possibility of easy transitions from time to time. But I would also maintain that, as often as not, there are serious dues that have to be paid. The Wakedown Shakedown is the installment plan for those dues.

The year following my awakening was one of the most difficult I've ever experienced, with the first two months being horrific beyond words. Saniel writes in *Waking Down* that the Wakedown Shakedown plunges you into your most primal insanity. In my case, this was not a metaphor. It was stark, living reality. I knew for certain why people who thought they might be going mad would kill themselves. It crossed my mind.

The experience is hard to describe. I was so raw, so exposed, so sensitive to every action and interaction that one might have thought my skin had been flayed off. The world seemed incredibly oppressive, as if every circumstance or event was designed solely to test the limits of my frail endurance. The level of anxiety was extreme. It felt as though I was hanging on by my last over-bitten fingernail, wanting to scream until I bled. All my long-denied feelings of worthlessness and self-loathing emerged full blown, and I was seemingly powerless to do anything about them as they laid waste to my carefully constructed internal landscape. I was constantly on the verge of mental and psychic overwhelm with no way to avoid what was happening or to shut it out. Life was an unending question, "Can I cope now?" "Can I cope now?" "What about now?"

Every waking second of every day.

Slowly, things began to improve. My bouts of overwhelm became less frequent. I had occasional moments where the sheer beauty and immensity of Creation was nearly enough to make me cry. Even so, I often felt pretty raw and exposed, and I still had a difficult time admitting that I had any kind of awakening or realization at all. About nine months after that morning in my bedroom, I had a realization of a different kind.

I was doing some reading in one of Saniel's books. He proposed that Consciousness is the baseline experience of a person in his/her awakened life. I stopped reading and considered this for a moment. I thought that it probably was, at least in my case. Then it hit me. That wasn't how I'd been operating. In all the time I'd been on the Dharma Circuit, my experience had been that I might have the occasional breakthrough or see something about Consciousness, myself, phenomena or have some semi-mystical experience. But such breakthroughs didn't last. They invariably faded and I returned to life as unending misery. At least that was how I saw my life anyway. The occasional revelations were small islands of joy in an infinitely large sea of depression and sorrow. I realized that I had formulated this notion early on and had continued to carry it around with me, so to speak, even after my Second Birth. This is what had made my claiming of my awakening so hard, if not impossible. I kept expecting it to disappear as all my other "breakthroughs" had. The moment I realized that this is what I'd been doing, the entire island/sea relationship reversed or flipped, as though it turned over somehow. It was as if I went from seeing small islands in a large sea to seeing a vast continent of land dotted by an occasional lake. I saw the truth of what I'd been doing, and in that moment Consciousness became the rule and the crap the exception. I sat on the sofa, smacking myself on the forehead, nearly in tears at what I fool I'd been in missing something so obvious.

Even so, old habits die hard. A year after my Awakening I was on retreat again. During the day off, I went to the beach with two other participants. While they strolled off to talk, I went by myself some ways down along the water's edge. It was very breezy and I stopped to watch the clouds, the surf, and the sand as everything rolled by. Suddenly, I could feel the whole scene as part of my body. I even had the sense that I could feel the curve of the earth as a physical, visceral reality. I was intimately, inseparably connected with all of the phenomena that I was witnessing, and at the same time I was a single discrete entity. It was the sort of experience that you read in books on mysticism about people having, but somehow think will never happen to you.

Despite this, the very next morning I found myself lying in bed, still questioning whether I had had any kind of Awakening or not. It seemed likely, for if I hadn't I'd fooled my teachers and a large number of other people. I'm just not that good an actor. "All right," I thought, "I'll test this a little." So I asked myself, "What is the relationship between Consciousness and phenomena?" My first thought, my knee-jerk response was, "What relationship?" There had to be two separate things in order for there to be a relationship between them , and there was no separation that I could see. For the first time, I really began to think of myself as really, actually, no-kidding Awake.

The final piece of this, although certainly not the end of the story by any means, came two months later at a retreat in Estes Park, Colorado. I was there as a mentor, assisting one of the teachers in small group work. My mornings were spent in a group meditation, which was being facilitated by my teacher, Sandra. During one of those sittings, I had the vision of myself as a Buddha sitting with perfect equanimity in meditation in some sort of carved niche or throne. I was the Buddha, the niche, and the vast open countryside that stretched out before me. It was a total change in perspective from my usual sense of myself, in or out of meditation. Usually, I have much the same sense that I had on the beach. I see the phenomenal world arising, existing, and then passing away. I am all of that and, paradoxically, a separate event—a part of the great Wheel as it turns. My experience that morning was one of a shift in perspective. That morning I was not only the Wheel, I was sitting at the hub, calmly watching all of Creation do its majestic, cosmic dance of birth, death, and rebirth around me. I came out of the meditation, looked at Sandra and said, "Sandra, I'm God." She looked kind of blank and said, "Yes," as though she were waiting for the punch line or the other shoe to drop. But there wasn't one. It was just that. Nearly thirty years of seeking and the piece I'd always wanted had finally dropped into place.

I started out all those years (lifetimes?) ago asking myself what was the best way to live, what it meant to be fully human. This work provides the best answer to that question that I have found to date. So now I have, after my "Second Birth," a "Second Life." The trick is going to be figuring out how best to live that life. I have the strong sense that I'm not going to be satisfied with myself or the circumstances surrounding my life as they have been. Changes are in the air and the status quo just isn't going to make it any more. But what those changes are or are likely to be I can't yet say. Getting to my "Second Life" was an adventure. Living it promises to be the really interesting part.

"All of a sudden, it felt sacred, all if it, from the very beginning of my life, every piece a gift to help me land here."

Shellee

Shellee Rae (01-04-60) relocated from the Boston area in December 2006 to live in Ashland, Oregon. A Holistic Practitioner since 1999, she shares her open, loving heart with clients through Reiki, massage, and nutritional and spiritual guidance. Shellee has been on the path of self-realization since 1986 and had her Second Birth in August of 2008. She has recently written a book about her life journey: Suffering—A Path of Awakening: Dissolving the Pain of Incest, Abuse, Addiction and Depression. *Email:* shelleerae@fastmail.fm. *Website:* www.shelleerae.com.

ARE WE THERE YET?

It's been a long ride home. I think it's important to give you just a little background on my raucous journey before I go into the story of my transformation. Life has not been easy; however, my recent shift has made this long and difficult passage all worth waiting for.

As a young girl, the world was overwhelming to me, and it didn't make any sense at all. I couldn't understand the tug in my heart for something more. I used to hold my breath until I fainted–it was such a great relief to slip out of this reality even if it was only temporary. That urge to escape became much greater by the time I was nine years old when my father began sexually abusing me and beating me. It did not take long for me to find drugs and alcohol to help numb the devastating suffering I endured every day for the five years that he abused me. As a little girl, I had no idea that the torment and abuse was becoming a deep wound that would not only become a hindrance in my adult life and relationships, but would also develop into an underlying reason to torture myself.

Fast forward twenty-eight years. I drank and used drugs to the doors of death, which was the ultimate convincer that I might have a problem. I was thirty-seven years old when I awoke on the fourth day in the hospital with this realization. I had attempted suicide in a drug and alcohol blackout. I was dying (not fast enough as far as I was concerned), and now hopeless, helpless and spiritually bankrupt, I was finally willing to try something different. Once released from the hospital, I began attending Alcoholics Anonymous meetings every day and managed to get clean and sober with the help of many people.

Once sobriety was well established, the calling of the heart began to stir again. For ten full years in my sober life, I searched and explored the meaning of existence and different paths of awakening. I was ready to give up, to stop all my practices, perhaps have a book-burning party, and maybe use all the CD's and DVD's as frisbees. Enter Waking Down.

As The World Turns

I've been told many times to be careful what I ask for–I just might get it. I had been calling for divine intervention, in whatever way it has, to come assist me in shifting to a higher perspective, an awakening for life. I have had many mini-awakenings in the past, but nothing ever sustainable. I would be in an altered state for minutes, hours or days, but it would not stick and I always returned to the status quo–me. Ugh.

Early in 2007, still chasing that illusive carrot of enlightenment, I ventured into a meeting of another "spiritual group" that met twice a month. However, I had all kinds of judgments about the way the meeting was run and about the teacher who was on speaker phone; it wasn't professional enough, or organized enough, etc., so I didn't think it was for me. It was their first meeting in the area and the last one that I attended for a while. Some months later something began whispering to my heart, and I had to go again to see what the calling was about. It was an entirely different event for me; I guess I was ready. There was a visiting teacher facilitating, and his words made sense to me. Rather than waking up, he was speaking of "waking down in mutuality." He was saying that he was aware of Consciousness in his body while at the same time experiencing an expanded state of Awareness. I hung on his every word as I had not heard any teacher or path speak of including the body in their awakening–not in this way, at least.

I was touched that evening by the honesty of the people who shared, and I was moved to tears identifying with the pain that was expressed, the longing for something more, something else; for me it was a silent screaming heart. I did not speak that night, but they certainly had my attention and I went back to the next meeting two weeks later. There was another teacher in attendance, and after she spoke, she looked right into my soul (I felt) and to the best of my recollection said, "And what about you? Do you have something you would like to say?" Crack! That was the sound my heart made. Something cracked and it all came pouring out. I don't recall what all I said, but I was crying and drooling and blowing bubbles, and I did not care–someone just kept handing me tissues.

The most beautiful part of the experience was the feeling of being held while I unraveled, not in a physical sense but energetically, so to speak. There was a feeling of such presence and attentiveness that it was palpable. As I finished the story of my "aching and longing heart," the people there began to give feedback, and I was again moved to my core with their words of support, compassion, identification and honoring. I remember thinking, "Wow, you mean you understand! And it's really okay to feel all these things?" There was a great sense of relief that ran through my body.

For my whole life I had great difficulty being here. As I've already mentioned, the world did not make any sense at all, and I could not seem to find my purpose or place on this planet. I was certain that something had gone terribly wrong somewhere, and I just landed on the wrong planet–lost on this desert island, completely misunderstood by the world and with such a longing to be home, an ache in my heart that couldn't be satiated with anything.

Things began to really stir once I began getting involved with Waking Down in Mutuality. At times, that longing inside turned into cyclones of energy that made me feel as if I would spontaneously combust if I did not find a release valve. Looking around at my life, it all seemed so meaningless, and I really wished that I could find a way to the exit. That "back door" was like the contingency plan; I always took a bit of comfort in knowing that if life got any worse (this longing, desperation, emptiness), suicide was always an option.

At one point, someone handed me "*Waking Down: Beyond Hypermasculine Dharmas*" by Saniel Bonder. I flinched and wanted to drop it and run. As the knot in my belly got tighter, something from within made me reach out and let it land in my hand. Even though I was breaking a promise to myself (no more books, paths, teachers or gurus!), I dove in and began reading that book and soon many others, attending workshops and going to all the meetings. In January of 2008, my partner and I even began hosting the meetings in our home because our prior host moved to California.

I read and re-read things. They spoke to my heart, and I knew on a deep level that I was finally onto something, something Big. From one of the books I was reading, *White Hot Yoga of the Heart*, also by Saniel, I turned the words around a bit to make them into a prayer or an invocation, stating: "I pray for, intend, even insist upon whatever is necessary for my realization of Being to come to fruition as directly and rapidly as possible." Again, I will warn here to be careful what you ask for. Words this powerful, spoken from the heart, can really turn up the volume on life! And it did! Very soon after that my whole world began to change.

Falling In—The Journey Home

The first big occurrence: I had a kundalini experience in April. With that came such a feeling of purification, lightness. So much burned off. It was incredibly intense and not something that I would recommend to anyone given a choice! It was right around that time that my partner of four and a half years started backing away from our relationship. He began house-sitting (we had been having some relationship issues), and he was gone for weeks at a time. I kept falling deeper and deeper into every feeling, every experience, and I slowly came to realize that something very profound had shifted. I was no longer in the same relation to pain as I had been for so many years.

My eighteen-year-old cat, Tigger, passed on June 30th, my partner ended our relationship July 2nd, and that evening I was bit on my right leg by a brown recluse spider, which caused great physical agony and fear as I watched the skin continue to deteriorate as if acid had been poured on it. It took a couple of months to heal and has left quite a scar as a reminder of my initiation.

As I began to experience the losses, the first thing that happened was the heartache, great sorrow, deep misery that felt like it might be endless. Mentally I kept making my list over and over of all the things that I had to feel pain-filled about, which had been my modus operandi for most of my life. What was different with this grief was that I was not fighting any of it. I was just falling right down into the middle of it, feeling it deeply, fully, expressing and venting it by crying, primal screaming, or punching pillows: whatever was needed in the moment to allow the feelings to fly freely. I kept "greenlighting" everything, allowing and welcoming it all, even my judgments about not being able to accept whatever in a particular moment. I was speaking openly, passionately and vulnerably to my newfound waking-down-family about my feelings. At times, the bottom of the emotion would seem to drop out, and I would either land in a pool of peace or bliss. I remember thinking "Wow, you mean pain can be blissful or peaceful too?" Not resisting anything, everything began to change.

The double-whammy of losing Tigger (and not having him to console me for the loss of my partner, our house, the recently built cottage for my clients and my garden) and also of losing my partner (and not having him to console me for the loss of Tigger) created a volcano inside of me that felt like it imploded. Once the implosion subsided, I landed right smack-dab in the middle of me: someplace I'd never been before: home…complete…nothing needed. All of a sudden, it felt sacred, all of it, from the very beginning of my life, every piece a gift to help me land here. Here. As I cried, now from a love that was alive in me, I wanted to thank my partner and Tigger for the gift they gave me. This heart that I thought was shattered and taking on one more battle-scar was washed clean and filled with amazing gratitude for life and all its dips and curves. Love like no other.

Another thing that I noticed as I was spinning from the one-two punch of loss was that there were no thoughts of suicide. I kept looking over my shoulder wondering, "Hey, where's my back door?" No back-up plan at all. Just here. What an incredible sense of freedom living in this Heart space! How did I miss this all these years? So close, so far, so beautiful, so very sacred.

Before the grief turmoil began, I had planned a trip to New York for a six-week Shamanic/Herbal Apprenticeship and then to move on to the Boston area for two weeks of work and a family visit. I ended up staying only one week in New York before moving on to Boston. I recall a sense of wondering why I was there, as the seeker that had been so much a part of my being seemed to have vanished. During the apprenticeship, I had many lessons in such a short period of time, mostly to listen to the inner guidance, always so wise. The trip so soon after my awakening was like the grounding of my transformation or cementing Being into this human form.

Here are some of the details of my experience, my reactions to them and how I felt supported by the universe through the whole process. To begin with, nothing looked at all like what was advertised on the website for the apprenticeship. The workload was unfathomable. My apprentice partner and I would start at nine a.m. and not finish until some time between eleven p.m. and midnight–we got a thirty minute break around five p.m. on one day. There were usually five or six apprentices doing the work that the two of us were doing.

As it turns out, the weed in the woman's name probably has more to do with the amount of pot she smokes rather than parsley, sage, rosemary or thyme, which is something else that I would have chosen to not be around had I known.

She also failed to mention, on her website and during the phone intake that she has Asperger's Syndrome, and if it were not for my young apprentice partner Liz, who was scared to death of our new "teacher," I would have left on the first day. Bizarre is an understatement of what we were living there. Within our first couple of nights, we removed two wolf spiders almost the size of my hand from our mold, dirt, web and bug infested living quarters, and on our first night we were visited by a snake about two and a half feet long. Liz almost stepped on it as she was making her way to the bathroom and screamed. I tried to catch it, but it was too fast and disappeared into the wall…holes and cracks everywhere.

Our first day we only got breakfast because we went up to the house and mentioned that we did not have any food; we were given a box of stale crackers, eggs, moldy bread and goat yogurt and milk–no lunch that day. The days following, we only got lunch to take with us during our goat watch because I demanded it; goat cheese, more stale crackers and some very old olives.

All the goat dairy was causing a real mucus problem with me–I had not had any dairy in many years, and I was forced to eat a "no-thank-you-size" portion of fish one night. I'm a vegan. Interestingly, though, there was such a pervasive calmness present and alive within me while all of this was taking place that nothing seemed to rattle me. I would lay down at night and snuggle deeply into my sleeping bag (after checking for spiders and snakes) with every ounce of my being aching of exhaustion, and I could not find a place inside me that felt upset, bad or sad about any of it. As a matter of fact, there was a sense of resting and being held in the arms of a loving and nourishing universe. Even after only a few hours of sleep, I would get up in the morning to begin another seemingly insane day and have a smile in my heart and a feeling of exhilaration for being graced with another day of life.

Wandering in the woods with the goats (we watched eight of them for five to six hours a day on fifty unfenced wooded acres), a wave came over me that said, "You are here for Liz to get grounded/started so she will not be alone for her first week. Let go of the money and move on. It will all be okay." Then a feeling of complete peace came over me. I checked with my inner guidance that night before bed and got that it was time to leave. Another thing I had noticed in the woods was the opportunity to work with Liz and give her some exercises to connect with her inner power, inner guidance, her breath and heart. It was beautiful to see her taking it in and to see her grasping the techniques so quickly.

The next confirmation from the universe was when I called the person who was going to be housing me while I worked in the Boston area to see if I could come five weeks earlier. I got him on the phone, and he said, "Where do you think I am right now?" He was pulling into Saugerties, New York, (which is where I was) for some work that weekend with a dance company and was heading back the next day. His home is almost four hours from where I was staying in New York, and he just happened to be in the neighborhood? That was definitely a thumbs-up from the universe for making the right decision at the perfect moment. All guidance is there when I listen.

One more interesting thing I noticed about my new persona: Our teacher could not get in. I don't know if she was trying to scare me, to break me, or to shake me, but none of it touched me. I am not sure if it was her Shamanic teaching or symptoms of the Asperger's Syndrome that underlay her actions, but there was no fear or anxiety while I stood there with her face in my face screaming like a banshee and spit flying everywhere. I felt love as I looked in her eyes, love like when I look at the trees and other things in nature, and I am pretty certain that it was showing up as a smile on my face. I left the next day.

Arriving in the Boston area, I spent five weeks visiting with family and working with clients and students from the practice that I had left behind when I moved. Everything was so different for me. Visiting with my children and siblings was such a joy. Where previously my mind would be analyzing and judging how well they were all doing, having expectations and disappointments, this visit was experienced from an open heart and a quiet mind. I just felt love–truly unconditional–and from that place came total acceptance with no effort, a complete resting in the arms of life and "what is."

Many clients and students asked me during that visit what had happened to me, and still others commented on the peace that was exuding from my being and the light emanating from deep within my eyes. I didn't know how to answer or how to explain to them that it was the smallest of movements that took place, a tiny shift that altered my world. Words...

The Fall

I once saw a leaf
Its graceful flight into the unknown
Flying free from its home

Not seeking to the future
Nor clinging to the past
Dancing in the moment

I watched its wild ride on the cool wind
Caressed by the warmth of the sun
Flitting by and touching the evergreen

Swirling in the scent of a rose
Before its soft landing in a stream
Joining others

In the many turns
Of the labyrinth's current
On a journey to a new world

And I understood letting go.

Is my life perfect today? The answer from the divine perspective would be, yes; however, from the world perspective, the answer is an unequivocal, no. I continue to have challenges and emotions. I still see pieces of the ego surface from time to time. The difference today is that I accept it all as perfect, even when it doesn't feel good. There is freedom from identification with my past, a relinquishment of sorts. It's beautiful to be conscious of everything as it appears and allow it to be there—to actually take it right into my heart, but not have it own me in any way. Love seems to dissolve or transform all the pieces that no longer fit who I am.

It is amazing to be so alive in this body. What a gift. Today I can't imagine missing one moment of this sweet gift of life...so precious. Awareness has expanded so much at times that the local self seems like such a funny trick that I am playing on myself. An example: I went to Mount Shasta to pick up some class supplies, and on my drive there, my awareness expanded. Gradually I became aware that I Am so Big. I am all of it, and nothing is moving separately from the whole. It seemed so funny to have all my attention on this "little me" driving in this little vehicle, moving around in myself and not really going anywhere at all. I felt like I should have a sign displayed on my vehicle: "*Caution. Driver under the influence of God and may be in an altered state.*" It would be like "little me" walking around all my life funneling all of my attention or awareness totally on just my navel and thinking that's all I am...this navel moving around all by itself, collecting a little lint from time to time, feeling a little sun, nothing more than this–me the navel–and then Someone removes the blinders and the navel becomes aware of this incredible and Huge Body, who's been carrying me–the navel–all along. Silly example, I know, but it seemed to paint the picture a bit more clearly in my head.

I've had other expanded states and blissful experiences since the awakening too. Recently, as I was out walking, all of a sudden, whoosh, I entered into stillness. I had to slow my walking and breathing down because both were making too much noise in this amazing state. I continued to float down the hill where I encountered three deer, a mother and her young ones. As we all stopped and our eyes met, instantly my heart became an inferno. The tears streamed down my cheeks, and the love I felt could have consumed me whole and left behind just a pile of ashes as far as I was concerned. I was frozen in place with them for what felt like eternity but must have only been minutes.

My older brother in the VA home came to mind. Years ago as I was relaying a story to him about seeing some deer on a trail while I was out jogging, he said, "If you could sit in their hearts, you would know something." That's what it felt like–although I'm not sure if I was sitting in their hearts or if they were sitting in mine. We were all in the One Heart.

There is a difference today with the way I feel after the spiritual experiences pass. Previously, I would search for more, long to be there again, examine my surroundings and make mental notes so I could recreate it. In some cases, depression would set in for days or weeks. Today, I marvel at them, fully accept their comings and goings and no longer need to have more close-encounters to be full.

Such staggering love, it keeps bubbling up and spilling over, sometimes almost into giggles, as it's too big to contain. My heart just wants to hug everyone, my mouth just wants to say I love you, and instead I stand there with a giddy grin on my face.

One last point: Most of us in this very confused country (world) have been wired to think that just because we feel deep love, intense love, breathtaking love, that it means we are "in love" and the next natural move would be sexual intimacy. While there is nothing wrong with sexual intimacy (it can be such an incredibly beautiful experience that enlivens the soul!), once we find that love resides in us, as us, we will never need someone else to provide it for us. There is no void to fill, and all aspects of relationships become so much richer. You are love. Truly, that's all there is. When we can get to the other side of our judgments about what life is and the story of what happened to me, we land in love.

Thank you, God, for life experiences, for my teachers and the whole divine plan–I bow to You with such gratitude and love. Words cannot express what I feel–unbound comes to mind, free. This is love that is unbound by concepts, beliefs, wishes–no limits. Everything in life feels like a YES. Each thing is so new, like the first time I've ever really experienced it. I've been here, but never Here. It's hard to tell where I end and the other begins.

This infinite love is what we are up to here. It is what we came to experience: love for all beings. What is really amazing is when we find it in the self, the heart shatters into a dimension that is unfathomable by the mind, and love without limits is experienced. Like a baby experiencing the world for the first time, when here, truly here, completely and fully here, life can be breath-taking.

God's Wings

Kayaking at Field pond, state forest
Sweet love filled the air
Filled my heart
And carried me about
As I made the motions of paddling
God's wings carried me to such beautiful expressions of Life.

The geese came together, gathering, honking
One by one, rounding up the others with their calls
My heart was touched when I discovered they were not just saying hello
But protecting the nest
All of them
Together as One.

Drifting in love, moving in grace
The turtle saw us
The camera

And she posed with assurance
And posed, she let us get so close
Then one last pose before her dive amongst the bursting water lilies.

All so magnificent, so splendid
But the great blue heron stole the show as she teased
Dipped and hid, and then took flight again and again
With my heart on her wings
She carried me to You
And through You God, to me…Beloved.

God, Life is beautiful.

"Since this awakening, I have felt a transforming fire rising that is burning away so much of the person I have been all of my life."

Steve

Steve Boggs was born and raised in suburban Los Angeles, but fell in love with Northern California while attending the University of California at Santa Cruz. His affiliation with the Transcendental Meditation movement led to years of world travel teaching TM, attending advanced courses and working at TM retreat facilities. For the last 25 years he has lived in Fairfield, Iowa, where he operates an electrical contracting firm along with his wife, Winifred, who is also an artist and poet. His participation in Waking Down in Mutuality has allowed in a relatively short time the completion of a quest that occupied his entire adult life.

THE SPILLING OF THE RUBIES

"You know, Steve, all those great spiritual ideals we have held for years? Those are actually real things, and they can be experienced by ordinary people like you and me." These words were spoken to me by my friend Max in 2002 and, needless to say, they got my attention. His voice was so matter of fact and confident, I had to find out more. When he told me this normally takes two or three years, I thought to myself, "I can do a couple years standing on my head. That's nothing." Decades of spiritual quest trailed behind me, and I had to find out about this Waking Down in Mutuality because, although it sounded too good to be true, it came from someone I knew well and was spoken with sincerity.

One thing that stands out from my first meeting with Saniel and Linda is that Saniel asked everyone in the room to "check in" by saying something about themselves and why they were in attendance. I had been expecting to sit and listen, not speak before everyone, and so felt pretty nervous and immediately started casting about for what I was going to say. Well, I came up with something I felt was sufficiently respectable, but when it came to be my turn, I became so overwrought and tearful, I could only blubber something about being tired of swinging back and forth between hope and resignation. It was quite a surprise to find myself emotionally aflame, but Linda just looked at my embarrassment and helpless plight with such tenderness and compassion, I felt reassured. Little did I know at the time, but this was just the beginning.

A month later two women came to Fairfield to lead what was, to my mind, a rather grandiosely named workshop called "The Human Sun Seminar." They were Sandra Glickman and CC Leigh, and both were quite impressive: queenly and self-possessed and yet just themselves. CC in particular I remember as broadcasting a call to love that was palpable around her. The seminar contained a lot of information, mostly around using new language for spiritual topics. In one exercise, I had a particularly clear experience of myself as Consciousness which was distinct from anything I had experienced before despite years of meditation practice.

At home, after the weekend seminar was over, I became so restless that I could hardly sit. I couldn't read a book, I couldn't watch TV, I was pacing like an animal in a cage. I called my friend Max to see if he could shed any light on what was happening to me. He was on the road, but his wife said to me, "This probably isn't going to sound like good advice to you, but I think you should just feel it as much as you can. Be as restless as possible." I did the best I could with that strange and unsettling advice. I didn't sleep very well that night, and the next morning, to my horror, I couldn't stop crying. After some real struggle, I got myself together and went to work. As it happened, that day I was replacing some fluorescent bulbs and ballasts in the produce coolers of a local whole foods store, and in the first twenty minutes of work, three people approached me and asked, "Steve, are you okay?" I thought I was putting a good face on my distress but was clearly failing miserably. The seminar presenters never said anything about stuff like this happening, so I decided I needed to talk to someone before they left town. I was squeezed into Sandra Glickman's morning appointment schedule just before she left for the airport.

As I sat in front of her in a small upstairs bedroom, she said, "Okay, just look at me and tell me about what's happening."

"I'm not given to sobbing and blubbering, but this morning I wasn't myself. I couldn't handle that many tears with a sponge in each hand."

She gently interrupted saying, "Keep talking but just look at me." After about fifteen minutes of what I later realized was an extended gazing session, I felt remarkably steady and at ease.

The following three weeks were characterized by an effusive and seemingly endless happiness, freedom, delight in each moment, and a freshness and desire to engage others. I found that when I spoke, I felt I was hearing the words at the same time as whomever I was speaking with rather than having them pass through my mind on the way to my mouth. To be so continuously content and exuberant for weeks was a surprise, but in the midst of it, somehow, it felt natural.

A few months later, I found that I had stumbled into some kind of orchard of love where I wandered for a long time. This wandering left me so enamored of the bits and pieces of daily living that each moment seemed to present itself anew: fresh, close and dear and, in some way, pregnant with meaning. I felt a kinship and affinity with everything that I experienced. I found myself tearing up two or three times a day with the poignancy of life. The best way I can describe this feeling is to say it's like a parent's love for a child when the extended family is gathered for the child's birthday. The cake is brought out aglow with candles, and when the singing stops, the child looks up and says, "Mommy, why are you crying?" His mother replies, "It's okay, honey. I'm crying because I'm so happy."

At times this feeling became towering and left me as if assaulted, like I'd been rag dolled across the ocean floor by a huge wave that crashed over me. Most times, however, it consisted of little tremors that came unexpectedly at odd moments during the day reminding me of how this life and this world are so achingly beautiful. I didn't know how or why this was happening to me or how I would feel when it was gone, but I did know I had never been so fervently alive.

At one point, I came across a painting of Saint Augustine by the medieval artist Father Lippo Lippi which spoke directly to me about this passage. It depicted Augustine sitting in his cell, pen and paper in hand, writing about a vision he was in the midst of where the Trinity appeared before him and filled him with its divinity. The part of the picture that arrested me was the three large arrows sticking out of his heart. It so clearly captured this piercing quality of love that kept penetrating me. This experience was further clarified for me by my primary teacher during this time who, at an open sitting where I was tearfully describing what was happening to me, responded by saying, "Yes, the Sufis call this broken-hearted hemorrhaging of love 'the spilling of the rubies'."

On the subject of awakening, for months I had been adamantly and maybe even a little bit defiantly insisting to my teachers, CC and Sandra, that I was not going to intuit, assume, conclude or deduce this awakening. It simply had to be clear, stark and unmistakable. CC would typically respond, "Well, good luck with that." An uninspiring response which somehow didn't even make a dent in my resolve. This was simply not going to be ambiguous.

I had been working with Sandra on the phone for seven months, and during the time she was out of the country for six weeks, I began to feel an indefinable angst that was quietly pervading all my days. It didn't really interfere with my daily life, but it was distinctly uncomfortable. I felt off my game, unbalanced, restless. I began talking on the phone with CC with whom I had always felt a tender connection, but the anxiety continued.

At the end of one call she said, "Steve, I want you to consider a question as homework."

I said, "Okay. What is it?"

She said, "What if your life as it is right now is all you could ever hope for in terms of spiritual realization? If that were true, would it be enough?"

"Hell, no!" I protested.

"Steve, it's homework. Just ponder it for two weeks and call me back then."

When I called her back, I reported that the enoughness or not enoughness of my life as it was right then seemed to vary quite a bit. Sometimes "yes," sometimes "no."

As I was talking, she interrupted with the question, "Steve, where are you located?"

I felt myself feeling uncharacteristically nervous and said, "What do you mean? I'm talking to you on the phone here in my office."

So she fired off another question, "What is your understanding of Consciousness?"

Now the panic was rising in me, and I felt like someone on a submarine when fire has broken out and red lights are flashing and warning klaxons are blaring as I fumbled through some non-answer about sentience. As she asked a third question, there was a feeling of her moving a chess piece into place, and this was going to be checkmate. The terror moving in me peaked, and I felt like someone running down a hall screaming, not knowing which door led outside to safety. Whatever it was that was unsafe, it was going to be the end of me. The person that I had been throughout my life was facing annihilation in that moment.

Then, in an instant, it all stopped, and there was this peace I had never felt before despite a lifetime of "good experiences" in spiritual practice. I felt as if I were in outer space with no up or down or means of orientation even though I knew I was lying on a bed in my office. There was only silence, emptiness, endlessness which had never been touched by anything and, wonder of wonders, I was that!

Sensing something significant had happened, CC waited, saying nothing as I lay stupefied by this recognition. Although it sounds pretty dramatic, it was a very quiet moment actually but, at the same time, completely sufficient. It needed nothing and was utterly unmoved. I was unmoved. I, as That, had never moved. These words don't really convey the reality of this because they sound both grandiose and contradictory, but it was neither. It felt natural and ordinary, and yet it was so mind boggling that I never could have conceived of it before. I tried to say what was happening but couldn't begin to express it satisfactorily.

She said, "Yes, you can't really say this, but you know it in the depths of your being." Since that moment, I have never been the same, although in many ways I am unchanged. I am wondrous, majestic and changeless and, strangely, I am also constricted, ambivalent and afraid. While I am all these qualities, I am undivided and simultaneous.

My expectations for this awakening were both unmet and exceeded. I had compiled a long list of qualities in response to a question asked of me by a mentor which I felt to be necessary for me to consider that I had awakened. As it turned out, none of these qualities had anything to do with this awakening because it is not a matter of thought, emotion or perception. My identity is no longer the product of my thoughts or my feelings, but of my Self. Like many people, I had grand ideas about how perfect life would be when I knew my infinite nature. However, it is clear now that measuring sticks based on any part of my life that changes cannot begin to define this unnameable freedom. When my spiritual seeker friends would ask if I witness sleep, I would say, "Yes, but not in the way I thought I would, not as something distinct but in the same way I witness everything." The constrained parts of myself haven't become free, but what was always free is now authentically alive. I am that One without a second. I have no history because I never began. I am ceaselessly creative and eternally identical. I am motionless, silent and whole. Changeless and impervious, I move and become. I am that self-interacting dynamics of Consciousness which constitutes all that is. A quantum physicist, in describing this movement within the unified field, might speak of spontaneous, sequential, dynamical symmetry breaking. The universe doesn't emerge from the unified field, it is the unified field.

Moving and changing, it is eternally the same, and I am that.

It might seem a bit counter intuitive, but this realization didn't blow out of the water all of the attractions, repulsions, attachments, hopes and regrets of my life. Indeed, I am more impassioned, more ardent, more fervent than I was previously. I care more, I feel more. I rise and fall on a grander scale. I am easily moved to tears, I am angered by social injustice, I commune with the natural world, I inflate in the presence of joy, I feel deeply the suffering of others. When I leave the house for work in the morning, I am momentarily intoxicated by her smell as I nuzzle my wife's neck. I turn to reach for the back door and I feel the silk turtle neck I'm wearing caress my arm. I step down and feel my cushioned thermal socks settle into my new Christmas boots. The bracing air tightens my skin and waters my eyes. As I open my truck door, a crow calls in the distance. I am alive to the world in a way that is continually new.

My acquaintances who have had awakenings through a less tantric and more advaitic lineage speak of the experience of their life as an open, spacious attention without past or future leanings: no fulfillments or regrets, no hopes or dreads. They say it's just a steady presence in the midst of the motion of their lives, a kind of nothingness that implies there's nobody home in the house of their individuality. To me, there is definitely someone home, and that someone is more intensely engaged in his existence than ever, but he is also that with which he is engaging and the process of engagement as well.

Since this awakening, I have felt a transforming fire rising that is burning away so much of the person I have been all my life. It's as if all the habits, assumptions, prejudices, intuitions, beliefs and understandings have to be reconfigured in the face of this new reality that so confounds the previous presumptions. Throughout my life, I have tended to be an accommodating, acquiescent kind of character. Even though I was looking pretty good and being well-liked, this strategy was costing me a lot in terms of personal integrity. It was also based on fear of conflict. To avoid conflict, I was prepared to and did give up a lot of my own desires, interests, needs without even being particularly aware of it. By seeing everything from everyone else's perspective, I was saving myself from ever having to stand for anything. To use an analogy offered to me by a friend, it's like I have abandoned parts of my own house, and in my absence others have taken up residence on my deck and in my backyard. It has taken time, but I have come to see the need to reclaim what is mine and have found that the property line is a better place for a boundary between myself and others than the doorstep.

I was attending a six-session workshop on myth and archetypes to which we would each bring an object to place on the altar every week and say how it spoke to something deep in us or inexplicably moved us. As the weeks went by, others would bring a different object each week, but somehow the image of a sword was haunting my days and nights. I didn't have a sword, so every week I brought the Cub Scout knife I still carried in my tool box after all these years. I went up and put my little knife on the altar as a symbol of the sword I was sensing. After four weeks, it was clear that the disturbing forcefulness that the sword image represented wasn't going away, so I went online and bought an inexpensive sword which I brought to the last session. When I pulled it out and spoke as the object I was bringing, I heard myself say, "I am that which will cut to pieces the life you have created to serve the life that is waiting for you." Since that time, a resolute quality has been growing in me that balances the placating habits of my previous life. This new energy is still a work in progress, but I am confident that, in time, the pendulum of timidity and aggression will find its steady mid-point.

There is so much more to say about this astoundingly potent process. There could be whole paragraphs on how deeply music now moves me or on inhibition versus exhibition and introversion versus extroversion, particularly with respect to parties and dancing, or on experiences of communion with the natural world or on tears and their place in the life of a man or on the sacredness of the ordinary in life. This path can be profoundly challenging and indescribably fulfilling. If it seems to be calling you, may you find for yourself the realization of your heart's desire to know and live the changeless reality that you are.

"It is such a relief to finally embrace and enjoy being fully human,
and such an amazing mystery that, in finally doing so,
the endless depth of my Being is increasingly alive in my life.."

Deviki

Deviki Shioshita lives in Boulder, Colorado, with her two children, Ana, age fourteen, and Tanner, age eight. She works as a registered nurse for an investigational drug research center, and loves to hike and camp in the beautiful Colorado mountains whenever her busy life allows it.

LETTERS TO BELOVED FRIENDS

September 12, 2002

Dear CC,

I just had an experience driving home from taking my son to school about a half hour ago, and I feel drawn to write to you about it, maybe just to write it, to clarify it in some way or maybe because I see the possibility of my mind minimizing or dismissing it and just going on with my life, and it seems important not to do that. On the other hand, I'm not sure that I can put it into words in any adequate way, so we'll see... Anyway, I was driving and listening to some music and the snow on the trees was quite beautiful. I was thinking about this paradox of being limited humanness and at the same time absolute Limitlessness. I was thinking about the relationship between the seeming two, about how it feels as though the limited one longs for and reaches for the Beloved, and amazingly, seemingly impossibly, how the Beloved longs for and reaches for the limited one, and how at the place where the two meet, they Are each other. Saying that they disappear into each other or are transformed into each other isn't quite right. Perhaps to say that they are consumed in each other and that they consume each other so that there is nothing left except this amazingly alive "Is-ness" is close to saying it, yet still inadequate. So, I was thinking about this, not in quite as much detail as I just wrote and I looked up and saw the snow-covered trees and my awareness went to the Beingness present everywhere and in everything around me. There was a relaxing into the seeing and experience of this. Then, suddenly, I was nothing but this huge Awareness, looking at Awareness, all the same, nothing but That. It was so huge, so open, just this Hugeness seeing Itself everywhere. Forms were still there, not a problem. There was no awareness of a limited "I," just myself as this huge Awareness. It only lasted a few seconds and it had a strong bodily effect. I looked for a place to pull over, but there was no immediate place, so I kept driving, which may have shortened the experience. Thoughts came afterward, "Would it be possible to live like that? Could the body withstand it? Is this the experience of no self? What was that all about? Oh, it's no big deal." So, I really don't know what to make of it, except that I am grateful for it and hope that more will be revealed. Also, I wanted to mention another brief, but seemingly significant experience that I had last Saturday. You know the last few weeks there has been such a deep plunge into the pain of the wounded parts of myself, childhood experiences, shame, self-hatred. Anyway, Van and I went for a hike on Saturday and I was feeling just sort of this low-grade depression all day but not trying to do anything with it, just letting it be there. So, on the hike I was still feeling it, but I sat down on a rock by this little waterfall, just kind of sinking into this melancholy and then there was just this awareness of the "richness" of what felt like the underbelly of existence. It's like the darkness, the shadows, are a dark facet of this amazing diamond and there is incredible depth to be discovered here. It was like, "who would have ever thought that this deep richness would be here in this that I have been wishing to be rid of? How amazing!" Not that the strong habit doesn't remain of wanting to get rid of the darkness and discomfort or hurry up and get through it so that I can get back to the lightness, but there was a seeing that there is something else, something that can only be discovered here. I am quite curious about it. I thought I might like to talk to Max about this, as perhaps he might know more about this. Anyway, I am quite grateful for this continuing unfolding and quite curious, even though the ride is quite intense lately. So, I am getting very wordy here. Thanks for listening. I miss being with you and all the folks up in Fort Collins, so sharing this is a way of connecting with you I guess. I hope the Transfiguration Retreat is going well. I will see you when you get back.

My love to you,
Deviki

September 18, 2002

Dear Friends,

I was asked if I might be willing to relate my recent personal experience with the Waking Down work, of which Saniel Bonder is the originator. I have felt compelled to share what has been happening with me, but imagined that I would do so in some small setting when the time felt right. This broader, more public exposure feels very vulnerable, but I feel drawn to do it, so here goes…

All my life I have had an unshakable sense that at my core I am irreparably defective. Even though through incredible grace I had been shown so clearly by my teachers, Gangaji, Papaji, Ramana Maharshi and others, that the Truth of my Being is pure, unlimited Conscious Awareness, and I had known this to be unshakably true for many years, I still could not reconcile this with the sense that at the core I felt irrevocably "bad." There were periods of time, especially after being with Papaji, where this haunting defectiveness seemed less palpable, yet it was only a matter of time before it would come undeniably into my experience again. I believed that it was just a thought, and not who I really was, but it felt like "original sin" that could never be erased. I also had tried many times to dive into and experience this defectiveness, but there was such huge defensiveness and resistance in my psyche that I was never able to do so. In the last year there was a somewhat hopeless resignation to the possibility that this might never change, as well as to the possibility that I might die and never fully live the Truth of who I Am in this lifetime.

This spring, I heard about the Waking Down work from friends, and although I wasn't looking to explore any other paths, and in fact felt some disloyalty to my teachers in doing so, I found that somehow I had no choice. In June I attended a "Human Sun Seminar," where the ground of this work was presented and discussed, and in July I attended a "Waking Down Weekend," which was primarily experiential in nature.

At the Waking Down Weekend the afternoon format consisted of a small group of participants working with a teacher and each sharing from the deepest possible place whatever was "up." When it was my turn, this defective feeling was very much present. CC Leigh, the teacher facilitating my small group, suggested that this defectiveness, instead of being just a thought, was true about me. This possibility stopped my mind, and I fell into an inquiry of whether this could possibly be. In this exploration I saw without a doubt that this defective, imperfect "me" is as completely and literally who I am as the endless sky of Being. I saw that in our humanity we are inherently imperfect, that it is truly the human condition. With this seeing, my heart broke and I cried uncontrollably for the whole world, for all the pain, war, hate, prejudice and horror that springs from this seed of imperfection. From this heartbreak arose a huge compassion that embraces all the deepest horror and the most exquisite beauty. I saw that it is from this seed of imperfection or separation that the world is born. I also saw that before multiplicity, there is only one. All is literally the same one. Before this one, there is no thing. Yet, mysteriously, in That, which is less than one, all is seen and all is held, intimately and so deeply held, in the endless perfection that is all there Is.

Since the Waking Down weekend there has been a continued unfolding of this realization. It feels like some tension wire was cut and that as a result I am finally able to just fall into and experience whatever is. Presently, this fall feels like a huge roller coaster ride. There has been a resurfacing of traumatic experiences from childhood as well as other repressed experiences and feelings. At times I feel completely overwhelmed and crazy, and then at some point there is a curiosity about and a relaxation into my present experience. Afterward, my heart is often bursting with love and compassion and everything is so beautiful I can hardly stand it. It's a wild ride, but I am so grateful for all of it. This is what my heart has been longing for forever. I feel like I am truly alive for the first time.

My surprising experience is that I am awake just as I am, with all my human limitations, faults, survival patterns, neuroses and wounding. Everything is included, that which I was most ashamed of and most defended against, as well as that which shines with brilliance from my unblemished endless Being. It is such a relief! I can finally be here fully in the world just as I am, nothing excluded. There is no need for transcendence, improvement or perfection, just the opportunity in each moment to fully be with what is.

It seems important to note that, for me, a vital component of this process seems to be that this Waking Down work happens in a context of "mutuality" or open, honest, true and supportive relationship. I have a strong pattern of difficulty trusting and feeling safe, and I think that I needed to know that there were arms to hold me before I could really let myself fall. I don't think I ever felt safe enough before. This mutuality is truly a beautiful thing. Authentic relationship is not always neat and tidy, but there is a realness to it that I realize I was starving for.

I have such a strong desire for all of humanity to know this, and to fall with me deeper and deeper into this mystery, which is both so ordinary and natural and at the same time so absolutely extraordinary. I am eternally grateful to Gangaji and Papaji and all my teachers, and I am eternally grateful to this Waking Down work, which for me has provided a crucial missing piece. Surprisingly, my experience is not uncommon. By some mysterious grace, this embodied awakening seems to be happening for many people who participate in this work.

It is such a relief to finally embrace and enjoy being fully human, and such an amazing mystery that, in finally doing so, the endless depth of my Being is increasingly alive in my life. I wanted to share this with you so that if you feel drawn, you can take the opportunity to see if there is something here that touches you.

With love and gratitude,
Deviki Shioshita

July 23, 2005

Dear Reader,

The above letters were written soon after what I would call Part II of my awakening in July 2002. Prior to that time, I had deeply known and experienced my/our Conscious nature for many years, and yet in day to day moment to moment life, I could not reconcile this greater knowing with my often painful human experience. My identification would flip flop between the "two." I would dissociate from my human self in order to identify with my Conscious nature. However, I was not able to maintain that identification.

The realization that I had in July 2002 clarified for me the relationship between our human and "Divine" natures. I realized directly that we are the full spectrum of Being. We are all of it, all at the same time, and there is no conflict in this. I have heard it said that this human experience is just a story created by thought, that in truth, it has no reality. It is a dream, an illusion. This is not my realization exactly, and certainly not my day to day experience. In my experience, Essence, Beingness, Nothingness, Everythingness, "God" is That in every form, just as it is. We are unblemished perfection, as well as inherently, humanly flawed. Living consciously in our day to day lives is potentially a moment to moment knowing of ourselves as both/all. There is a very real, and vulnerable "landing" in the body in very real everyday life, and there is the possibility of living the moments of that life consciously, with deeper Seeing, deeper Knowing, more openness, and more heart. Transcendence is thus not necessary or, in my experience, even possible for any extended periods of time.

Having said that, I now have to say that living in the body more consciously is really difficult a lot of the time. This awakening really is only a beginning. It truly is comparable to when we are born into these bodies as human babies. A birth is the beginning, not the end of development.

I believe that there are stages of development in this second, awakened life, just as there are stages of our first life. The only problem is there hasn't been much research to predict what those stages are. This awakening has not seemingly been accessible to the masses until recently, and thus we are bushwhacking our way through the territory. We can support and assist each other, but except for a relatively few advanced souls, we are groping our way through. There is thankfully much Divine help available, which can take many different forms.

So, I speak to you from the middle of the woods, from having landed consciously in a body that I spent most of my life trying to dissociate from. I don't have a clear perspective at this point, and I really have no idea where I'm going to end up. In the last couple of years, I have encountered deep cellular places in my body that hold much more trauma than I was aware of. My most core issues around trust, and shame have been deeply encountered. I have dealt with significant depression, and my desire to engage in conscious, intimate relationship has pushed the wounded parts of my personality to their limits.

My friend, Van, says I'm like a department store that's all boarded up, with a big sign posted outside that says, "closed for remodeling." I do feel that way. I feel like this big reconstruction project is going on in me, and that the builder really had no idea what she was getting herself into when she took on the project. It is actually a much bigger undertaking than she ever realized, and at this point she has no idea when or if it ever will be finished. Additionally, the project is happening in the midst of a very busy, everyday life, with kids, and job, and responsibilities. I think we really do need to acknowledge ourselves for what we have undertaken in this lifetime, where we do not have the luxury of living in the ashram, the cave or on the mountaintop. It is truly challenging.

Amazingly, however, I wouldn't trade it. I am forever grateful for the grace that has allowed me to know who I am, and that continues to show that to me, and I am grateful for all of you who are on this path with me. May the Divine Heart, which is not separate from ourselves, guide us and bless us on our journeys, and may we hold each others hands along the way.

Part of my personal journey has involved being touched by the Divine Feminine or Divine Mother/Divine Heart aspect of who we are. So, in closing, I feel drawn to share with you a reflection of this that I wrote along the way.

Many Blessings,
Deviki

The Heart of the Divine Feminine

You are Divine, Feminine Beauty, inseparable from Absolute Consciousness. You are simple, gentle, Radiant Presence, which calls you deeper and deeper into Her endless embrace, until the embracer and the embraced are indistinguishable from one another. You are the open Heart, the eternally welcoming, open and compassionate Heart, which embraces all that we are, all that is without preference. You arc deep, quiet Stillness, Aware, Alive Silence, which is always present, even when your attention is occupied elsewhere.

Yet in the mysterious paradox of human existence, we cry out to, we pray to, and we are desperate for this Love that we Are. We so desperately need to feel ourselves held, to know that we are not alone, to feel that all of who we are is OK, even those aspects of our nature that we most despise and are most ashamed of. The world is in desperate need of this Love, this Heart, our love, our hearts.

It is our birthright both to know ourselves as, and to receive, this Love. So, receive what is your birthright, everyday, in the smallest of ways, in the simplest of moments, in this moment. Receive this Love, and know that the Heart from which you receive is none other than your own.

"And I laughed, and I laughed, and I laughed. Because it did *make sense, even though to the limited capacity of my mind it never entirely would. It made sense to my* body*."*

Jon

Jon Mattingly has lived his life variously throughout the Pacific Northwest, the Mid-Atlantic, Northern California, and New England. He currently makes his home in Portland, Oregon, where he works as a massage therapist and writer. Also, he holds an M.Ed. in Marriage and Family Counseling, and in addition to spiritual counseling he offers his services as both a relationship counselor and intimacy coach. He also provides counsel as an abundance and personal fulfillment coach. Jon can be contacted at jon@easeandfreedom.com. *His phone number:* 503-956-4085.

HERE AND BACK AGAIN

One afternoon in mid-summer 1996, due to a remarkable (and dastardly) sequence of events, clearly determined to leave me in an overwhelmed state of dull shock and bewilderment, I found myself lying in bed, reflecting yet again on the recent loss of my job, my girlfriend, my social life, most of my money, my car, my personal pride, and—oh, yes—my overall faith in the rational order of a beneficent Universe.

Thankfully I still had my apartment. And my bed. Because what with one thing after another, it seemed most appropriate to hunker down into one long, silent week of hermitage, where burrowing down deep was obviously the only sane and rational course of action (or non-action) available to me in the face of a world seemingly determined to disillusion me in every way it could think of. It's worth mentioning that my existential crisis went beyond a mourning of the mere trappings of personal success. I'd also, and as it turns out more significantly, just about run out of patience with another matter which had occupied much of my time and attention recently, that being a focused investigation into the timeless and alluring mystery of...spiritual enlightenment. An investigation, I was disgusted to admit, that had so far come to naught. Ha! Who was I kidding? Spiritual *enlightenment*? I couldn't even get my car out of the impound lot. As far as I could see, the prospect of effecting my own liberation wasn't much more likely at that point. All in all, I was pretty much fed up with the whole thing.

Not too hard on myself, eh? I'll admit it. I was green. Pretty damn cocky too. And maybe just a little unrealistic. I mean, here I was 27 years old, no more than four years into any serious enquiry of human spiritual potential (if that), and yet I'd been absolutely convinced that I really had a shot at figuring it all out. Never mind we're talking about the supposed penultimate goal of human evolution. Never mind that far greater minds and personalities had been striving and searching and meditating for thousands of years for this self-same Self-realization, with really very little to actually show for it apparently and certainly little in the way of widespread consensus. Never mind that practically everything I'd managed to figure out up to that point was stuff I'd only pieced together from books and the occasional New Age expo. Never mind all that. I did. Somehow, I was actually convinced that I had a shot. Me. Mr. American privileged, upper middle-class, over-educated, Joe-schmoe white boy, with a reasonable chip on his shoulder, a remarkable lack of life direction—and, oh sure, a heart of gold. (I had at least that much going for me anyway.)

Well, oh well. So much for figuring it all out. As I said, life for poor Jon was essentially a mess at that point. I was pretty well flattened, and none too motivated to do much else about it, thanks very much. And though the idea of continuing to cocoon myself in grousing and self-pity held a certain appeal, at one point that afternoon I abruptly felt the urge to get my tuckas out of bed and at least make the attempt to be a part of the world again. Can't say I really wanted to be the life of a party or anything, but the idea of at least being around people sounded tolerable, and probably wise. So off I went, down to my favorite neighborhood café bar, book in hand. Imagine my surprise and consternation when I found the place to be absolutely *packed.* There was one seat, and one seat only, available at the bar, and so—oh, well—there I sat myself, diligently burying myself in my book, trying very hard to be *in* the world, but not exactly *of* it, know what I'm saying? Didn't work though. See, as it happened there was this rather beautiful woman sitting at the bar next to me. And I was flattened, yes, but I wasn't dead. Actually she started it. She commented on my book, which was some spiritual treatment of something or other, and pretty quickly we fell to chatting about, well, spiritual stuff. I threw out a few choice gems which seemed to get her attention and got her talking, and pretty soon she was regaling me with a rather glowing description of this *guy* she'd been spending time with, this spiritual teacher type she'd found out in Marin, who was just absolutely *incredible*. Just fantastic. Someone I really just had to go see, she could tell, based on everything I'd told her so far.

Uh-oh. Some teacher-guy, huh? Hm.

What had I told her? I don't recall exactly. Probably something about my interest in Tantra. (Y'know, to sort of test the waters and all.) But more than that, I think I spoke of the frustration I felt at not finding a spiritual path I could really get behind, something that made sense to this poor modern Western boy, something that wasn't so unwieldy, or so political, so hierarchical, or so ridiculous, or something that wasn't so *non-relationally biased*. Or for that matter a modern tantra that didn't seem too esoteric or too overly focused on sex. Because sure I like sex, but that wasn't really my fundamental attraction to a tantric path. (Really.) I told her I was looking for a path that didn't aggressively dismiss or discount the material reality we lived in, that took into account and honored the relationships we have and develop with the world and the people with whom we share it. I think that's probably what did it. Not that it got me laid that night. No, actually, it got me something far more valuable. It got me my first ever, genuine spiritual teacher. And then more besides.

Three days later I found myself making my very first spiritual pilgrimage, literally hiking from California's I-5 freeway and up the suburban, condo-speckled slopes (or, OK, maybe the foothill slopes) of Marin County's sacred Mt. Tamalpais. To the apartment and the afternoon sitting of the amazing gentleman my new friend insisted I go and see. A man by the name of Saniel Bonder. Because, sure, at that point what did I have to lose? And it certainly seemed like somebody Up There thought it was a good idea that I at least go and meet this guy, hear what he had to say. I was a little nervous, I admit. I had no idea really what to expect, having never *had* a spiritual teacher before, having never really ever *wanted* a spiritual teacher before, and having never really met one before. Well, OK, I did have ideas, you always have *ideas*. I figured on probably a rather kindly, perhaps portly, grandfatherly-type character, who was welcoming, gentle, and somewhat beatific-seeming. Right? That's what made sense to me. Mmmmmm...yeah. No. I found an elderly gentleman all right. But he was sitting *with* Saniel, who himself was a considerably younger man, mid-forties maybe, lean, sharp-looking, *intense*. I mean energetically this guy had a lot going on. Nothing soft or mellow about him. Heck, he looked like he'd be just as comfortable up on his feet discoursing at length as he strode purposefully around and around the outside of his apartment complex. Which is about what I looked like I'd just done, standing there breathless in my sweat-soaked t-shirt, shorts and knapsack, ready for revelation, transformation and, hopefully, a glass of water.

That's when I heard the first words I would ever hear from a man who would soon become my first-ever spiritual teacher, guide, guru, and eventually very good friend: "Uh, hi. Would you mind very much taking your shoes off and leaving them at the door before coming back in?" Oops.

Heh. Poor Saniel. If he wasn't what I was expecting, I'm pretty damn sure I wasn't what he ever expected to see walk through his door. Frankly I think I pissed him off at first. I mean I was young—at least by his reckoning I was young. A mere pipsqueak. What was I doing showing up on his doorstep, expressing a sincere interest in this revolutionary, advanced spiritual awakening yoga he was trying intently to forge into a well-respected and seriously-considered new spiritual path? I couldn't possibly be ready for the level of investigation and enquiry this work required. He was fond of saying things like I hadn't worn off enough tread from my tires yet for this to be of any real value to me. Looking back, ten years later, I can see what he meant. I mean comparatively I really didn't have much life experience to work with, not like the people he was used to working with. That was true. Didn't matter to me though. Well, yeah OK, I thought it was a little obnoxious of him. Truth be told I wasn't entirely sure I really liked Saniel at first. Oh, he was courteous enough. Let me hang out, sit in on a few of his sittings, get a feel for what he was doing. He didn't really pay too much attention to me though, not initially. But that suited me. I've always been much more comfortable in new situations hanging back and getting a lay of the land, rather than getting in close and mixing it up, testing and challenging, making my presence known. So that's what I did. I came to a few more sittings, hung back, got to know a few people, and watched what he did.

Which was about all it took for me. It didn't take long for me to realize that there was something about this guy that *really* got my attention. One of the first things I noticed was just how well he really paid attention, even when it didn't seem that way. The way he held a conversation together, for example, regularly attending to the needs and issues of several different people simultaneously, with an uncanny knack of bringing things around and tying them all together into a nifty spiritual discourse that seemed relevant and inclusive to everyone present. Heck, that alone was impressive to me, something I very much wanted to learn if I could. But beyond that, there was no denying that what he had to say made sense to me like nothing I'd ever heard before. For that matter it appeared that it made more than just sense to me. It was downright enlivening. And I mean that literally.

Please understand: up until this point my experience with spiritual matters was somewhat...rarified. In other words, I had an almost entirely intellectual relationship with the subject. Lots of books, lots of concepts, lots of *imaginings*. Ideas, mostly. To be fair I had more going for me than that, but let's just say that at the time I wasn't particularly in touch with the more experiential potentials of my spiritual makeup. No evident psychic powers, no energy working, no astral traveling...no, certainly not. Nothing so "woo-woo" as any of that. (Foolish child.) But also really, I had no particular spiritual discipline, no community, no formal path, no practice, and, therefore, no real context for spiritual experiences. No facility with meditative states say, nor for that matter with any other states of consciousness that weren't otherwise, uh, facilitated by more, mmm... "recreational" agents.

Imagine my surprise then, when within my second or so sitting with Saniel, I found myself spontaneously experiencing a distinctly energized *vibration* running throughout my entire body. And I do mean distinctly. Nothing subtle here. I remember the first time I noticed it; I literally stopped in my tracks. It was like, while I'd been sitting with the man in his apartment, we were contained in something of a pressurized environment, one which once relieved into the open air, revealed to me the fact that my body had acclimated to a certain frequency or sensitivity that I was suddenly extremely aware of. That's an analogy. It's not really what was going on. But it's something close. My body *felt*...alive. Like, *more* alive than usual. It wasn't really, mind you. But I was suddenly aware of it as such. Or rather, *it* was. Aware of it. Aware of itself. That is, I, as my body, was suddenly that much more aware of myself, in and *through* my body. Tangibly. Cellularly. Sensationally. Buzz buzz buzz. Like, Zzzmmmmmmmmmmmmmm.... Whoa, dude. Whoa, whoa, whoa. What was this? This was...outside...of my normal...experience. This was really quite extraordinary, and most definitely a little wild, maybe a little crazy—certainly nothing I should call home and tell Mom and Dad about. (Though, God help me, I think maybe I did.) More importantly it was very reminiscent of many of the things I'd been hearing Saniel talk about as his own experience of awakened "Being-force." Now mind you, according to him, according to what I subsequently learned, I shouldn't have been experiencing this myself. Not yet anyway. Hm. Well...apparently not.

Which was when I figured out that as much as I loved what I was hearing in that apartment, no matter how much I appreciated suddenly working with someone who seemed to have a genuine grasp on what it was I wanted to learn, I was still going to have to figure a lot of this out for myself as I continued. Because by then it was certainly clear—I wasn't going anywhere.

This was good for me, I believe. This need for an independent, personal validation of my own process. As, indeed, it is in life. Saniel talks about grasping the means of your own Realization. Claiming it and owning it for yourself. Taking responsibility for your own progress, your own understanding of it. Well, I stepped into that mode from the get-go. And it served me well. Basically it emphasized for me that I would always know more than anyone else about what was really true for me in my experience, in my relationship with myself. A good thing to affirm in the face of uncharted territory. Not that I also couldn't learn a lot from someone who had already claimed that expertise for himself. So I sat back and absorbed as much as I could of what Saniel was saying, watched what he did, how he did it, what he did with us all in his sittings. And then I'd critically compare all that to my own perspective, my own experiences, my own opinions and convictions, assimilating what felt to me to be on target and dismissing what simply didn't work for me. The balance worked well. It allowed me to engage and increasingly involve myself with a teaching that served me profoundly, while keeping a certain healthy distance from any biased opinions of the teacher.

I loved it. Rather quickly I came to realize that almost everything about this teaching was remarkably suited to me. The openness of it, the down-to-earth honesty of it, the common sense brilliance of it, the quality of the people I found there, the magic that seemed to surround it, that had brought it into my life—even my life as it had been when I first encountered the work appeared consistent with what was to be expected, a well-nigh perfect description of the physical and spiritual ennui which Saniel said serves as a critical gateway into this work. Huh. So much of what he had to say made sense to me straight off and seemed to fit my own experience.

It wasn't just what he had to say though—it was how he said it.

I mean, sure, it was gratifying and exciting to be in a room where a primary point of interest was our individual awakening as non-finite, eternal Consciousness. But, unlike any of the sources I'd come across before then, Saniel had a way of keeping the subject both very acceptable and very accessible. True, he seemed prone at times to make comments that could be, uh, perceived as self-inflated and grandiose, but then he'd immediately extend that same context out to us, those of us sitting with him. He'd bring it down to a language that spoke directly to us, to our interests, our understandings, our conditions, with a perspective that was simultaneously practical and transcendent. He used language that was down to earth, and he spent time addressing our very real material and worldly concerns. Our *relational* concerns. He didn't diminish or dismiss them. He *embraced* them, he invited them. He worked *with* them to provide yet further material and conversation for the clarifications he was trying to get us to understand for ourselves. He didn't use them as encouragement for us to remove ourselves *from* the world or to hold ourselves back from our relationships. He honored them as legitimate issues, coming from legitimate perspectives, and he made it clear that those perspectives deserved to be seriously considered in a process nonetheless orchestrated to show us that ultimately we were not served by identifying exclusively with them—even as we learned what it was to really encounter ourselves, to know ourselves, to *feel* ourselves, *in* the world. We were them, those issues and conditions, yes. But there was also that part of us which was not them–that part of Who we were that was not affected by, not defined by, not identifiable as those issues and conditions—*at the same time*. A paradox that when spoken into, as Saniel continually did, allowed us gradually to relax into ourselves while simultaneously opening ever further to the Freedom of our divine nature.

As far as I was concerned this was revolutionary. And utterly wonderful. My God! Finally. Someone who seemed to actually know, first hand, what that Transcendence was and who championed it, someone who nonetheless also kept things tangibly, meaningfully–even sometimes uncomfortably–*real*. Here was a path of Self-realization that wasn't focused on denial of the physical world, but rather on a sober acceptance of it; a path that allowed for a reality that was divinely Perfect while at the same moment riddled with pain, loss and sorrow. A path that allowed us to be imperfect and to grieve the separations in our world, while learning to appreciate the non-separate foundation which made it possible to transcend *through* that pain and integrate the sorrows we encounter here. This was yet another of the aspects of Saniel's work to which I responded instinctively. The understanding that we didn't have to be perfect or have to perfect ourselves to realize Who we were and to become established as That–while also experiencing ourselves in, as and through any imperfections that continued to arise. Talk about liberating. And relieving. *I* certainly wasn't perfect. That was clear. Neither clearly was Saniel. Something *he* made very clear to *us*. Sometimes with an exasperation approaching belligerence. Sometimes with outright relish. Very strange. Very empowering. But *always* real.

No matter what I felt about the way he presented himself, how he chose to relate to certain people or certain subjects, or the vagaries of his, uh, temperamental personality, that was the one thing I got, quickly and clearly, from the very beginning. Saniel was never going to be anything other than intently, intensely, unstintingly *real* with us. Honest. Un-mediated. *Vulnerable*. I had to respect that about the man. And I did. I respected it. I appreciated it. And while I didn't always *like* it, it nonetheless gradually became clear to me, that in point of fact—I loved the man for it.

And I loved what I learned from him. I remember when he presented me with a copy of his first book, what was then the primary vehicle for his teachings: a large, substantial looking Kinko's-bound volume that was something of a dream for this wide-eyed spiritual bookworm. I took it home that first week and practically inhaled it. Everything I could want in the way of detailed explanation, clarification, encouragement, permission, empowerment, insight, history, anecdotes and parables–all run throughout with Saniel's own experiences, a personal story that put it all in context, made it a living, breathing reality that also suggested the very distinct possibility that I could claim this same integral awakening for myself. Like I said: a dream. But quite the reality too. Because if you haven't heard by now, and as I was finding out myself by then, this awakening we're all going on about here is an inherently visceral, *body-centric* awakening. It's one of the reasons I think of it as a "tantric" awakening. It's the reason I had started experiencing flashes of enlivened awareness throughout *and* as my body whenever I'd leave Saniel's apartment or when I'd finish reading a section of his book (yep, then too). The Being-transmission appears to extend outward as an innate expression and communication *between and among the cells of the bodies*, between the organisms.

A fact that made all the friendships I made during this time all the more profound. There was only a small core of us back then working with Saniel, but those few quickly became something of a family for me. Certainly we came to know each other very well. Our dreams, our losses, our yearnings and our private anguishes—the inherent emphasis that the work placed on *relationship* inspired us to be very vulnerable with one another. And it became necessary to navigate that intimacy through some fairly rough passages at times. So we learned to trust one another too. And then also we were all actively engaged in an enlivening that was quite literally waking us up. There is no doubt in my mind that we each benefited from the synergistic working of that process, each of us coming to understandings and insights in our own time, each of us interacting and sharing our experiences. We learned from one another. And then, too, there were a few there who, like Saniel, were already where we wanted to go. People whose presence and encouragement galvanized us to the conviction that this was something we *could* achieve, something we could claim for ourselves. People like Van Ngyuen.

I met Van my second sitting, I think, and before long we fell into a friendship unlike any I have ever known before or since. Our relationship really took hold a few weeks into my involvement when, following one sitting, Van graciously offered to drive me back to San Francisco where we both resided. Oh, little did he understand exactly what he was offering me. Up until then I saw absolutely nothing about losing my car that was anything to be happy about. Suddenly, though, I found myself, once a week at least and soon more frequently, with a very captive, if moderately willing, divinely Awakened audience with whom I was able–finally–to download all the here-to-for unexpressed thoughts and ideas and impressions and questions that were coming up for me regularly at Saniel's sittings. This has much to do with my certain conviction that Van is a saint. He was soooo patient and available with me and my newly uncorked and enthused ramblings and conjectures. For that matter he actually seemed to possibly enjoy it. We had so much fun in those car rides home, buzzing and blazing forth with all this activated (in his case established) "Being-force," cruising down the highway and across the Golden Gate in a state of boyishly gleeful bliss. Oh, the joy of it. Hee. Ha! It quickly became a regular routine and a cherished time of camaraderie and friendship for us both. I will always, *always*, be grateful for the movements in Being that landed me in the passenger seat of Van's car all those many weeks of summer and into the fall of that year.

Always. Blessed be.

One of the things that became abundantly clear to me about this work is the innately organic nature of the process. Because this awakening is a full-Being transformational process, it makes every sense that it will show up in every aspect of your life, and further, that it should be engaged with in as many ways as possible, as many ways as you are drawn to investigate it. Frankly, that tends to happen spontaneously, especially when the channels and opportunities to do so present themselves. This was happening to some significant degree for me in the more structured classes that Saniel was conducting. But it also occurred in all the *informal* activities and meetings that I was fortunate enough to encounter with Saniel, et al–whether that be in the form of a hug or the form of a madcap car ride. This fact should have been more obvious to me from the first, but I think the point really drove home some several months into my association with my new family when Steve and Tara Plocher threw a party.

Steve and Tara were perhaps the most 'normal' of our little clan. By which I mean they were married, had already raised two children and were raising a third. They owned a home in a pleasant Marin suburb and lived a comfortable lifestyle made possible by the success of Steve's accounting business. They were very worldly, very of the world, and they'd made a real success of it. Not that the rest of us weren't doing or living well. (Well, other than *me* maybe.) But there was a certain...solidity that Steve and Tara provided. And they shared that solidity and that sense of family with us every chance they got. They were fond of providing us all with opportunities to come and associate together outside of the norm—this, at that point, being Saniel's apartment for the most part—something which I sincerely believe served us all very well. The first time I had the pleasure of doing just this was quite the experience for me. The reason for this is that Steve and Tara are naturalists. Nudists. Very self-assured nudists I might add. Their household is, for the most part, clothing free, and Steve in particular is an avid hot-tub enthusiast. And so, some number of weeks into my involvement with this work, I attended my first Plocher hot tub party. And before I knew it, all the fine and lovely individuals with whom I'd mostly spent time discoursing intently, in relatively cramped quarters, on matters of revolutionarily transformative spiritual dharma, were suddenly running around starkers in Steve's back yard, jumping in and out of his pool and hot tub.

Uh-huh. Now for me this was intensely liberating. Frankly, I think that was true for everyone there. Though probably I was less familiar with the practice than many of them at that point. I wasn't entirely unfamiliar with clothing-optional recreation mind you–just not with all my new family here. It may be worth mentioning that on the whole I was a good fifteen to twenty years younger than most of these folks. So regardless of my prior experiences, this really represented something new for me. More of a lifestyle experience. A very *California* lifestyle experience it seemed to me, though that's perhaps unfair to naturalists everywhere else. But for me that's what it was. And by good golly, if *that* didn't just jack the Being-force up a couple of notches right there.

All in all, I was getting a crash course and a crash appreciation in revolutionary California divinely awakening spiritual considerations 101. Who'da thunk it? Moreover—it was working. And as amazing as it seemed at the time—as amazing as it was—it really didn't take all that long before I had my own Awakening. Of course, I was impatient for it. And it a felt like a lifetime. (Well, maybe several lifetimes.) But I mean, c'mon. When all was said and done, we're talking no more than a couple of *months* here for things to shine through for me. And as impatient as I might have been, at one point that fall I realized that the occurrence of these consciously enlivened Being "flashes" I'd been experiencing were increasing both in frequency and intensity. And before long it occurred to me that as things were progressing, according to everything I'd been learning, this Awakening thing was pretty much…inevitable.

Which wasn't to say that it had all been a cake-walk exactly. No doubt—the entire process had put me through my paces. Life had become *very* interesting that summer and fall–for months, all manner of happenstances and occurrences had presented themselves with alarming frequency to, sort of, test my resolve and to test my resistances. Sort of like me as Consciousness testing my all-too-human boundaries, I suppose. Getting a real good feel for them. I have to say I don't have any shining examples of this in mind at the moment, possibly because the trials and tribulations of post-awakening life have put any of that time to shame. Perhaps at some point I will be asked to expound further on that point, but for now please accept my assurance that there was as much grace and magic and awe running throughout my life in those months as there was any discomfort or challenge. The whole process was nothing short of amazing. And the whole is what you get. Good, bad, happy, sad, challenging, blissful—all of it. And that pretty much continues. Not really unlike how life normally is. What's different is that once you get a real taste of this, and it settles in, well, at that point it's off and running. You *will* encounter, consciously–ever-more consciously–all the many conditions and limitations and every "apparent" nature of your existence. Because that is the only way you will clarify where, or in what way, you are also *un*conditioned, *un*limited, *un*changing, *eternal*. Free.

It happened for me Thanksgiving Day 1996, lying in the same bed I lay in all those months ago, in almost exactly the same position I'd laid in then. I believe I was contemplating my navel. Or, actually, I was *trying* to get a grasp, finally, on the essential *paradox* of our nature. The paradox that I had been told held the key to this realization of Conscious Embodiment. The Paradox that our existence consists *equally* of *both* that which is conditioned, limited and changeable *and* That which is unconditioned, unconditionable, infinite and immutable. The Paradox that we exist simultaneously *both* as human form/matter/energy *and* as divine Consciousness/Awareness/Presence. A paradox, I told myself, which must be realizable. Except that…my mind…couldn't get it. It just didn't make *sense*. Laughably, I kept trying to find a way to figure out infinity. But I couldn't conceive, practically or mathematically, of any way to encompass it. Which of course is the point. You can't *conceive* it. It's not conceivable. How can the mind, which is finite, hold infinity? It can't. It can't experience that infinity directly, because the mind is a mediated perspective. You can't imagine that direct appreciation. You can't figure it out. You can't. You have to become aware of it directly. You have to *feel* it. You have to recognize yourself as that paradox, as that undifferentiated, unmediated awareness arising in *simultaneous communion* with every*thing* you also identify with. Every thing, every experience, every phenomenon you also feel yourself to be in relationship with. *Everything* that You as That Awareness can be, and are, related to, or can be identified as, whether in your individual body or in the body of the World. A World that is felt by You, in and through the body. As your body. *Feeling* that is aware of itself in your body, as your body, in relationship with All that is, arising in All that It is, simultaneously, as Awareness, as living form, as you, as *You*.

And somewhere in there, my mind just…gave up. And it fell back. (Gibbering.) And suddenly, that same spontaneous abiding awareness of Being which had flashed through so many times over the previous months, arose in my experience, as my awareness of that experience, as Awareness itself, in my body, through my body, as my body, like thousands of billions of tiny effervescent bubbles rising to the surface of a new Relationship with my world, one which established my normal awareness, my everyday appreciation of myself, throughout my body, throughout my sense of self, irrevocably and consciously in and as That which is simply and always Present. Here. Now. Moment, to moment, to moment. On and on and on. Consciousness forever and always married to, and mutually inter-dependent with, All that It is aware of, experienced here, now, through and as me.

And I laughed, and I laughed, and I laughed. Because it *did* make sense, even though to the limited capacity of my mind it never entirely would. It made sense to my *body*. I realized it in and through and *as* my body—the awareness of my body—the many millions and millions of sensings of my body. It was sense itself. *I* was that sense itself. That which arises as sense. Infinite Consciousness arising in individuated form as individual awareness. Individually experienced, but always and everywhere arising as that same Awareness. That which Is, always and everywhere present. Presence—eternal and infinite. A Presence that was Alive. In me. As me. *Both*. Simultaneously. Forever.

The appreciation of that moment has lasted ever since. It has moved forward from that moment into every moment that has followed. It is a recognition and an appreciative awareness of the essential Truth of my existence, which in the simple, quiet, open, moments of living arises as appreciation, spontaneously and effortlessly. The ever-present, abiding feeling-awareness of my own individual existence sourced in and as That which Is aware of and forever married to, All that is, is itself a bliss unlike any I can name, incomparable to any individual, particular experience I may have. The words that really come closest to describing it for me are love and gratitude…and appreciation. And these days those are the words that make the most sense to me. The open exposure to life that I experience now—the raw, unmediated vulnerability to its presence and its qualities—is sometimes pleasurable and sometimes very joyful. Sometimes it is a source of great pain and sorrow. But throughout it all is an abiding appreciation of the simple Truth of it, the radiantly effortless Being of it. Throughout it all there is Love.

(For a complete version of the story that appears here, please check online at *prosperitypages.com/story.html*)

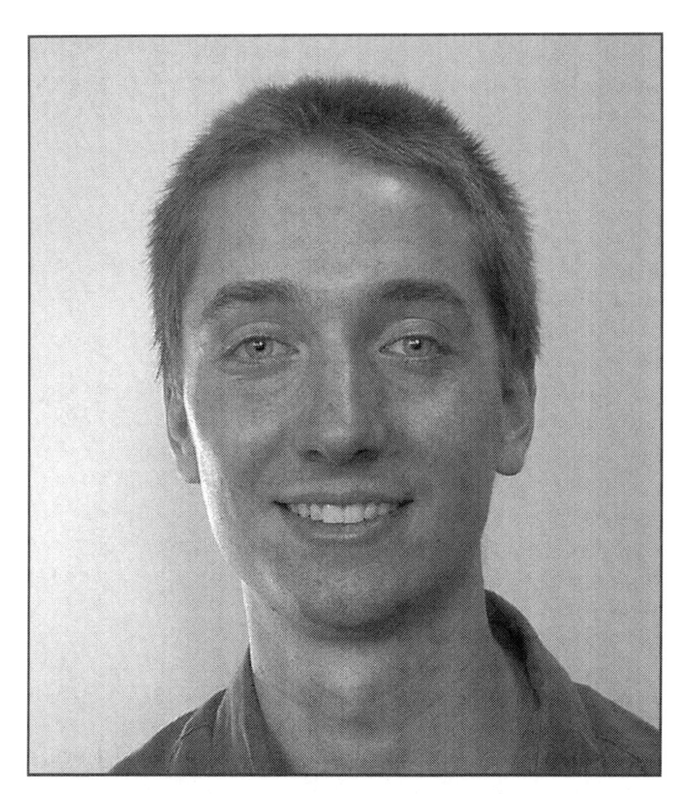

"This wound, this wound, this wound, this wound."

Sean

Sean Arnold was born on December 4, 1980, in Eugene, Oregon, where he was raised. For the past five years he has lived and worked in a number of locations throughout Oregon and Northern California. In 2009 he lived in Canberra, the Australian Capital Territory, working in disability support and helping initiate and establish an Australian Waking Down in Mutuality ("Waking Down Under") community. Currently he's the youngest mentor in the Waking Down in Mututality work. You can read more about his personal journey on his mentor page at wakingdown.org. *His email address:* sean_arnold@hotmail.com.

AWAKENING AS THE ALL OF ME

"Joy and pain are siamese twins sharing a brain." Stuart Davis
"Thank you very much." Suzuki Roshi

04/10/03:
The world seems to have turned upside-down. I feel as though I have lost and continue to lose my mind. I think this is going to take some getting used to. I don't actually really understand what's going on; it's just happening, that's why it feels strange.

08/02/03:
First night of the Human Sun Seminar (free intro). Upon walking into the room I almost immediately felt this unmistakable energy—hard to describe, but I'll just say that it felt like the energy of conscious embodiment. I can't tell for sure, but I think I might have had my "Second Birth" awakening during the meeting—I suppose time will tell!

08/03/03:
Second full day of Human Sun Seminar is over. The whole weekend was really rewarding and challenging for me. Last night I felt so, to speak poetically,

drenched in Being, that I could barely talk at dinner. Or maybe I should just say it took some effort to speak; it was interesting.

08/09/03:
What does it mean to accept or embrace All *of* who I am?

08/15/03:
I've been feeling kind of "sick of it all." I think it is related to the winding down of the effort to be different than how I really am, and the effort to try to make other people different from how they are. I'm just sick of it. It's getting harder and harder to muster up the energy to oppose what is actually going on, in me or in others or in life. I'm just sick of it. It was kind of funny. Today I was noticing how there's a part of me that's basically a real asshole, and it's getting harder and harder for me to distance myself from that, as in, "That's not who I really am, that's not really me." Bullshit! It is me. It's not all of me, but it's part of who I am. I'm just getting really tired of denying this sort of thing.

08/16/03:
I'm realizing more and more that I'm really ready for this Waking Down work, or at least that's the way it seems. I probably don't know what this even really means, but I feel this deep urge to be crucified on the limitations of this body/mind, this human culture and society, my relations with others, and life itself. I want to be crucified by/on all of that so I can be resurrected as All of that, All of what I am.

08/24/03:
I feel some trepidation about the path ahead of me. I sense there will be many challenges in the passage Saniel and others refer to as the "Wakedown Shakedown." I feel that much woundedness, and much that is now hidden from my view, will emerge, and I want to have sufficient help to cope effectively with this passage.

08/31/03:
I'm not sure, at this point, whether or not the shift in Being called the Second Birth has, or has not, occurred in my case. I am remaining as open as possible to both of those potential realities, but I will have to see over time what unfolds. Either way, there is a lot moving in me, a lot of changes and apparent quickening. I have been listening to Waking Down *(audio-book version) a lot, and it has been, and continues to be, a great help and inspiration.*

10/16/03:

I spoke with Krishna today and told him that I thought I might have entered my Second Birth. I'm feeling pretty confused and strange today. I didn't really feel like I was able to communicate with Krishna very well, which I think is part of the reason I'm feeling sort of distressed. I'm going to have to think about what it is I need from a relationship with a Waking Down teacher and what I might have said differently with Krishna in order to feel like I was communicating.

11/02/03:

Man, I'm feeling pretty shitty. Frozen fear and distrust, or, maybe more accurately, un-trust. The Waking Down people I'm beginning to connect with are people I think I will be able to talk openly with about these kinds of things, but, well, this is just really hard. I feel boxed-in, frozen, fearful, and pretty full of despair. But I don't really want to run from all this anymore. That's a big piece of why I'm getting involved with the Waking Down work, I think: to have people in my life who are willing and able to support and affirm me in these parts of my being and who have also gone deep and learned to fully inhabit similar areas in themselves. But it really just sucks.

11/08/03:

Just saw the Matrix Revolutions *and Holy Shit! Something crazy was happening inside of me! I was noticing something different at work earlier in the day, but it intensified a whole bunch while viewing the Matrix movie. I'm guessing it might be my first glimpse of the "White Heat," but really I don't know what the hell it is. It has the quality of an explosion, though, and it seems extraordinarily difficult to try to comprehend with the mind. I guess it's just the next phase in my awakening process, whatever the hell it is. I'm really interested to see what happens next.*

12/02/03:

There's part of me that just wants out *of here. And there's also part of me that just wants to* get *Here! I'm experiencing a lot of tension in my being from feeling these two impulses simultaneously. I sense that the part that wants out is gradually diminishing and being replaced by the part that wants simply to be here, with what is, the part that wants to Incarnate most fully.*

12/03/03:

This wound, this wound, this wound, this wound. I think I actually have had my Second Birth awakening because I feel like I'm becoming a fundamentally different person, a different being, on the basis of that awakening. The awakening is realization of myself as this wound of being, both infinite consciousness and a finite, mortal, frail human animal. I am both*—they can't be separated in any ultimately meaningful way.* I am both! *I am God and I am a single human animal, simultaneously. Both. That's the wound, and that's the awakening.*

12/11/03:
Talked to Sandra. Wow! She confirmed my Second Birth. I can't believe she confirmed my Second Birth! This is really an amazing confidence booster, and a great gift.

12/12/03:
I'm trying to grok the implications of having entered the Second Birth, but it's not so easy. I definitely am different than I was before the shift, but it's difficult to say exactly how. I guess it's not really necessary for me to know every little consequence of the awakening, and I think it would be a good idea for me to follow Saniel's advice in Waking Down: *"Congratulations on your Second Birth (now, take some time to be a baby again)." It really does seem as though I am at the beginning of a whole new life, and I think it's a good idea to take things kind of slow, especially now, at the beginning. One thing I notice is that a sense of deep dilemma that was always present before is now gone. I think it has to do with the sense of falling into myself as a totality rather than being broken up with one part of me that is the Self, and one part that is the body, and one part that is the mind, and one part that is the ego, and one part that is the soul. Now, what I am includes all of that as* itself, *and not merely as parts of itself. I am all of that, and, curiously, I also transcend all of that, as the Self, apparently. Free of and free* as. *The strange thing now, though, is that I don't feel that those two flavors of freedom are really different. It's the same freedom in both cases.*

12/15/03:
Well, seems like the infamous Wakedown Shakedown is getting underway. Last couple days at work have been pretty tough. It just feels like there's no separation between my essence and other people and my own manifest expression. This is actually a pretty uncomfortable state of affairs much of the time. I notice that there's a certain strange pressure in my body as well, and tension, especially in my shoulders and neck. It can be sort of hard to breath sometimes also, almost like my whole torso is getting squeezed. There's also some weird stuff going on in my head. There's pressure and heat and various sensations.

12/28/03:
Today there's a sense of peace, of relief, of trust and ease, deeper and more profound than anything I've ever experienced. There's a quality of acceptance and presence with things as they are that's quite exquisite.

01/03/04:
Today, and recently, I've been feeling the sense of "crucifixion" a lot, especially in relationship. I often feel almost terrorized by the presence of others. I realized today that I've gotten so used over time to not having my needs really met that the idea of having them met is almost scary, because it's such a foreign idea. I've been noticing that there's a growing demand in me to find ways to get my needs met, for real! I'm looking forward to the day when I can fundamentally stand up for myself and my own real needs, and I'm committed to finding ways to help make that possible.

02/24/04:
I'm feeling really bewildered, perplexed, disheartened. I see that I must begin to face and deal with myself and my life more and more directly, and that is a painful realization, but it is also somewhat ecstatic, because it's what I want. Instead of, "I want to wake up!" now it's, "I want to grow up!" I want to find out what the hell my life is really about, really.

"It was necessary for me to much more fully feel the sensuality, strength, and delight inherent in my male body in order to fully inhabit who I am as an infinite being."

Peter

Peter Reed grew up in the sixties, i.e., he never really grew up. He never really inhabited his body either, despite the many years he spent practicing yoga, rebirthing, vegetarianism, following a guru, and keeping quite fit swimming and running on the beach near his home in Florida. It wasn't until he moved back to California, gave up his nice pool home, his girlfriend, the guru, and 95% of his "stuff," that he discovered the Waking Down process. This allowed him to let go of all his seeking and spend time in nature on the wild Northern Coast beaches, the rivers, and the mountains that enlivened in him the natural appreciation, joy and bliss of what real embodiment is. His life is a mosaic of various artistic and healing expressions having to do with facilitating consciousness on the planet. His art can be seen at www.holysmile.com.

SEXUALITY AND MT. SHASTA: TWO PASSAGES TO AWAKENING

During my 50th year I experienced two incredible passages that led to my Second Birth embodied awakening. I'd like to share them with you. The first one was a sexual passage.

Even though I had thought a lot about (i.e., desired) sex and felt sexual energy in my body throughout my life, I had not had very many girlfriends or much sexual activity with women. My last girlfriend, six years previously, provided for the most part a totally dysfunctional relationship, sexually and otherwise. The previous three decades of my sexually-enabled life were not that fulfilling either, to say the least. So it was a great pleasure and joy to meet and be with a pretty woman twelve years younger than I. The second time I met her we made out with each other most of the night, kissing, hugging and touching. The next evening we made love for half the night. It felt so natural and truly nurturing the way our bodies came together in feeling so much pleasure and joy. She expressed to me that no man had been with her and touched her the way I had and also conveyed that she had led a rather active sexual life. We spent every night together, except for one, that first week in equal amounts of passion and embrace. The following three weeks things gradually subsided to where we were together only two or three evenings a week. The length of our lovemaking also decreased to a couple of hours, yet were just as enjoyable. It's as if our bodies hungered and fed each other on a nurturing level as much as a pleasurable one. One of our last evenings together, on my birthday, was a beautiful sweet time, making love to a melodious mantra, both of us climaxing simultaneously with the ending of the mantra.

Even though our wonderful sexual communing didn't last that long, being with her opened me up to more of who I am as a man and allowed me to own much more of my maleness. As a sensitive artist type I had been out of balance in the way I identified with and allowed the more feminine sides of my nature to show up. This imbalance led to passivity, lack of confidence and fear of self-expression. Also, in relating to women I experienced fears of performance, of not being good enough in other ways, and of rejection and abandonment. As a lot of my fear and inhibitions began to dissipate as a result of being with this loving woman, I became more attracted and attractive to women. I had another brief sexual encounter with a sweet woman soon after, and began to feel more comfortable around women and enjoyed more fully looking at their beautiful faces and bodies.

This releasing of fear also played a big part in another embodying passage I experienced that fall on Mt. Shasta. Even though I was healthy and fit and a lover of outdoors, I never considered myself an avid hiker. And even though I had always been enamored of mountains, I never hiked anything higher than 7000 feet. Yet something drew me to Mt. Shasta and the desire to hike to the top of its 14,161-foot peak. I did some homework, reading and talking to people, bought the necessary camping and hiking gear that I didn't have, did some practice hiking and tried to prepare myself physically and emotionally. Yet the second time to the mountain, on the fall equinox, none of that seemed to matter. I felt for the most part totally intimidated, anxious and fearful.

That night at base camp (10,500 ft.) the stars sparkled brilliantly in the cold air and gave me an even greater sense of my smallness and my aloneness. Not only did I fear failing my summit attempt, I feared for my life. All the rangers that I had talked to earlier said it was one of the most dangerous times of the year to be on the mountain and climb. The heat, by that time of year, melted a lot of the ice that held the mountain together. The dryness and lack of rain loosened up the smaller rocks to where your foot slid backwards as much or more than it stepped forward. The potential for rock falls was also at its highest, where large rocks could come flying down off the mountain at great speeds. Helmets were strongly recommended. They also suggested it would be better to come back next year at a safer time.

At a certain level I felt they were just doing their job and trying to keep the expensive helicopter rescues to a minimum. (There was one earlier in the season.) However, there were other campers on the mountain, and that morning I ran into a half-dozen sleeveless and shirtless testosterone-laden young men on their way to the top, non-stop. That afternoon I saw most of them again on their way down, separated in groups of two. None of them had made it for various reasons ranging from not navigating a mildly tricky traverse at 13,000 ft. to just plain running out of time. The rangers gave a turnaround time of 1 P.M. to give enough time to make it back all the way down the mountain . Two men stuck it out until four before turning around. All the hikers I talked to confirmed the odds of what the rangers said and what I had read about—one in three summit attempts were successful.

So without much sleep, awakening for the umpteenth time to the sound of my tent door flapping in the wind, I arose, packed, coffee'd up, and was hiking up the mountain in the dark predawn hours. A sense of newness and exhilaration immediately fueled my body and awareness with a delightful presentness. Taking one step at a time, I felt empowered also by my remembrances of others. My normal sense of I as the doer with all my petty predicaments and worries was totally eclipsed by the feeling that this hike was so much more than "my" hike. I felt a presence of Beingness that included those great beings that came before me in my life and on my spiritual path, including my mom. This empowerment never diminished the whole way up.

A young kid in his twenties was following me from early on. My finding a frozen streambed where all the stones and rocks that would normally be loose were iced together facilitated our relative sense of ease and swiftness up the beginning of one of the steepest parts of the mountain. There were no marked trails on this part of the mountain. Every man for himself. Yet in my case there were others guiding me.

Our sense of exhilaration only increased as we traversed the tricky 13,000 foot threshold at Red Banks and on up into the thin icy air blowing with pure oxygen. We were treated to the most incredible of views of below and beyond. The glacial crevasses gave off a color of blue only seen at those elevations. Up Misery Hill, across a large snowy plateau and on up the last pinnacle of the mountain, we both screamed as we reached the top. The maximum time I had anticipated for myself to summit was around six to seven hours. We made it in less than four! Three weeks later I led three others to the summit.

What summiting Mt. Shasta gave me was a sense of confidence in myself. I had never met such a physical or emotional challenge before, along with a much greater confidence in being, in soul nature. A confidence that resides more in a surrendering and in an allowing to happen what's to happen and a knowing and being OK with it. It also allowed me to be exposed and vulnerable to the raw and awesome power of nature and gave a sense of awe and wonder about that power as well as the power of my own being. My fear gave way to delight. My anxious mind and sense of weakness gave way to strength.

This experience, just as much as my experience in being with a woman, allowed what Saniel terms "the sensual delight of being alive" to be truly felt and embodied. It was necessary for me to much more fully feel the sensuality, strength, and delight inherent in my male body in order to fully inhabit who I am as an infinite being.

At the "Old Timers Retreat" a few weeks after my Shasta trip, Saniel talked about this sensual delight in being alive, embodiment, and the Waking Down process. He also acknowledged that my hike up Mt. Shasta was no small deal. I knew then that my awakening, in whatever form it was to take, was not separate in any way to my feeling and inhabiting this aliveness. Being more comfortable in my own body and my ability to receive comfort was freeing and liberating for me. The increasing amounts of joy, pleasure and strength I felt also released a lot of bound energy and attention that allowed Consciousness to inhabit, with more frequency and intensity, the darker and shadowy areas of my life.

This gave way in about two months to my finally landing in the all of me—to my being able to hold in total recognition all the despairing parts of myself, bound as well as unbound, free as well as trapped. It was a great release and relief not to have to use the energy and attention I had normally used to keep all the parts of myself and the world separate and at bay. This was a revelation at a subtle, yet fundamental and cellular level. The wound of being, the feeling of separation of body/mind from Consciousness that I had always feared to fully feel, I now fully felt and became. This paradoxically gave way to feeling and being in communion with all the heretofore separate parts of myself and my world. In communion with whatever arose in the present moment, I felt a fundamental sense of ease at the core of my being. I was free in the seamless Consciousness of myself to be present to anything that arose . This was truly liberating, yet very subtle. And it was only the beginning. That's why it's called the Second Birth.

"Awakening was a big unknown with no guarantees of what life would be like afterwards."

June

June Konopka was born and raised in the Midwest. After college she spent many years traveling and teaching meditation around the world through an affiliation with the Transcendental Meditation organization. She later obtained a Master's degree in Nutritional Sciences in California, and currently uses that knowledge to help people with addictions and other nutritional concerns. She is also a teacher of Waking Down in Mutuality and holds regular sittings in Fort Collins, CO. Her supplemental training in the Shamanic arts, trauma therapy, and in the Hakomi method of body-centered psychotherapy enriches her teaching and healing practices.

LETTING GO

My life has always appeared to flow easily in an ordinary way without a lot of drama or excitement. I oozed slowly into my awakening, having been fascinated with meditation, enlightenment, and spiritual teachings since my early twenties. There was nothing in my outer life that distracted me away from my awakening process. I always made time for meditation and self-exploration, and yet it was a very slow process that didn't come to fruition until my mid-fifties. Part of the slowness of the process was a result of being naive about what awakening really was. Consequently, some of my spiritual concepts and practices were actually keeping me from realizing myself as Unlimited Consciousness. But a bigger, more primal obstacle lay deep in my psyche. Far inside, I was afraid to awaken. Part of me was afraid that moving toward an embodied awakening would take me on an uncontrollable ride. It is one thing to meditate and kiss Infinity deep within, and quite another to be Infinity while living the challenges of ordinary life. Awakening was a big unknown with no guarantees of what life would be like afterwards.

I was given this lucid dream which seemed to convey the underlying fear and the inevitable letting go:

I am driving my car to a very important event, but I get lost. I don't know which road to take, so I pick up a passenger who is going to the same event and who says he knows the way. Soon we are going down a hill and the brakes start to go out. "Faulty brakes" is a very old theme in my dreams, but for the first time I can actually see what awaits me at the bottom of the hill. It is a river that has flooded up over the road and has become a raging swift current. This feels like certain death, and I try with all my human power to make those brakes work and turn the car around. The passenger in the backseat is unconcerned and encourages me to keep going, letting me know this is the way to get to where I want to go. He assures me we will be fine. Suddenly, and unexpectedly, he calls me by a new name that I recognize as the name of my deep Soul Essence. I look around at him in the backseat, his words capturing my attention. The distraction causes me to forget my fear and efforts for a moment, and I move inevitably toward the water. I wake up just before being caught up by the river.

I met Saniel Bonder and his future wife, Linda, in 2000. After hanging out with them for awhile, the possibility of awakening in this lifetime was rekindled in me. And, as in the dream, my life events started to intensify. From the outside, no one would say, "Oh, June is really going through a rough time." It was such an internal process that very few people, besides my husband, really knew what I was going through. I was presented with many circumstances, especially at work, that I couldn't control or run from. The pressure was on, and all my old "fix it" skills and survival strategies weren't working. I was beginning to conclude it was hopeless to try to control anything. There was no way to fix these situations. I was also frustrated that I couldn't make my awakening happen faster by fixing myself. Maybe I would just have to let happen what was happening. Maybe I would have to give up and let go of trying to control my life, even though this meant anything could happen in the end. "Hopeless to fix anything" were the words that landed in my mind from what seemed like somewhere outside myself. There was relief in believing those words and in starting to give up. I realized later that what I was giving up was just my defended state, born of eons of living in a reality that only knew separation. This state couldn't hold up as the reality of Unity was dawning.

Just like the passenger in my dream, others in the Waking Down community who had already awakened came to my assistance. They reassured me that I was on the right path, even if it was scary and hard. My Divine Being was continuously enlivened through the remarkable transmission from Saniel, and the other Waking Down teachers I grew to trust. This took my attention off my fears. It took two and a half years after meeting Saniel and Linda before I felt comfortable enough to let go and slip into the river of awakening. I awoke to myself as the Unbounded Infinity that penetrates and interconnects All That Is. I also knew, ever so subtly, that this penetration included this human life I was living. I wasn't sure what that meant completely at the time, but knew even my deeper psyche couldn't resist it any longer.

I didn't awaken because I finally understood, resolved or overcame all my deep fears and pains. It didn't happen because I fixed something in me. It didn't happen because I did something better. It happened because I desired deeply to awaken. It happened because I gave up any hope of controlling life. It happened because I was superbly held and reminded of my true nature. It happened because I was willing to risk whatever was going to happen to me. I realize now that any resistance to the penetration of All That Is into all parts of my life is futile. I have given up the primary struggle to stay in control, even though there are parts of me that try to control things for short times out of habit.

I have now been in the sometimes raging, sometimes blissful river of awakened life for almost three years and wouldn't have it any other way. This reminds me of a second recurring dream:

I am floating without a boat down a peaceful river. Here, I am quite blissful, enjoying the scenery and the bodily sensations of the moving water. I let the water carry me, doing nothing, trusting the water completely. But I notice a vague anxiousness when I sense the ocean downstream. I wonder what might happen to me when the river eventually opens into the ocean and the water becomes deep and powerful, without shores.

I am deepening into the understanding of how unique and precious this fragile human experience is, while simultaneously embodying the Immortality and Oneness of Life Itself. Sometimes I sense my Divine Soul, which I intuit through my heart. It keeps calling me home to the Beloved Unbounded Ocean, while simultaneously showing me which currents of activity are mine to express along the way. My unique self is unfolding as I travel down the river of life, and I intuit that any hidden fears and pains that mask my creativeness and love cannot stay hidden much longer. This particular union has never happened before, and somehow it feels important to be all that I am meant to be, by the time this union completes itself.

UNRAVELING

It has been almost six years since my Second Birth awakening. Much that was unconscious has found its way into consciousness. The unraveling of unconscious shadow material has occurred through the simple reflection of the mirror of daily life, through conscious direct methods of self-discovery and by the loving presence and transmission of others. The backdrop for this entire process has been Self Awareness continuously deepening and growing in my life. I absolutely know that I could not have let the core of my inner unconscious shadow unravel and become conscious without knowing that I was Limitless, Unchanging, Immortal Being. It is the ground of my human existence.

My core inner shadow was bound together by a belief that permeated every cell of my body (probably the DNA itself). This belief was "I am not safe." It manifested as a child who was extremely shy. It manifested as a student that worked really hard to get the right answers. It manifested as an adult who was afraid to express her creativity or opinions. This sense of lack of safety may have been planted in me from growing up with an alcoholic father, or maybe it came in my genetic maternal make-up (possibly dating back to the witch burnings). Who knows the origin, but "not feeling safe" was at the root of all my ego defense structures. It was as if I had an agreement with myself, my mother, and my grandmother to not take too many bodily risks, not show too much creative power in the world, and not be too different. I mention these agreements and defense structures because they effectively cut me off from my physical, intuitive, and spiritual power. And, my post-awakening story has been, and continues to be, about finding, trusting, and reclaiming this power.

I have gained the ability to trust life again. I know now I don't have to stay vigilant and in control to be safe in this world. It would take many pages to report all the events, insights, processes, and integration that occurred over these last six years that resulted in this knowing, so I won't. What was common at each stage, though, was a deeper willingness to feel what I had been unable or unwilling to feel before. This willingness grew as the trust in life itself grew. At a retreat in June of 2008, I suddenly knew that I could let myself feel the grief and terror of life's worst expressions of separation and still be held by the Wholeness of Life Itself. This climaxed for me in one particular moment. Feeling deeply held by myself and a few good friends, I spontaneously let myself feel and express the bodily terror of being burned alive. I had no idea this energy was being held in my body, or how long it had been there. I do know that by letting myself die, another part of me came back to life.

I am amazed how much safer I feel now in the world. But most importantly, a space has opened in my heart that previously was closed. With the help of my Shamanic teacher, this space has become a portal through which I have begun to consciously commune with more and more of my Soul. The impact of this reconnection has been so life-changing that I have at times referred to it as a Third Birth. I look forward to this unfolding of my multidimensional being, and can only imagine what this will look like down the road.

"I had, for all practical purposes, committed suicide in the south of France."

Gerardo

Gerardo R. Cantu has was born in South Texas, where he was influenced by two great cultures: the Mexican and the American. Having interests that range from Atlantis to Zen, Gerardo had a hard time picking a major, and eventually graduated with a BA in Communications and, in 2003, a Master's in Spiritual Psychology. In 2006, together with Rev. Dr. David E. Ault, Gerardo was an integral part in founding The Conscious Mile Center for Spiritual Living in Mobile, Alabama. Gerardo currently lives in Hawaii.

THE ONE I CALL BELOVED

Before my Second Birth I had, for all practical purposes, committed suicide in the south of France. I did everything I could to check out, but for reasons unbeknownst to *moi*, I was rescued and spent a month in a hospital.

When I came back to L.A., I realized I was suffering from co-dependency and joined a 12-step program (CODA), which I attended regularly for two years. Towards the end of my second year, I put a personal ad on a website for dating people, and someone who was doing the Waking Down work contacted me. I started going to satsangs where Saniel and Linda presided.

When my friend asked me to come see Saniel for the first time, I was open and had no preconception of what it would be like. I remember people were cutting a tree down just outside the house we were meeting in. We were trying to ignore the sound of the buzz saw, but it was impossible. Suddenly Linda started wailing. I thought it was very dramatic until I processed someone else's pain in much the same way. She expressed the agony of this life form being destroyed. It was very moving. Still a part of me was wondering if this was all an act.

Then the gazing...this was also very strange for me. I wanted to be seen, yet was apprehensive at the same time. In spite of my skepticism and apprehension, the love was palpable. I could dive into the pools of love that were Saniel's eyes. Also, he shared much information with us, and I read his *The White-Hot Yoga of the Heart* and *Waking Down*.

During one gathering, Saniel spoke about taking a snapshot of the person one is right now; this is the one who awakens. This really sank in. I understood that I didn't have to be a special way or do anything to get there.

I was carrying a lot of shame around having committed suicide. During one of our gatherings, I asked the adepts if an Enlightened Being can still be Enlightened and commit suicide. They affirmed that they knew of one who had. I guess this was the "permission" I needed.

A few months later I attended a satsung with Holly and Renie and spent a half hour with each. That day I was my usual self: I was open and skeptical (I feel a certain amount of skepticism is healthy). I have tended to judge people who charge for bringing light into the world. And though I still feel that sharing the light ought to be something we do naturally, as a given, as an integral part of being human, we pay for food and even to have our waste taken. It is where we are on our evolutionary path at the moment. So with reservation I paid for my time with Renie and Holly.

In hindsight I'm glad I did.

I refer to Renie as my Second Birth midwife. During the half hour I spent with her, she sang to me and gently caressed my body. Suddenly my back arched spontaneously and my body got very hot. They had to get cold towel compresses for me. They said there was a smell in the air of a new born. My experience with Renie was frightening and exciting. I felt shaken to the core and at the same time a vibrational aliveness that I don't remember ever feeling before.

It took me a while to recover, and then I went outside to sit and gaze with Holly. We were not gazing for more than five minutes when I felt a voice enter through the right side of my face that said, "You are divine." I started smiling more and more broadly and my eyes were wide with awe. Holly broke the silence to ask me what was going on. I told her that I got that I was divine, and she slapped my thigh and said, "Welcome to the club."

For a week I felt like a lighthouse. A beam of light was pouring out of my eyes and forehead. And then it settled down.

Today, I am and I am not the same Gerardo I was then. I am the same and different at the same time. It's hard to explain. It's easier for me to be here even when I feel pain. It's easier to feel it. I get that it's just a part of being human. It's hard to be infinity in the flesh. I think the "crazy" episodes I was having in the past were just part of my being partly awake already, but not knowing what was going on. I think I was going through some kind of initiation process or settling in, but for me it was very difficult to accept because I've had a bad case of culture shock for as long as I can remember—and by "culture" I mean being human.

FOR SANIEL, ALL ADEPTS AND ASPIRANTS

Oh wakened child, oh radiant one, I am the one I call beloved.

Created form which was first a mother's thought of having someone to hold and love, so here I am come forth to feel, to see, to touch, to be.

I've had hard times. I've hurt so deeply and through it all I thirsted for what I felt inside my heart was past all pain and suffering; a place where I could stand and witness my Self being unshakeable and unaffected. This thirst led me to a well whose water was alive and spoke to my true essence, hearing it not with my human ears it said, "You are divine."

As I was meanwhile being held in the consciousness of others who had gone before me to the well and had recognized their truth; a touch, a song, a gaze into my soul—two gentle, loving women helped me open my heart's ears to hear my own.

My thirst is quenched for now. I know I am divine; a finite being whose true essence cannot even be described because there are no words.

It is with reverence that I bow to my authentic self and when I fall, I know I'm there witnessing and reminding myself of who and what I truly am.

I yearn to let this light shine through me burning bright and right through all the darkness, helping others shine their own; being a well of living water for all who thirst. In exaltation and delight I greet you and welcome you and hold you in my heart. It is great joy, gratitude and pleasure that I feel to behold you and to serve you.

Oh wakened child, oh radiant one, You are the one I call beloved.

"In the gazing meditations with the teachers, I felt how much I needed and wanted to be seen. At the same time, there was a deep shame in being seen in all my jagged glory: Deep shame, yes, but also profoundly liberating relief."

Jen

Jennifer Mayol lives in Mill Valley, California. She loves working with people as a Senior Waking Down in Mutuality Teacher integrating Transpersonal Hypnotherapy and Somatic Experiencing, a trauma resolving process, as well as Creative Coaching, nurturing people's unfolding creative expression. She has degrees in Art and Textile Design. She enjoys painting, writing, singing and toning as part of her own deep unfolding process and self-expression.

JAGGED GLORY

I was born in 1959 and had a "normal" upbringing in a "normal" American family. Amidst that I was always interested in the metaphysical, what is beyond the ordinary way of seeing, thinking and being. I also had and have a strong devotional nature towards God. At an early age I began having this existential fear that would arise when I would find myself spontaneously contemplating the nature of God and infinity: If God is infinite, then what created God? How could something be infinite? What preceded the infinite? Could anything precede the infinite? A barrage of thoughts like this would storm in my mind until I would become exceedingly overwhelmed and confused. At some point I would have to stop this line of thinking because I was afraid if I continued I would become unhinged. It was something, however, that I felt impelled to do over and over again throughout my life. I never shared this questioning with anyone. It was my own private cauldron that I stewed in.

I began meditating at the age of sixteen, learning Transcendental Meditation, a huge Godsend for me. Coming out of my initiation and first meditation, walking outside, I noticed how bright and beautiful the colors were around me, how distinct the forms, how fresh and alive everything seemed. Meditating curtailed my desire for high school partying. I voraciously read Maharish Mahesh Yogi's teachings and began to consider the possibility of some kind of enlightenment for myself. I attended Maharishi International University in Fairfield, Iowa.

The sense of spiritual camaraderie I felt with the group of students there was wonderful for me, and the atmosphere of the campus from everyone meditating was very relaxing. For at least the first two years I was there I bought pretty much hook, line and sinker the general paradigm of TM is The Only Way, or certainly the Best Way. Around my third year I found this thinking to be too narrow and insular for me. I couldn't fully buy into the whole dogma. I found myself doing what I needed to do, what I felt was right for me, outside what was accepted if you were to be "on the program." I went for some readings with a local psychic channel knowing that if I was found doing this I could have been kicked out of school and not been able to get on any TM courses. I didn't want to have to hide what I was doing in order to persevere with my TM explorations. But, I also couldn't risk being kicked out in case it really was The Only Way for me to awaken. There I was, divided in myself: Devotion on the Path doesn't include questioning and seeing what feels right inside for me, does it?

There was an intimation that after being at MIU for four years that one would "get enlightened." Well, I finished my B.A. in Art and I definitely was not "enlightened." I moved to the San Francisco Bay Area and studied with a variety of teachers, read many books and attended different workshops and seminars through my 20's and 30's. There was a continuing exploration of ascended states, levels and realms in which one could be in contact with all sorts of Beings and realities. I was hopeful, though, to find an ultimate person or teaching—something pure and trustable, the highest truth where I could become enlightened. I would immerse myself in various paths, but then find I needed to differentiate, discerning what was true for me. That quieter voice inside me always had to make itself heard even more strongly at those times, serving as my own personal rudder navigating dicey spiritual waters. The naturally flowing current of my own inner process necessitated my leaving a few different spiritual communities over the years. This was difficult and painful, and yet, initiatory and important in my overall development of myself as an autonomous human and spiritual being.

Amidst all this exploration "spiritually" and living my adult life, I sometimes dealt with depression, anxiety attacks and paranoia. This seemed to stem from early challenging and traumatic experiences in my life and also some genetic factors. At times I thought about commiting suicide—considering this as a possible option seemed to serve as a relief valve for me, but I knew I could never actually do it. Along with my need to escape the pain of being in this physical life was my deep desire to awaken, to know myself in the most fundamental way. I did hope, that maybe enlightenment would give me both those things—relief from pain and fulfillment of my spiritual search. That seemed to be what was "advertised." I am always amazed in reviewing my "spiritual history," how much I was willing to believe and put up with in this pursuit of mine.

Case in Point: In 1992 I met a "crazy wisdom type" teacher with whom I spent five very difficult years along with a small group of fellow students. There was constant testing by him and an encouragement to be emotionally detached, equating that with spiritual detachment. This teacher, as many teachers do, taught that the student must totally surrender to him in order to awaken, that he knows what is right for the student even more than the student does. I lived with a knot in my stomach during all those years from trying to manipulate my inner state so severely— basically trying not to have human reactions, swallowing this teacher's directives to a pretty extreme degree. I tried to embrace what he was telling me was right for me, tried to surrender, yet there was my inner voice untouched by his sense of things. I had such a split in myself. I continued on down this path, but always there was a place in me that couldn't buy his whole way of teaching and being with his students. Something felt so wrong in my guts.

In 1996, I found a hard mass on the right side of my torso. I knew it wasn't cancer but I didn't know what it was. I was fearful of going to a regular medical doctor because of some past experiences. I did a cleanse that I thought would help but it debilitated me. So, not feeling well and against my better judgment, that inner voice telling me, "Don't go. You don't have to go," I traveled to Romania on vacation with my mother. I ended up in the hospital there because of a severe health breakdown and was given a diagnosis of a life-threatening disease. My time there was an experience of extremes. Being in a hospital in a not very developed country was no picnic. I was in some of the darkest, most painful states I had ever been in—a dark night of the soul—as well as some of the most ecstatic and heart opening. When I returned to the States, I couldn't work because I was too weak and sick. My romantic relationship ended and the decision whether or not to leave this spiritual teacher and community had come to a head. I had reached the end of my rope physically really and in every other way as well. I could no longer manipulate myself to detach, to go into alternate realities or bliss states in the ways I had been doing for so many years. Sometimes those states would come just naturally without my trying, but I couldn't seek them out, try to make them happen. In my illness and utter fatigue, with so little energy, I literally couldn't do what I had been doing anymore.

I realize in retrospect that that spiritual path with that teacher was the ultimate "rot-making machine" for me. The trying to not react to things, trying to detach and manipulate my inner state, trying to go into these "higher" realities was so extreme something finally broke in me. I finally had to let myself be the way I was in some basic way. I had to have my plain old human self (I never really succeeded in having anything else anyway!). I began to let my thoughts and feelings be rather than trying to manipulate them. There was some magic about allowing my own humanness and relaxing in my body that started a deep unwinding and resting in myself. I would sit with myself not as a practice but because that was what I was drawn to do, all I could do really. I needed a sense of my own integrity back. I had given over myself in so many ways that had felt violent to this quiet inner part of myself. I had to feel clearly what was true for me in the deepest part of me. The time with this teacher could be seen as a radical betrayal of my autonomous self. But I guess I needed to enact this pattern to that degree for me to see the whole dynamic clearly, so I could finally begin to trust my own authority first and foremost. I'm not saying now that I won't or don't listen to the wisdom of another—of course I do—but not at the expense of my own integrity and my own inner truth.

During that year I was trying to decide whether or not to leave this teacher and community. I started to read ads in a spiritual magazine called Common Ground and saw Saniel's ad and picture there. He claimed his students were awakening. Hmmm…that stopped me in my tracks. Is it possible? I had mostly lost hope of awakening and yet that desire still burned in me somewhere. Are these people deluded? After much consideration over some months and repeatedly looking at that ad and Saniel's picture, in January 1998 I made a call to their office number. A Waking Down teacher, Ted Strauss, answered the phone and a two and a half hour call ensued. I felt so at home, comfortable and welcomed in talking with him. We ascertained that we both had done TM as part of our early spiritual life, and the conversation rolled on from there. I purchased Saniel's book, Waking Down, which I read twice within a couple of days. It spoke so deeply to my experience and inner process. I planned to attend a sitting with Saniel later that week. In my heart I was hoping, since everyone in my other community wanted to awaken too, that maybe I could share with them what I might learn in the Waking Down dharma. This was not to be.

A few days later, feeling hopeful and apprehensive, I attended my first sitting or, in my case, lying down. I was still very debilitated physically. During the sitting I noticed an unusual transmission that wasn't like anything I had experienced so far in my spiritual search. It had a density that I could feel which definitely was a bit strange to me but somehow okay; it was intriguing and relaxing to me as well. That night as I was going to sleep I saw in front of my eyes an undulating mandala composed of fur. There was an intense initiatory presence to it that as it continued to stay in my vision started to scare me. I had a friend staying over downstairs and was tempted to run down there for help! Then that one abated, but then another one appeared. It seemed to be made of blood and muscle. This one was even a little more intense and freaky than the first. I had seen many weird things in my years of exploration, but this was different. Instead of visions that were more ascended in nature this was so profoundly earthy, intense and rich. I thought, "What I have gotten myself into this time!" Yet I found myself impelled to explore further with Saniel and the other teachers. In retrospect, these visions seemed to me to be an initiation into my primal human animal body. There were other experiences as well along the way that were further explorations of this primal side of who I am.

At that first sitting and some of the ones following I tried to ascertain who was claiming they were awake among the people there. Initially, I remember thinking things like, "That person claims they're awake—give me a break. They look pretty neurotic and uptight to me." I had definite ideas of what you were supposed to look like in a post-awakened or enlightened state, and this definitely wasn't it! And yet I kept being drawn to attend these sittings. There was something about the way the teachers and also some of the other students were being with me that was different. There was a quality of compassion for my human story that I desperately needed. I felt inherently encouraged to be and express myself: my agonies and ecstasies, my superficialities and judgments, my beauty and worthiness, my neediness and victimhood—to explore all these different aspects, to embrace and let myself be all these aspects. I felt a welcoming of both my infiniteness and my natural human limitations.

I attended many teachers' sittings for many months. Sometimes I would feel such a deep peace and connectedness, and with that, such gratitude; Other times there was a profound sense of separation and confusion, as though a giant magnifying glass was intensely fixed precisely on this feeling, so much so that it would be almost unbearable. In the gazing meditations with the teachers I felt how much I needed and wanted to be seen. At the same time, there was a deep shame in being seen in all my jagged glory: Deep shame, yes, but also profoundly liberating relief. As I continued my exploration, there seemed to be a natural, continuous stripping away of conceptualizations about myself, my life, the nature of reality and my ideas about enlightenment. With that occurring, I began to notice something about the people who had had their Second Birth: a kind of soberness, freedom, presence and truth about them coexistent with all their human peculiarities. The impact of their transmission was profound for me.

My process to the Second Birth awakening was so jam-packed and it's been awhile, so I can only recall some of the significant experiences, sign posts along the way. Writing about this process feels frustrating to me and inadequate on so many levels. Words can just barely touch on the richly layered, multi-dimensional landscape and the riveting, initiatory and transformational power as I navigated my landing in the Second Birth. Given that, I'll try to convey in words, as best I can, some of those significant aspects of my process.

In the first week or so that I started attending sittings, Saniel started a class to study his new book, Waking Down, which had just been published. As he was speaking that first night of the class, I started to notice this sharp, needle-like pain on the right side of my chest deep inside. It was a sensation I hadn't had before, and so I was a bit alarmed but I just sat with it. The class continued, and then at some point Saniel spoke about the right side of the heart being significant in this process. I felt intuitively that that was what the pain was on my right side. This was something that came and went during the nine months leading to my Second Birth. Then a kind of spiritual explosion happened that emanated from that precise point in my chest much later in my process.

One time I found myself standing motionless in my living room being struck with a memory or vision. I didn't know which it was. I saw and felt that somebody I had been was absolutely being beaten to death. As this pummeling continued mercilessly I began to notice I was witnessing, completely untouched, unaffected, free, neutral, observing the event. I wouldn't even say it felt liberating. It just was. My mind was quizzical that there was this "noticer" untouched by this beating. This sense of witnessing began to "stay with me" more regularly over time. I say "stay with me" in quotes because that was how I perceived it initially. My witnessing was definitely not coincident with my physical form. I seemed to be noticing from a vantage point behind my head and body. I began to realize that this noticing presence was always there in every moment of my life. Sometimes the witness was more subtle and understated, and sometimes it had as though a more striking blown-out infinite quality to it taking me at times into a no self state. As my ideas and mental concepts about Consciousness were stripped away through the process of deeper rotting, the reality of the continuity of the witness became obvious to me. Later, as my process deepened, my sense of the witness began to change. I remember one day my lower belly area became awake as this witness. It was quite an odd experience and hard to describe. I was as though noticing, registering the world from that vantage point. I didn't think I would want it to be that way all the time though! It was a passing experience and a sign of the feeling-witness consciousness coming to roost in and as my body.

Around this same time period, I ran into my former teacher at Whole Foods grocery store. I was pushing my cart in the produce section when he approached me and started wheeling my basket, talking a mile a minute while walking with me. I remember the Witness Consciousness was so strong and established in me that I could see him in a whole different way. I remember thinking, "Oh, there was never any room for me to come forward, to come into my own natural rhythms and wisdom. I really needed to leave." It was a rather neutral observation without much charge, just what the reality was for me while being with him right then. I think other students might well have had a different kind of experience with him. Based on my own patterns of wounding this is what it had been like particularly for me. The relationship with him had been complex. There were many powerful, beautiful moments, but that general dynamic of him being the final authority could never work for me. Running into him again was clarifying and helpful so I could relax even more fully into my process with Waking Down.

One Saturday morning I went to Ted Strauss' sitting. As luck would have it, I was the only one who showed up that day, an unusual occurrence. So we started talking, then gazing and then talking again in a free form, organic kind of way. At one point as we gazed, I started to notice and feel this familiar horror at the core of me. I remember thinking, "Oh, my God, not this too. Oh, no…is this what I have to face?" Just then we heard this dog howling in the distance in the most haunting way— a perfect reflection for the flavor of what I was beginning to allow myself to feel more fully. This horror was what was underneath the confused insanity place I would feel when I would think of God and infinity. It was always with me waiting at the core, waiting for me to be ready to embrace it, land in it. Over time, as this reflexive need to escape this most dark, insane, horror feeling began relaxing more and more, something began to be born in me. I began to be able to bear the pain of being human in the most fundamental way, down at the very bottom. This was my gateway.

Something Saniel said about his own awakening process, "Dare to grasp the means of your own realization," became a naturally arising inquiry during the last month or so before my Second Birth. Dare to grasp the means of your own realization. Dare to grasp the means of your own realization. What the hell does this mean?! How can one grasp the means of her own realization? How is that possible? During this time where this was an ongoing trajectory of exploration, there were a number of images and considerations that were related to this inquiry and significant in my process. One image was of a table with one leg. As I would "gaze" upon this internal image, I, at some point, had the impulse to kick out the last leg of the table. It sounds a bit strange, but to do that kick in my inner vision took intense energy and focus. It felt like a ritual passage to take that action of kicking.

Another image that came spontaneously to me was of a house with a peaked roof where the sides of the roof were ready to collapse into to the center of the building. I felt that this symbolized my own internal structures and conceptualizations getting ready to give way. I felt as though I was getting ready for a large scale collapse to make way for something very different—along the lines of the zen poem that goes something like, "My barn having burned to the ground, now I can see the moon."

There was another recurring image that held a great deal of intensity and stayed present with me for about two and a half weeks: a tall, dead male who had a slice of flesh cut out of the side of his body so I could see the different layers rotting inside—imagine a slice of brie cheese and you'll get the right feel for it. When it first appeared, it was quite viscerally overwhelming to me. But as I stayed with this vision of mortality, over time the intensity lessened. There came a kind of restfulness in looking and being with this image. It was strange to be going through my normal day with this image embedded inside, staying with me in whatever I was doing, a constant companion—just as my own life threatening disease diagnosis was also a constant companion for me. That diagnosis, feeling the squeeze of time, my mortality, was definitely fuel for my process. It could also explain the resolve that occurred in me around an important consideration about the repercussions of living an awakened life.

Historically, some people who awaken and then begin to speak from that level of truth get killed for it. This was one of the things that I would ponder over the years when thinking of whether I could or would awaken. It felt to me that if I was not willing to face that possibility, pay that price, then I wouldn't awaken. Whether this is actually true or not for me or anyone else, who knows? However, for me it was a crucial consideration. Anyway, one night as I was drawing a bath, "Grasp the means of your own realization," was roiling through me as well as this consideration of being killed if I awakened. Before the answer was always the same for me: basically, the price is too high to pay and I'm too frightened of that possibility of being killed, so I guess I won't awaken. I guess I don't want it enough to pay that price. However, on this night, as I was about to enter the bath that I was drawing, what came up in me was, "I don't care. I don't care if I get killed for this. I have to know who I Am and if that is the cost well then So Be It." With that resolve in place I stepped into the water. This resolve was new.

Another significant moment in my process was around the many visions of Gods and Goddesses that would come from time to time. On one particular day it was a regular parade. After awhile of this, I must admit, with some irritation and impatience, I spoke to "the heavens," "This is all well and good. I'm enjoying this celestial display very much, but can you tell me what the hell does this have to do with awakening?!" Immediately, the whole celestial parade inverted into and as my body. They were no longer outside and separate from me. I felt, now that's clear, I'm all of that too. I'm both a human and divine manifestation. I felt myself to be this whole continuum of creation. It was another clarifying piece in my process of landing in and as the non-separateness.

One day while I was driving in my car, getting onto the freeway via one of those circular on-ramps, I felt this miniature explosion originating from a pin point on the right side of my chest, as though something had given way. It was a white-heated energy and was blowing outwards from my heart in concentric circles of light out into infinity. I kept driving the tight curve I was on while having the experience. I had some fear that if what was happening intensified even further I might lose control of my car. I didn't and the experience concluded and I kept driving north up Highway 101 to my destination.

September 9, 1998: the day started in an ordinary way. I had been feeling a sense of suspended animation. Mid-morning, as I was walking to the store to buy some lettuce, I saw a young guy whom I knew to be a bit attracted to me in the past. I was nursing a painful heart from being rejected by someone who I thought I was going to be with in an intimate relationship. So I thought to myself, "Oh, good, some male attention." As if in a tightly choreographed dance, he came wheeling his bike perfectly in time to join me in walking down the sidewalk. A moment later and with the same sense of orchestration, two other women crossed our path and he, without seeming to miss a beat, joined up with them and kept walking. I kept walking, too, without looking back to see if he wanted to say anything such as, "Good-bye." I said out loud, with resolve, "Perfect." My relationship with men couldn't touch what needed to be fulfilled in my Being. There had been a way that I used relationship and my sexuality, and many other things as well, to cover this pain at the core of me, the pain of the Core Wound. It actually became more painful, really, creating distractions and not feeling this place than finally being ready to face this place, to relax as it. Don't get me wrong. Relationship and sexuality has been a big part of my life and remains so, but fundamentally I wanted and needed to awaken. That was the strongest hunger in me. Saniel has a saying, "Don't seek from relationship what only Consciousness can give. And don't seek from Consciousness what only relationship can give." That was the crux of it for me.

Anyway, later that day I went shopping. One could call it binge shopping. I would feel as though in a trance as I was hunting for the perfect bargain. I was noticing my shopping intensity was ramping up as well as my usual guilty talk. As I noticed this, I decided to embrace this part of me, to explore the feeling of shopping frenzy, this need in me. I hunted with focus and boldness, finding some great things—a faux fur purse the best find of all. It was my kill. I gloried in my finds on the drive home. Letting go and laughing maniacally, really having fun with myself, as two lanes merged into one, something popped or broke. It was very distinctive. When this membrane popped, it was very clear to me that there was no way to reconfigure whatever had just broken. The membrane of separation was gone. This sense of pressure I had felt my whole life, at the core of myself, just gave way. Inside was outside; outside was inside. They were on the most essential level the same thing.

It wasn't a sense of infinity that came, rather continuity of all. It was also odd and confounding to realize that this most intimate communion was not something that I wasn't already being. The first words out of my mouth were, "This is dumb." That made my heart twinge a bit in pain. "No," I thought, with a feeling of poignant tenderness in my heart, "This is silly." It was just the obviousness and simplicity of It All.

I didn't know at the time, mentally speaking, whether this condition I found myself Being was the Second Birth in Waking Down terms, but I knew something was complete; something fundamentally had changed —whether there was validation for this or not from anyone else.

In the following couple of days after that defining moment of my Second Birth, there was a profound reconfiguration going on in me as well as my mind trying to figure out what exactly was going on. As my mind started kicking in to access the situation, spontaneously what came up mentally was the idea to do the inquiry, "Who am I?" As I stopped to take stock of my condition, I just found myself laughing at the obviousness of Being. For me this was It, such a relief in my heart. I also remember at the time my mind registering that there was no longer a seeking impulse going on. I began to, with some panic, search for the seeking impulse. The hunter became the hunted, so to speak. My identity had been so wrapped up in being a seeker. It turned out to no longer be functioning. Oh dear, nowhere to go, nowhere to be, other than just Here, effortlessly. What would I do with myself now? My mind began to grasp the reality of what had occurred. The relief on this most basic level, to not be searching either outwardly or inwardly; to know myself as Being, my body as Being, all other manifestation as Being, all One, is hard to convey in words.

Somewhere in those couple of days, when I was lying in bed one morning, an initiatory power exploded in me. One way to express or describe it was that the most exquisitely painful and the most excruciating pleasurable force was "cooly" burning me through and through, like a massive blowtorch of Being. Transmogrification was the word that came to me as my experience was lessening. I thought to myself then, "Oh my God, if this is going to be an ongoing event or lived moment to moment reality I won't be around to tell the tale." I now know it was part of the whole integration into the new condition.

Before my Second Birth there was such a sense of many parts at war with each other. Afterward, there became less and less internal war with what and who I am. For instance, there was this part of me which felt like a victim. In other teachings I had been involved with, it was considered taboo to feel like a victim, a sign of less evolvement. It wasn't spiritually correct to feel like a victim. Yet, in Waking Down, I found myself able to fully embrace that part—hear its voice and truth, then as time rolled on, that voice found its proper, relaxed place in the landscape of my human divine self. I didn't have to cut it off. Another example of this was the wonder of not being told that I shouldn't have the desire to awaken. I know in some schools it's considered a taboo and a block to becoming awakened if you want to awaken. It's believed that you have to let go of that desire. It was such a relief to not be manipulating myself to not want something that was natural for me to want—another way that I didn't have to divide myself.

All this relaxing into the different voices and parts over time, really helped me to allow the fundamental split and tension I felt at the bottom to be finally navigated and rested in. The meeting point of consciousness and matter, finite and infinite in continuum, core human and divine mystery, this is what I am. I no longer have an impulse or need to ask, "Who am I?" There's a fundamental relief I feel from that seeking impulse, from the separation and confusion at the core, of not knowing who I am. That is resolved definitively. All phenomenon and consciousness are really one event or non-event, including me. It's all made of the same thing, so naturally I live in a state of non-separateness. Fundamental integration of Consciousness and matter has occurred. Onlyness is the word Saniel would use to refer to it and that has always felt to me a fitting match to my lived reality now. I'm amazed at the poignancy of this condition I find myself living. The utter heartbreak of feeling what it is to be here in human limitations and the utter ecstatic freedom living in that same Heart. I do feel the relief in others as they navigate into this fundamental landing in and as Being: The kind of sober sanity and integration that occurs over time as they realize and rest in their own Jagged Glory.

If this path turns out to be a part of your destiny, it is my honor as a teacher and as part of this Waking Down in Mutuality community to welcome you, hold and witness you in your awakening journey as well as the profound, ongoing integration after the Second Birth. My own integration after the Second Birth is really a whole other story so I'll leave that for now...

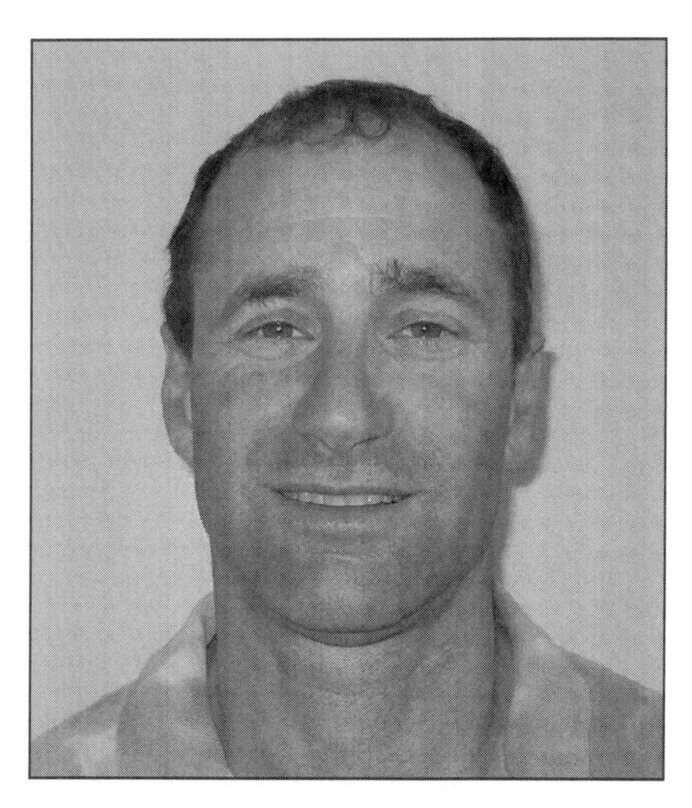

"No, officer, I am not on drugs.
I am having a spiritual experience."

Phil

Phil Cotton was born in San Francisco, growing up around his parents' deli and his father's real estate brokerage. Raised in Marin, he had a generous offer from his dad to go to the school of his choice. Phil chose to start a tow truck business in San Rafael (now run by his older brother). Phil currently lives a quiet life managing some rental properties in Oroville, California. His hobbies include biking, boating, and motorcycles.

WHO'S DRIVING?

The day after Thanksgiving (November 25, 2000) started out like most Saturdays. I woke up, looked at the clock, and went back to sleep. Around 7 a.m. I rolled out of bed, ate some fruit, put on my bike clothes, and went out to the garage to put my road bike together. I was thinking the last time I rode was before we went to Pengiua, a raw food community in Hawaii. There's a knock on the door. Frank is here early for the bike ride.

As we are riding I feel the cold, moist air on my face. I have to wipe the drops from my helmet every few minutes. We ride around China Camp discussing our lessons, our lives, past relationships, and some of the painful times in our childhood.

When we turn right on Mabry Way, Frank says, "See you later."

I tell him, "I'll be home. So stop by if you get a chance. I'll be working on my truck in the driveway." I thought to myself that I'm glad we made it back without getting a tow call.

I started working on my truck when I get a call from the Marin County sheriff. "We have an abandoned car. Do you have a truck?"

I said, "Is it in civilization?"

"Yes. Reed Boulevard, Mill Valley."

"I'll be there in twenty. Thanks."

The phone rings again. Marin County sheriff. "Make that Dolan at Morning Sun."

"10-4."

I get on 101 and take Highway 1 and turn right on Dolan. Man, what a narrow street! There is the patrol car. They want me to tow that big, old, ugly Olds wagon. I back up to it, drop my wheel lift, and start hooking on the straps. I'm thinking to myself this car is worthless. What a drag! Then I thought again. The sheriff gives me all those nice cars from in front of Strawberry Safeway. I don't mind this car. This is part of the deal.

I am all hooked up. The only thing left to do is climb under the car and put the trans in neutral. I go to set the e-brake on the car, and the e-brake pedal won't stay down. I wonder if it has anything to do with the coat hanger coming out of the dashboard where the release lever used to be.

I ask the officers, " Could you put your push bumper against this car? I have to release the transmission and I don't want to die."

I sign the 180 and ask the officer the best way out. He says, "That's a dead end and Morning Sun is pretty narrow."

"Thanks. I'll just do a 20 point turn to get out of here."

I pull the car up. Then stop and reset my straps. I'm impressed I got the big-ass Olds Custom Cruiser station wagon and my '99 Ford F450 Super Duty turned around and down that hill without knocking over a mailbox.

Coming down into Tam junction there are four road bike guys. I think, "I don't want to run over one of those guys."

The next thing I remember is pulling up to the stop sign at the Old Fireside Motel. I started feeling different. Am I here? Is this a dream? No. Why am I feeling this way? Is the heater turned up too high? No. Should I be driving? Am I everything? Am I everybody? Does anything matter? Do I care? Is it OK to get on the freeway?

Probably not. But I think I really like what is happening, so I'll keep doing what I'm doing. But turn down the heater.

Then I feel this orgasmic flow of energy flowing through my body from head to toe. I start having this wonderful feeling all through my body. This is great. I don't want this to stop. Do I just keep driving? No, I have to go to the shop. Should I call Pascal and tell her what is happening? No, don't use the phone. You can't. Stay with this flow of energy. Don't mess it up.

I've felt energy before but only in my head. Or for a few seconds after an intense yoga class. But what do I do?

I get myself together to dial the phone. Did I dial my home number or did I just dial the phone I'm holding? Should I be driving? Could I be arrested? No, officer, I am not on drugs. I am having a spiritual experience. Yeh, sure. Come with us.

Then I get my answering machine. I leave a message for Pascal. I turn left on Baxter's Court and see about eight guys waiting at the end by my gate. I think to myself, "I have to talk to these people? What do I say? Will I be able to talk? Do I have the keys to the gate?"

I get the gate open.

"What car do you want to pick up?"

"The bug."

"OK." I add it up. "$1039."

The guy says, "Can you do better than that?"

"No."

"All I brought is $800."

"No, if you want to get the car it is $1039. Otherwise I sell it to someone."

"How about…"

"No, I told you to bring about $1000 and it's $1039."

"1, 2, 3, 4, 5, 6, 7, 8, 9, 10, 11."

Wow, I thought they were going to try to hand me only a thousand. Do I look funny? Will people notice that I am different?

"Here's your $41. Let's go get your car."

I release another car. "That will be $419 plus $75 for a tow out."

"Four hundred nineteen! They said it was $310 yesterday."

"Yes, it probably was $310 yesterday."

On my way home should I buy a new truck? No, don't make ANY decisions for a few days. I turn on the radio. Wait! I don't like that music. Is there any Lynard Skinner song I can stand right now?

Who am I? What is important?

The customers leave. I lock the gate, hit the three speed bumps, turn left on Francisco Boulevard and head home.

*"I am listening to the deepest impulses of my Being now,
even when they contradict the prescribed ways of being "holy" and "righteous"
that I've learned from the past."*

Jonathan

Jonathan Labman was raised in Eastern Pennsylvania, attended an international high school in the U.K. (Wales), and after graduating from college in Georgia, settled in a Christian fundamentalist community in Southeastern Pennsylvania. After seven years there, he "came out" as a gay man and lived alternatively in New York and Philadelphia for thirteen years. During those years he studied acting, became a massage therapist, and then an energy healer. After returning to Eastern Pennsylvania in1996, Jonathan earned a Master's degree in counseling and became a Yoga instructor. Jonathan now lives with his committed partner of thirteen years, Ray, in their home, "The Wild Woods." He has a private counseling practice and works in a Fortune 500 company. You can reach him via e-mail at j@simplyawake.com or find his website at www.simplyawake.com.

AWAKENING FROM THE SLEEP OF COMPULSIVE "FOLLOWING"

The weekend of July 13th 2001, I awakened to my nature as Divine Consciousness embodied and intricately entwined with my human, ego-driven, animal self. To me it was a culmination of nearly 40 years of religious education, psychological investigation, and spiritual work. And, at the same time, it was the beginning of a whole new set of investigations and struggles.

To be sure, there was shift in me and my life and body. In physical terms I lost the chronic tension in my left iliopsoas muscle (though the right side would be revealed as an issue seven years later), a muscle deep in the abdomen that connects the front of the spine to the thigh. This muscle had been screamingly tight since I was in my early twenties. This release corresponded to a certain relaxation and a new confidence in Being...that I was finally really okay; the fundamental uneasiness I had felt in my guts was finally exposed, explained and healed, or so I thought.

Yes, we really are Infinite Consciousness crammed into a mortal (and, alas, decaying) body that's going to die. We can have intimations of immortality because we are immortal (or as they say in the East, "We are That"), and we are also, paradoxically, this limited, human and finite body.

Immediately prior to my Second Birth I completed a year of intensive Yoga Teacher Training, attaining the 500-hour teacher certification. Through Yoga and meditation I had begun to awaken as the Witness in early 2001, but didn't really have a clear map of the territory of Awakening. I had been studying Yoga and Tantra since 1997, and the latest forms of an interest in the Eastern path toward Enlightenment that I had pursued since 1989. However, although I pursued many Yoga practices and a lot of philosophy and teaching, I didn't understand Awakening, nor did I experience it. I continued to perpetuate that sort of violence against myself that says, "I'm not good enough, I have to change myself." In the world of Yoga that began to translate into "I've got to cripple, annihilate or destroy my ego."

I found Saniel Bonder's work through *What Is Enlightenment?* magazine, and as soon as I started working with his school, I delved deeply into his work and put everything else on hold. Fortunately, my formal training in Yoga ended about then. From May through July 2001 I read, spoke, listened, meditated, contemplated and generally devoured the Waking Down teaching, until my Awakening the weekend of July 13, 2001.

I might have been better off had I dropped my Yoga practices immediately after my Second Birth. However, the major event of my early awakening life has been a plunging into a meta-pattern or what Saniel Bonder calls a "governing sentimentality." All of my life I had been assuaging my Core Wound, the feeling of confusion and separation in my identity and relationships, and other deep wounding, by trying to win the approval and favor of "special people." These were people whom I considered religious and spiritual leaders and my ontological superiors (e.g., they were superior by their very nature). These people were those who perpetuated the subtle or not so subtle bashing of their students' egos with such counsel as "You're not righteous enough," "You must eat this kind of food to get enlightened," or "You must get rid of your ego, or you're not good enough for my advanced group of disciples."

Between this approval-seeking behavior, my desire for local and physically close community, and my ongoing confusion about whether spiritual people were allowed to have functional egos, I continued in my Yoga Tantra studies after my Second Birth. My teacher taught a synthesis of ancient and modern teachings, but ultimately I found them to be both confusing and unsatisfying because of a mistake about the Impersonal and the Personal. It seemed that Awakening was being confused with being "impersonal" and "ego less." But, because of my Second Birth, I had discovered that we are the Impersonal Absolute and our finite body, mind, and the ego that the mind generates. As Krishna Gauci, one of the teachers of the Waking Down work, writes, "Your personality, made of thought, is simply the way that Consciousness becomes a person."

However, in a surprisingly non-Tantric interpretation, my local teacher always valued the impersonal more than the personal. When I wasn't chosen to be in an advanced group of students, no comprehensible reason was given. It was said to be an "impersonal decision"—although those chosen were only those who had stayed loyal to her instead of wanting to work with another master she had brought to visit the school. Everyone who stayed loyal got into her "inner" group, those who were disloyal were in the "less than group" that I was put in.

An elaborate esoteric explanation was constructed, but at the time I harmed myself by taking the blame. I just asked, "Did you not choose me because I was too egotistical?" and her answer was, "Yes." Later I learned the truth: that I had made the unforgivable error of being disloyal and her pride had been hurt, so I was rejected from advanced worth. Her egotism was the problem.

However, I spent months hurting from that rejection, but having no opportunity available to talk about those feelings. Those feelings were referred to as being egotistical, too! "I, me and mine are unimportant" was the teaching I got that was supposed to deal with my hurt feelings. And it didn't help at all. I spent the next year and a half trying to prove I was "good enough" and trying to deny my basic human desire to be seen and heard. It was very painful.

It took nearly three years after my Second Birth before I woke up to the fact that I had been running my old gambit of looking to a charismatic and/or powerful teacher to make life okay. If I got the teacher's approval, my hope was, I would totally not feel the core wound, and I would not be afraid for my survival. However, after plunging into this pattern from December 2001 until May 2004, I finally figured out that this was not true. No one's approval or disapproval would take away the experience of the Core Wound, that continuing and uncomfortable dance of the finite and infinite inside of me. Nor would approval assuage the deep survival fears coming from my early youth from unknown origins. Not only that, seeking someone's approval would mean that I would invariably do violence to myself, or let others do it to me, as had happened with my teacher in the above example.

Of course, this wasn't the only thing that happened to me during the years after my Awakening, and it was not the most intense. However, this was a major turning point in a debilitating pattern of my life finally being dissolved, and my Yoga practice finally being laid to rest. This is quite amazing considering that I spent my childhood intensely involved in seeking my family's and teachers' approval, my adolescence and young adulthood with the Christian fundamentalists seeking their approval (and running away from being gay and Jewish in our unwelcoming cultural environment), and my 30's and early 40's looking for the approval of therapists and then Eastern gurus and Enlightenment teachers.

My whole way of being in the world and all of my assumptions about what is true, what is right, and what to do with myself have been changing since my Awakening. I'm no longer willing to take anyone else's word that what is good for them is good for me. It's all got to be an investigation.

What this means is that I am listening to the deepest impulses of my Being now, even when they contradict the prescribed ways of being "holy" and "righteous" that I've learned in the past. This means that I have experimented with diet again, going back and forth from being a carnivore to a vegetarian several times: my conclusion is that meat is hard for me to digest and contributes to my insomnia. I don't think it's anti-spiritual to eat meat (though it may not be ecologically sound in the modern world).

It also means that I don't do a formal "spiritual practice" anymore; if I'm led to practice, I do; if not, I don't. All of the ways that I've been taught to conform to the unnecessary rules of society and spiritual community are being investigated and many of them discarded. I am learning to accept whatever shows up in my inner world of deep impulses and my external circumstances in each moment...something I could only imagine before my Awakening. Now it is actually happening.

WAKEDOWN SHAKEDOWN BREAKDOWN

At first, after my awakening in July 2001, I was "blissed out," thrilled, and dazzled by the experience of The Transcendent aspect of Consciousness. After a while, however, I thought, "This can't be 'it.'

There must be something more." But seven years of sitting with teachers, and even world-renowned masters like Mata Amritananda Mayi Devi, also known as Ammachi or "The Hugging Saint," proved to me there is nothing else. She appears to have a special gift for the Transcendent side of Consciousness, but being with her does not alter my normal mode of life except temporarily. What I experience now is apparently all I get; my experience of the Transcendent side of Consciousness hasn't changed much in seven years. Consciousness has incarnated as Jonathan as he is: gray-haired, soft-spoken or loud, gay and partnered with a man, and with a history that is full of near-fatal missteps.

In fact, bathing "oneself" in Consciousness and letting everything be as it is reveals more pain, conflict and limitation than I could ever have imagined. Saniel and the senior Waking Down Teachers were right to warn us about "The Wakedown Shakedown," and I would say their terminology is not strong enough. After these last months I would call it "The Wakedown Shakedown Breakdown." The desire to know and experience Truth, and the diving of Consciousness into all the dark corners of this body-mind, has led to the most difficult and shame-revealing truths: that this incarnated Consciousness was betrayed by my own authority figures and sexually abused as a child. Does that shock you? It should—it shocks me still.

My glorious quest for Truth and full "enlightenment" has currently landed me into my physical, nervous, emotional, psychological and intellectual reactivity and damage from being betrayed by my own authority figures in their sexual abuse of me as a child. My ego, this creation of the brain's language-generation, has been running from these truths about abuse (actually verified in a letter from the perpetrator) all my life. Now the quest for "Total Awakening" or "Total Enlightenment" has landed me in a quagmire of damage. I am anxious, don't sleep at night, and my body bears the residue of the extreme damage in the form of habitually tight muscles deeply embedded along my spine, in pain from holding down the terrible truth of past abuse: a terrible secret, indeed.

Oddly enough, the only antidote that relieves the held panic and reactivity in my nervous system is letting Consciousness feel and become this damaged body and mind (with thanks to Linda Groves-Bonder's Recognition Yoga). So the Non-Dual becomes the dual, and both exist (thanks to Ted Strauss). Since awareness surfaced of these events, I have worked (by phone) with Sandra Glickman, a Senior Teacher in the Waking Down in Mutuality and the woman who mentored me into awakening in 2001 and has been my friend and guide since. She has helped me to understand how the stable Grounding In and As Consciousness makes the difference between being able to cope with these awful memories and emotions or succumbing to madness or dissociation. As we work with a technique called Somatic Experiencing, Consciousness is invited into these wounds to embody Itself as them. The Consciousness that I thought would be the escape from these painful memories and body sensations is paradoxically what helps me to inhabit them and heal them. As the awareness almost literally "seeps" into these held and dark places of the body, they are liberated from the isolation of having been pushed "out of mind," and they are brought back into integration and wholeness.

Embodying this damage is a difficult process whether the ego (I cynically call it "the chatterer") resists it or accepts it. "I" am now in the midst of accepting the damage that was done to me by the perpetrator, and the two cults that I was part of, by the simple act of feeling it with my conscious Awareness. As far as I have read and experienced, nothing other than the simple awareness or allowing of the damage to be as it is works to heal. To heal it, I have to feel it, and All of Consciousness feels it through the ephemeral "me."

The damage from abuse must be felt to its depths and incorporated into the larger awareness that this damaged person and survivor is the form that Consciousness chose to take! Consciousness incarnated into this person who was sexually abused, deceived, betrayed and emotionally abandoned not just by the original perpetrator, but by several other group perpetrators (the cults). I thank my lucky stars that because of the democratic approach of Waking Down in Mutuality, I wasn't victimized once more: instead there is healing.

I can fight, scream, cry, complain and resist this truth and this healing process—and I do! I have to succumb to the need to take sleep medication for the time being (since I was abused at night), which I resist; but it is necessary to my functioning and healing. And simultaneously and increasingly, I am accepting this pain in my body, pain in my heart, and this complex of grief/fear/rage now emerging as the long-suppressed darkest corner of my soul. If I were to return to my Christian theological education for an analogy, it would be to say that the one most needing redemption at the deepest levels, eventually has the most complete experience of redemption and Grace.

Consciousness, incarnating as the "finite," the "chatterer," and the "me," must embody and inhabit this damage from sexual abuse, psychological abuse, and betrayal, in order to redeem and heal it. The nervous system itself (with its sleeplessness, anxiety, and restless energy) must be embraced as completely as is possible in this moment-by-moment experience of this life, along with the things it likes embracing: like tasting a good cup of coffee or having a hug.

This is the paradox of Awakening. The very last thing that I thought a search for Enlightenment would lead to is this set of memories and identities: that I am a survivor of one of the worst forms of human abuse, trauma and betrayal. And not just once, but three times: growing up with sexual abuse, and experiencing the psychological abuse of two different religious cults: one Christian, another one Hindu-based. Yet that is the reality of the "me" that I am today.

I would also add that the last thing in the world this "I" would have wanted would be to rely on other people (mutuality). I learned that it was safe to trust no one. And yet, in my Mentor's phone work with me, or my life partner Ray's being there to hold me while I shake or cry, I find the deepest form of human, personal healing that I've ever experienced. The healing is not only dependent on my direct perception of Consciousness in its transcendent forms, but is also dependent on how It expresses itself through these kind and wonderful people. This is Mutuality.

Awakening and Consciousness have produced awareness of the darkest corners of my own soul, and by extension, the knowledge that those I loved and looked up to in my early life and my later "spiritual life" were the originators of the deepest kind of human darkness and tragedy that anyone can know as a personal tragedy. I am suffering the breakdown of all the myths of normalcy, spiritual "sincerity," religious meaning, and security as part of my "Wakedown Shakedown Breakdown." My one remaining hope is that integration and wholeness can still emerge, like the Phoenix, from the conflagration of all my illusions. Already I see this emergence in: the love of my partner Ray, the support of my close friends, my mentor Sandra, my therapist Mark, those remaining from my childhood and past that I can still trust, and the refuge I take in the present moment—which is, after all, where I am now free from harm.

I wish all those reading this an easier time than mine. But if you have this same level of suffering, I want to reinforce your hope: healing is still possible. I wish you awakening, healing, love and many blessings, plus a crystal-clear knowledge of the Truth: it really does set you free, even if the freedom isn't what you had imagined it would be.

"When I am right there in the present moment, all is spontaneously related to the specific situation, person, time and event. All speech and action is perfectly adjusted."

Sandra

Sandra Glickman, a senior teacher of Waking Down in Mutuality, recently moved to small-town Fairfield, Iowa, after forty years of exhilarating fast-lane living in the San Francisco Bay Area. Continuing to teach, lead groups, and practice psychotherapy, she has been infinitely blessed to enjoy the ordinary and very lucky life of work, relationship, children and grandchildren, as well as the extraordinary and very lucky life of spiritual practice and awakening. She currently delights in exploring Heartland America, where friendships indeed grow intimate in the warm heart-heat, where conscious refinement blooms vast as the cool blue skies, and creativity is as rampant as the wind and the corn. She breathes a sigh of relief that life here with her partner Don and new friends is at last local, balanced and humanely sane—much like a smooth free ride up atop the seat of her beautiful new bicycle on a must-ride day!

Spontaneous Revelation Speech: Shift in Sense of Self

The Fairfield leadership group is meeting. We are asked who will volunteer to make up a topic and lead a Sunday night group. The tension is thick. The space is begging to be filled in, but nobody wants to do it. Seems we'll have to let this event go. We're on to another topic, when suddenly from out of my mouth pops the phrase, "Spontaneous Revelation Speech!" The words have seemingly sneaked past my ordinary conscious awareness. I feel a "dangerous" split-second suspension in midair—then excitement and "juice." With an internal click I'm saying, "I'll lead the meeting. This is my topic!" Yikes! What am I doing?

I haven't a clue what this topic, arriving like a meteor from outer space, might portend, but I feel excited and certain that I'll love it! "Strange and exciting" promises a part of me that has executed this leap at apparently lightening speed. My "ordinary" self, hesitating, is a little more careful with its offers!

A few days pass as the topic begins to elaborate itself in my conscious mind. Many ideas come all at once. Could be fun to throw open the topic, calling forth incidents, people, groups, of every ilk and time, such as Quakers to rappers, which demonstrate this phenomenon. We can speak personally of the topic, recounting its presence in our lives, speculating on its function, confessing what it has gotten us into! Maybe someone will burst into a spontaneous revelation speech right on the spot! "Hmmm, potentially lively stuff ," I'm imagining.

To clarify my use of the term "revelation," it often connotes very big, far-reaching predictions about the future, the destiny of the world, the moral state of its peoples, and the path of redemption before doom descends. This is not the meaning I'm considering here. I am using the term to designate significant material emerging from currently "unknown" repositories in one's self. This meaning is more about short-term consequences having to do with immediate "predicting"—revealing what is deeper than the obvious, what is relevant in unexpected ways and what may have a strong, even decisive, impact on the next moment, the next decision to be made.

This form of "revelation" speaks to current personal and collective understanding in the social and world environment right now, which potentially bumps us up into new levels. This could change the future, though not necessarily in the grand—and often nebulous—speech and manner of the traditional "revelation." Take, for instance, my being seized by the idea for the meeting. Something about me had let loose into the unknown; amazingly, the outcome this time was thoroughly delightful. With a great sense of engagement, I planned and delivered the meeting, which gave way to a free-flowing, enthusiastic, and very original exchange among the people who came. I gained more confidence in what comes uncensored out of me, and we as a group enjoyed a lively and humorous evening!

Here are other examples of spontaneous speech which I have witnessed: Steve, answering an often asked question, surprises himself by bursting forth into a heartfelt, sophisticated, and inspiring pronouncement. The room responds with admiring "oh's and ah's." We who are present experience Divinity, passionate, eloquent and clear. Understanding and joy, for Steve and ourselves as well! Or, here is Sharon, languid warm mother pool, flowing effortlessly into another's confession of difficulty, easing with soothing murmurings the person's raw and ragged Being—minimum speech, maximum nourishment. Grace and Beauty!

The others and I are quietly stunned. Or Winifred, suddenly open and powerful as a pristine mountain scape, receiving another's disturbed and chaotic words, returning them with poetry (yes, literal poetry), empathic, enlivening and humorous. The mountain has spoken! Recognizing, we bow down to her gifts. Again, wonder and joy for her Being and for our lucky selves as we grow in our process of Waking Down. We are served and sublimed again and again by this Spontaneous Revelation Speech. I would say it develops organically with those maturing in Waking Down, noticeable especially among the teachers, but certainly not limited to them.

As I approached the evening of the topic, I found myself extending the notion of "spontaneous revelation speech" to the whole of my "second life" awakening. "Speech"is a regular means of externalizing my internal observations about the nature of life and being a person is—a very important tool when connecting with those who come to me. Speaking what I perceive begins to catalyze Being in both the person and the environment. It seems that words "happen," yet the one who is speaking enjoys the delivery and effect as much as if she or he is the one receiving it. I usually feel that "I" am not speaking, but am being "spoken through" by a more intelligent and knowing "me," a more risk-taking, fun-loving, or even whacky me. Almost always it is a satisfying, informative and fun experience.

Over the years, speaking up freely has become for me a far less fearful act—a surprising thing to my former self that nothing bad happens when I speak forthrightly. At one level I am always shocked that my honest speech serves! It's a relief to be freer now, less inhibited; in fact, it seems entirely natural. Some time after my Second Birth, I noticed that pretty much always I could speak at length on almost anything. Happily for others I don't do this very often, but this seems to be a gift of Second Birth Awakening.

For me, in the Second Life, the phenomenon of spontaneity is an important sign of moving into deeper trust in being, mainly in being myself, or even in being a witness to that which arises at the locus of myself. I've moved very far beyond what you read of me in the first edition of this book. In these "advanced" twelve-plus years of my awakened life, this spontaneity has become my main "guidance" for participation with others. This signifies a big shift in self-trust from a more cautious, studied, fearful, existence to what I call "attuned to Being."

I used to hold myself back through the habit of "analyzing." I have been the psychotherapist who analyzes everything and speaks in theories, comparisons, observations and the like. I no longer have such a strong tendency to be in the "psychological" mode, now preferring to relate from a broader, maybe deeper place. However, the habit dies hard, as I can't resist a "psychological" comment right now: maybe I am able to "free-associate," the proof from Dr. Freud that his patients were "cured" of defensive protections against their true integrity and being. Okay, I can't really get away from exercising my thinking processes, but somehow my thinking is less compulsive, open, more flexible and playful—in a word, spontaneous! I now have more choice between "thinking" and speaking "spontaneously," even in the therapy work I do with people.

Whatever it is, I find myself able to wait, by habit, for spontaneity to move me forward. My unconscious pattern in the past was fear of exposing myself to criticism and judgment, guilt over hurting others, and dread of being "wrong." I perceived my lack of "flow" as a shameful lack of capacities, which I imagined others had but that I did not. Thus, I promptly went into either envy or counter efforts, which consumed my free energy and diminished my pleasure in being. I worked hard trying to arrive at decisions and opinions through writing, internal gnashing of the thinking gears with talking to myself—and procrastinating. Now I've come to feel really okay awaiting the arrival of something spontaneous to act through me. Not that these old patterns are gone—they do still arise—but they don't have the same sway over me.

This is quite a change in my sense of myself, and reciprocally, it helps attune me to others, where I often sense the patterns and limitations that lie outside of their conscious sight. I've had the sense of being able to "penetrate" many veils. This in itself lends "depth" and pleasure to ordinary experiences, revealing new dimensions to life, new twists, which often mean new understandings of very old patterns and which, in turn, means I am more valuable in sitting with others and giving feedback.

I'll try to give you a further sense of ongoing transformation after the Second Birth. As an example of an old pattern, before I used to be pretty much a "two-sided" character, that is, always able to see both sides of anything. I realized that this could be valuable, but I often felt unable to make decisions, to act. Of course this was not always the case, and at certain junctures I even made significant "irrational" leaps into the unknown. However, to myself I mostly felt slow and sluggish. For example, when I was with my generous mother-in-law, she often wanted to buy me something "special" which I was to pick out, but she finally gave up on shopping with me because I couldn't decide, and it was too frustrating for her. I can still frustrate my partner, but I have learned it is no good to act until "spontaneity" announces the choice. So at least I'm not frustrated and adding to the problem.

For as long as I can remember, I wanted to be "creative" and somehow thought of myself as an "artist," but I really did not have an artistic medium of self-expression. In college I was vividly moved by the description of "artist" by Rollo May in *The Courage to Create*: taking up the brush and executing one's stroke on canvas being emotionally equivalent to bringing down the accepted world order—the artist as iconoclast, daring hero, courageous slayer of the past. I always wanted to be that one. But, alas, I seemed more the steady ordinary "producer" of stuff that had value, but no pizzazz.

Since my Second Birth, happily, this has shifted—either my self-concept has, or my execution of speech and action has, or both. Something has "let go," some internal governor, some caution about upsetting things, some roadblock to creativity. My artistic nature is not in conventional forms such as painting, writing, sculpting, playing music, etc., but rather I recognize that I am living a creative life. Now my sense of myself is that I am "moved" by the spirit of life that is endlessly "creative."

Before, I had a conventional notion of what constituted "creativity," which I didn't appear to have access to. I was imposing upon myself definitions from the "outside," and I didn't measure up. In my mind I was a condemned plodder. As it turns out, this creativity—or what I now call "spontaneity"—this playful intuition, this up welling of fresh ideas, words, lively sensations, re-arrangements of forms, just pours from me. A wonderful surprise of the Second Life!

I hope you are feeling how delightful this is to me! So delicious, so amazing, so energizing what I've grown into! Don't be misled by "I've grown into" it. It is clear to me that it is not "I," the ego self, the dullish person who longed to be artistic, but was unconsciously bound by rules and notions, who has somehow acquired this "talent." I can tell you that it is the Source Itself that infuses this particular being, me, for its work of creativity, supported by the fertile climate of my Waking Down Community. I don't even try anymore to step out of the way—something in me just steps aside of its own accord.

However, it is not exactly so simple as I'm saying here. I'm not completely all "new." I'm aware that my history, experience, study, and unique emotional, mental, and physical makeup, all this and more, is the "container" in which seemingly "divine" expression takes shape. And I do take human care of this precious flow, and especially take responsibility for it when I recognize that something more might be called for, such as restraint or modification. Life has a "shared" or "co-created" quality; it is not just "me," per se, but both myself and the "Divine." When I tune in and surrender to that which is flowing through me, life is rich and wonderful, and full of feeling, and I have the sensation that I am rising up to coincide with Joy, with Insight, with Love, which joins and enlivens the expression.

Another phenomenon I've noticed is that I appear to be losing the projection that the great "Other" is the Source of the Best that is known. Instead, although I do find satisfaction in being receptive to ideas and impressions and conclusions from "out there" and from gifted others, I prefer now to ponder them within my own experience and self-Source, coming to my own best conclusions about Truth, Reality, Beauty, and Goodness, trusting that all this can be revealed through the local "me."

Paradoxical to all this is that "I" am not simply just the localized one, but an open window for deeper, wider, more "elegant"—maybe even "wild" or "untamed"—expressions and perceptions, emerging straight from the Mystery. The tight core of "me" is more invisibly expansive, like a vast net formed by the environment itself, pulling in phenomena to be materialized—or not—as it will: "permeable," more open, more unknowing, not "doing," rather, being "done," "responding" to, or "surrendering" in and as the River of Life. I'm hoping this is giving you an idea of one person's unfolding Second Life. I feel it bespeaks a basic principle.

Spontaneous Revelation Speech has also shown me its subtleties. When I am present (rather than distracted and going on automatic), I notice the flow is always new, fresh and scintillating. Nothing repeats itself. Every situation and moment is different from anything that has gone before. When I am right there in the present moment, all is spontaneously related to the specific situation, person, time and event. All speech and action is perfectly adjusted. Spontaneously! Elegantly! When I am not present (as, of course, happens at times) things—that is, "I"—go dull, lacking life, lacking creativity. This is no surprise, right? But this deadening effect happens far less often now, and it has no "profound" significance to me, as if I inherently lacked "creativity" or some greatly valued gift.

Then there are moments of pure abiding, when even creativity loses its fascination, becomes tiring, and tiresome. Then I spontaneously rest, speech disappears, and silence prevails. I fast from thought and its outflow, released even from spontaneous revelation speech.

"The Second Birth process for me was finally landing me in my own shoes, my own skin and my own life. Simple and yet inexplicably profound."

Dan

From his first reading of Psycho-Cybernetics in high school, Dan Altman has been a seeker. He explored Consciousness as a counter-culture dropout after getting a degree from Case Western Reserve University in Cleveland, Ohio. Introduced to Prosperity Consciousness, he achieved worldly success with two software companies and eight years at Microsoft. Despite creating wealth, Dan did not find the peace he also sought. His success did give him the opportunity to continue his earlier quest. This exploration eventually led Dan to the Waking Down community and his Second Birth awakening. Dan currently lives in Ashland, Oregon, where he is writing a spiritual memoir entitled Microsoft to Maui: How I found peace that money couldn't buy. He is also writing software for the iPhone. You can email Dan at: danalt7@hotmail.com

AWAKENING AS ME or FALLING INTO MY OWN VAT OF YUM

Most, if not all, of my life, I felt separated and disconnected from the direct experience of living. This led me to believe that something was fundamentally wrong with me. Whatever I did or didn't do, feel, speak or think was never quite right, never enough. I needed to break the code so I could finally start living. I was a consummate, desperate seeker. My lifelong search led me to the Waking Down community. In spite of the warnings from the literature that awakening would not solve my problems, make me a different person, or fundamentally change my life, I still hoped and believed I would awaken magically transformed into someone new and exciting. The good news was that I didn't need to perfect myself or become a new, improved version of Dan in order to awaken. The bad news is I have awakened as me. Well, maybe not such bad news really. In my Second Birth I have landed in my life. I am here no longer waiting to live. What follows is the story of my awakening.

I began my Waking Down journey early in 2007 and attended almost every available retreat that year. In May I attended the annual Waking Down Transfiguration Retreat at the Joshua Tree Retreat Center, an aging, eclectic gathering place designed by Lloyd Wright in the 1950s. The mystery and magic of this high desert location near Palm Springs added to the adventure of my entry into the Waking Down experience. My small group, an important element of Waking Down Mutuality, was composed of four other seekers, Senior Teacher CC Leigh and mentor Winifred Boggs. During the sizzling desert afternoons we shared our souls as we sat in a semi-darkened room underneath the dining hall. An epiphany snuck into the darkness one afternoon as CC peppered me with a seemingly random series of questions. She asked if my life were to continue as it had been, even with the despair, would that be enough? Would my life still be worth living? The sudden, unexpected inquiry took me deep where I discovered to my surprise that, yes, my life would be enough, would be worthwhile. I dropped and inhabited my body like coming home after an exhausting trip.

Later that evening as I lay on my narrow bed in the wedge-shaped concrete cabin, I could hear an occasional car rocket down the distant highway. Previous evenings I enjoyed the silence and was annoyed by passing cars. This evening I marveled at the sound as it echoed off the desert floor and buildings. It was like a gunshot ricocheting through my consciousness, simultaneously outside and inside. I was present with the sound, not my judgment. Even though it lasted for only a few days, I tasted the juicy immediacy of Consciousness in my body.

A few months later, while I was reading *The White Hot Yoga of the Heart* in which Saniel describes his awakening process, my experience at the Joshua Tree retreat seemed to match what he describes as the Embodied Feeling-Witness Consciousness, and I experienced it again that summer. Naively, I had driven with friends into downtown Chicago on July Fourth. I had not realized a million others were also intent on seeing the fireworks over the water. Diverted by barricaded streets, we found ourselves lost and in total gridlock. Normally, I would have had a mild freak out, judged myself and fallen into despair. Instead of the hopelessness of the situation I slipped into the delicious experience of simultaneously witnessing, feeling and being in my life. As Embodied Feeling-Witness Consciousness, I was okay if we spent the entire evening grid-locked in traffic, enjoying a summer evening in a strange city with flashing lights and captivating people. We met our people, listened to the Chicago Symphony Orchestra play the "William Tell Overture" and watched the fireworks over the lake. This state and the accompanying sense of relaxation and peace continued through the week. I watched and felt my life unfold with ease. I loved it. Of course, it didn't last.

After attending a retreat with Saniel and Linda on Maui in August, I journeyed to Fairfield, Iowa, for a Mini-Transfiguration Retreat. In both retreats I descended into deep caverns of darkness and despair. In the presence of the Waking Down transmission and being held in the sweet arms of Mutuality, I allowed myself to feel the depth of my own pain. I returned to Ashland that fall, wondering if I would ever feel relief from the darkness in my soul.

Early in November 2007, I sat in Starbucks reading *The Second Birth* book, the first collection of awakening stories. Inspired by others' stories I found myself believing that awakening was really possible for me, too. In that opening I chose to greenlight my experience, to fully accept and say "yes" to even doubt and judgment. I didn't need to change anything in my life. Nothing was fundamentally wrong. I didn't need to fix myself, fix my girlfriend or fix the world. What a relief. I couldn't force my awakening – it would happen in its own time and its own way. My job was to relax and trust. Easier said than done. As CC Leigh once said to me: "You can try not to try, but you will anyway." As I sipped my Americano, I remembered a session with another senior teacher, Sandra Glickman, in which a deep longing sprang forth. With tears I shared, "I have been waiting forever. This is all I have ever wanted. Everything else pales in comparison."

In mid-November I found myself driving to Saniel and Linda's home for my final retreat of the year. The setting was exquisite: the Northern California wine country, rolling hills covered with a tapestry of golden yellow, orange and red grape leaves. I arrived Friday evening a few minutes before the session began. We introduced ourselves, each of us saying what we wanted to get from the retreat. We would each get twenty-five minutes of group time and could select the general time and day of our session. I chose Sunday morning and was scheduled to go second.

The energy transmission of the retreat catalyzed the sharing which moved many participants to tears. Inspired by the people who shared on Saturday, I found myself doubting my own sincerity. Did I have anything authentic to share? At times I felt empty and alone, even in the intimacy of the group. As I went to bed Saturday night in the comfy, but slightly run down Best Western Hotel in Petaluma, I had no idea what I would share during my group time.

Sunday morning I snapped awake at 5:30 a.m. filled with anxiety, then lingered in bed frustrated that I didn't remember my dream. It was supposed to be an auspicious evening for dreaming. Was I worried about impressing others and looking good? Yes, I did want to be authentic and feel included in the group, but in truth, I feared missing my opportunity to awaken. This was my last workshop of the year, my last chance to shift and drop into my Second Birth. I remembered my session with Sandra Glickman and once again experienced the anguish of unmet longing: a craving in my soul, my heart and my whole being. As I lay on the stale, hotel-smelling pillow, I wept. Slowly, warmth radiated through my chest as though my heart was pulsating with an orange glow, like ET in the movie. I held myself in this delicious warmth and fell back to sleep.

Bright colors. A parade. A celebration. A carnival. I watched a UFO land and ran to take a digital photo only to realize it was a publicity stunt, as marketing people emerged from the craft and began to leaflet the crowd. I glanced up to catch a multi-colored cloud textured like a Persian rug. Amazed, I thought to myself: "I must be having my Second Birth. I have never seen a cloud so hauntingly gorgeous."

Abruptly, I awoke, minutes before my alarm was set to ring. I quickly readied myself to check out, met my car pool companion and stopped at Starbucks. Immersed in the vivid, crystal clear dream, I was no longer concerned about what I would say in my session.

During the morning gazing in which each of us had a couple of minutes of direct eye-to-eye contact with both Saniel and Linda, I felt raw and vulnerable. When it was my group time, I moved to the front of the room and sat on a pillow. I shared my dream and my longing and asked to be held by the group. Having spent several days with Saniel and Linda in an individual residential retreat earlier in the year, I felt a deep trust in their presence. I lay on the ground, and Saniel directed me to move closer so he could place the heel of his foot just on the right side of my chest. Sri Ramana Maharshi, a famous Indian sage, said that the seat of Consciousness was two finger widths to the right of center in the heart chakra. Even medical science recognizes the origins of each heartbeat in that area called the sinoatrial node, although science can find no extrinsic neural and hormonal cause. The group surrounded me. Someone held my head, another held my feet, and others held my hands. As Linda toned, this longing I felt earlier welled up in my heart and I began sobbing. I had waited lifetimes to finally let go and feel the depths of hopelessness, despair, unworthiness and disconnection.

I dropped and dropped, my chest heaving, hot tears streaming down my cheeks. I gripped the hands holding mine and wailed a cry so haunting, from the wound of existence, the feeling of being crucified in my own humanity. My lost, longing, lamenting soul felt the aloneness of all time. Hot energy pulsed from Saniel's foot into my chest as he played the Native American flute producing a cavernous melody that resonated with the abandoned darkness trapped underground for eternity. Flashes of heat enveloped my body, and I began to sweat. My shirt dampened and my forehead grew clammy. I wept, sweated, wailed and held on for my life. The music finished, and my wailing subsided. I lay there, my moist body tender and innocent. As I breathed in the newborn moments of existence and released lifetimes of suffering and guilt, a peace descended. A woman named Barbara sang me a lullaby that brought more tears, this time soft, easy tears. New. Raw. Innocent. Vulnerable. The many hands helped me sit up, and I made my way back to my chair. I sipped my coffee. Who am I? What happened?

A few days later, back in Ashland, I noticed that something had shifted. During the retreat I dropped into the depth of what Saniel calls the Core Wound, the sense of myself as separate, empty and alone. Now something had changed. I no longer felt the pressure to seek. Was I awakening? I didn't know. When I paused to feel inside, I found that life was okay. Life was enough. I was enough. Life, at times, even seemed like an amazing gift. For so long I had experienced life as a curse, so fraught with despair and hopelessness that part of me did not want to keep living. I had expected that awakening would be noticeable, and yet I was not feeling noticeably different. I doubted that anyone would pick me out of a crowd. I didn't expect or even want to be noticed or special. Perhaps the underlying feeling of never having been enough had fueled my quest for specialness and recognition.

After Thanksgiving I took some time for reflection. I had completed spring, summer and fall with Waking Down. I had attended six retreats in nine months and felt myself engaged in the awakening process. I had spent hundreds of hours with teachers and mentors, in retreats, reading books and listening to recordings. I had worked, focused, intended, longed for, craved, prayed, begged and cried deeply for this shift. I had traversed despair, hopelessness, emptiness, separation, longing, sadness, regret and self-loathing. Sobbing heart-breaking tears, I had crawled on my hands and knees and wiggled on my stomach through the deep muck, sludge and grunge of my life. I begged for help. The Rot I experienced was at times a personal hell. Part of the awakening process and the Waking Down teaching was greenlighting my life exactly as it was. I had run the gauntlet, committed and given myself fully to this journey. How strange to feel complete with seeking. What might just living life as me be like? The Second Birth process for me was finally landing me in my own shoes, my own skin and my own life. Simple and yet inexplicably profound. But wait, wasn't I always in my life? How could I not be?

A few weeks after my Sonoma experience, sitting at another favorite Ashland coffee shop, the Rogue Valley Roasting Company, I looked up at the sky and flashed back into my workshop dream. The clouds had a texture and richness that abruptly halted my journaling. I was captivated, not sure what would happen next. There was a yumminess to the experience. I relished the sensual delights of my fleshy self. I remembered Saniel describing falling into the Vat of Yum. This was my personal dip into the Vat.

By late February 2008 I had barely left Ashland all winter. This was highly unusual for me, as I usually craved escape from the cold, gray, rainy weather of Oregon. Over these winter months, I had many more experiences of falling directly into the real time presence of my life. Particularly startling was having this awakening mid-sentence, while talking with someone. Suddenly, the words were gone, and I was there, really there, looking into another's eyes, seeing a universe, a richness of being. The more I dropped into being me, the more I experienced life with poignancy, gratitude and tears of joy. And I noticed a sadness arising. Yes, I had lived a good life, even extraordinary at times, and yet, in some fundamental way, I hadn't been present. It was as though I was trying to be someone else, hoping that one day I would have the key to truly begin living. Now I had the key. And I grieved all the wonderful times I was not fully present to savor and enjoy the blessings of my life.

In March I traveled again from Ashland to Sonoma for another retreat with Saniel and Linda. This time the retreat was called Heart Nectar and Meditation, not a traditional Waking Down retreat. It was Easter Sunday, March 23, 2008. At seven a.m. I sat at a small bistro table outside the Barking Dog Café in downtown Sonoma, California. The morning sun rose over the rooftops. It was a yummy, delicious morning. I asked myself, "Am I awakened? Or is the whole notion of awakening an illusion? Just another pursuit?" I wanted to experience a dramatic awakening that would leave me without doubts. On the other hand, if I felt deeply fulfilled and joyful, did it really matter if there was an awakening? In an instant, sitting alone in front of the Barking Dog Café, as an early morning jogger ran by, it was as if the veils of existence were ripped wide open allowing the bright light of truth to shine in. Right there, right then, resurrected, I surrendered to live life fully with passion and peace. I was Consciousness infused into matter. We were one. There was pure majesty in this marriage. Such joy. A gift. Grace. I thought to myself how I could even enjoy being a 500-pound person or struck in traffic or on my deathbed. So on that Easter Sunday morning, I felt deeply and profoundly awakened. Awakened as myself, fully present. I had given myself full permission to be completely in my life and in my body. Full permission to be alive and embrace life. In that moment, it seemed I could never be depressed or feel despair about life again. I really wish that would have been true.

It has been a year now since that Easter Sunday, the date placed on my Second Birth. I did the formal Second Birth interview with Sandra Glickman on April 8th and was confirmed in my awakening. Barbara, the friend in Waking Down who sang the lullaby at the end of my first Sonoma experience, shared her mentor's description of the post awakening life as Mr. Toad's Wild Ride, the classic Disneyland adventure. At the start of the ride, you climb into an innocent-looking car. You go through the swinging entry doors. Suddenly, you are whisked into darkness and swung around unseen curves in the track. Your nervous system is exhilarated with flashing lights, taunting laughter and eerie music. The Waking Down name for Mr. Toad's Wild Ride is the Wakedown Shakedown.

My transformation began showing up in surprising and delightful ways. A couple of months after my Second Birth, I was on my way home from the annual Waking Down Transfiguration Retreat, this time in Kansas City, Missouri. After two canceled flights and a night in the local Howard Johnsons Hotel, I noticed that I wasn't upset or distressed. I trusted life, I didn't resist. This was huge. I entered the experiences with ease and grace. Instead of making life wrong, I embraced the wonder, delight and surprise of the moment.

In the year since my awakening I am feeling some stability in the sense of well being and peace that I so desperately sought. Still, sometimes in this awakening adventure, I hold onto the bar tightly. At other times, relaxed into my life, I casually raise my arms into the air, laughing and having the greatest time.

One thing for sure – I am no longer waiting to live my life.

"At last I knew myself to be infinite, unchanging eternal Consciousness simultaneously in and as a mortal, finite human form. All seeking on the level of spiritual attainment blessedly came to an end."

Bob

Bob Bishop was born in New York City, but shortly after graduating from CCNY, he moved to California. Since then he has lived in the San Francisco Bay Area for most of his adult life (except for graduate school in Chicago and some interim time in India and Aspen, Colorado). Bob is the father of two grown children. He presently works for an international corporation, and travels frequently in Asia, Europe and Latin America. Bob may be contacted at www.allawaken.net

AWAKENING IN THE ARMS OF THE GODDESS

I was born in New York City and lived most of my early life in an Irish-Italian working-class neighborhood. Of my local gang I was one of very few to go beyond high school. Attendance at Hunter College in the Bronx and CCNY in Manhattan gave me a life-long interest in learning. Two years after college, in the mid-60s, I joined the Peace Corps and was assigned to India where I worked in small industry development and the training of science teachers. During this whole time I lived in India, I had no interest at all in the great tradition of Indian spirituality.

I returned to the USA completely ignorant, until a few years later when I experienced a spiritual life crisis. This occurred when I was in graduate school at Northwestern University in Evanston, Illinois. I was completely on scholarship, enjoying my studies immensely, in excellent physical condition and health, and my girlfriend looked like she just stepped out of Playboy magazine. What more could a young man want?

But, somewhere in the midst of all this, I started feeling there must be more to life than what I was experiencing and where it seemed to be leading. This feeling became stronger and stronger until I began to feel that life lived as I was living had no meaning whatsoever. One evening in the bedroom with my lovely lady, I began to cry uncontrollably. She became quite concerned and tried to console me in all the ways a beautiful woman can, but to no avail. All I could do was weep and wail about the meaninglessness of life.

Over the next few weeks my spirit continued to darken, until a friend of mine invited me to attend a lecture on transcendental meditation. This lecture fascinated me with discussions on the meaning of self-transcendence, and techniques to attain cosmic consciousness and enlightenment.

After this meeting I learned to meditate as soon as possible. This initiation opened the doorway to spirituality for me. Subsequently, I devoted most of my adult life to the pursuit of spiritual growth and ultimate awakening.

For more than twenty years I spent time in the company of spiritual teachers and engaged various spiritual practices to the best of my ability. Although personal growth and development certainly occurred during this time, I had become somewhat despairing of ever having a profound awakening myself.

However, in 1996 during the holiday season in mid-December, I gathered with several old friends who each had a profound interest in spirituality. During this gathering each man told of his own spiritual process, and I was very moved to hear what had happened for each of them. I was particularly interested in one man's account of what had occurred for him working with a spiritual teacher named Saniel Bonder. I had also known Saniel previously, as a fellow participant in another spiritual community.

Following this gathering I met Saniel personally one evening. We had dinner together, and I asked him many questions which he answered graciously and to my complete satisfaction. After this meeting, it was clear to me that something very profound had occurred in his life.

I began to read Saniel's spiritual writings with great interest, and all my "yes" buttons began to be pushed. Soon hope awakened again that I might actually awaken in this lifetime. This was a mind-boggling perception, as I had put all my aspirations of enlightenment to sleep. After all my spiritual work, no conclusive realization had occurred at all. I felt at this point, that I was a failure as a spiritual practitioner, and that it could take many more lifetimes before I would actually become realized.

However, after spending more time with Saniel, I started to feel that something great was happening. Saniel had obviously gone through a profound transformation himself and was doing truly effective spiritual work with those around him. I began to encounter others working with Saniel who were awakened and awakening themselves. This was amazing to me. After all I had been through, it seemed like a miracle. I soon found myself completely attracted to participate in this process.

In Saniel's gatherings my own spiritual process became alive in fiery and intense ways. Many changes began to occur in my life; the ending of one love relationship and the beginning of another, marvelous psychic openings, spontaneous reception of archetypal energy that moved me to create sacred ceremony for healing and protection of others. During this time I was blessed with visitations by Kali and Santoshi Ma—the former being one of the most terrifying experiences of my life, and the latter being one of the most blissful. Most importantly, a strong and lasting connection was forged with Hanuman, and it was then that I took the spiritual name "Han" in his honor.

During this time I also made a pilgrimage to India where I attended the Khumbla Meela in Haridwaar and visited many powerful temples of Hanuman and Kali. It seemed that every time I entered a Hanuman temple some ceremony was going on, and I would be invited to participate.

I also visited the ashram of a revered Indian saint, Ramana Maharshi, in South India. While attending a ceremony there, I realized most deeply that my time working with traditional spiritual practices was over. My spiritual work was now directly linked to the Goddess ("Big She" herself) and to all her human forms which were manifesting in my life. This was proved out some months later when my own awakening occurred shortly after the painful ending of an intimate love relationship.

The whole time immediately preceding this occurrence had been a nightmare. The shock of losing an intimate love relationship and the recognition of my primary responsibility for that occurring had been devastating. I felt stunned as if delivered an immensely powerful blow by an adversary.

And yet, in the midst of this nightmare whirling around me, I kept noticing a center within who I am that remained calm, balanced and untouched. It seemed odd since, at any other time in my life, I would have collapsed altogether for some time from the emotional effects of what was occurring.

I recalled Saniel Bonder's essay, "The Aikido of Consciousness," comparing the ability of a skilled warrior to stay centered in the midst of attack, to one identified as Consciousness staying centered in the midst of all experiences, no matter how difficult or terrifying. I began to realize that something was changing in me, and quickly.

On Monday, October 18th, I flew to Austin, Texas, on business. I spent that evening with friends who did their very best to distract me from the pain I was feeling. We ate a good meal, drank a few beers and smoked some cigarettes—actually "good medicine" to anesthetize my bleeding heart.

During part of of this evening we were playing pool in a downtown dive with loud rock music playing continuously. At one point, I spontaneously started spouting wisdom puns about Consciousness only in the midst of all experience and "being" the entire event that we were witnessing. I realized later that what I was speaking was not just humorous speech, but bearing witness to what I was actually experiencing.

Later that evening I went back to my hotel where a simple but very significant event occurred. I was in my room, still not sleepy, alone without distraction and feeling more intensely the pain of what had been happening in my life. I watched TV for a while, and then shut it off, sitting and staring at the blank screen, feeling so down I could hardly move.

Then the awareness came that somehow it made no difference whether the TV was on or not to who and what I really am. I simply and clearly felt my primary identity as Consciousness—that in which every being and thing arises unmoving, witnessing, never changing and timeless. It was so tacit and simple, yet subtle and most profound.

Many times before I had experienced the Witness Consciousness present, but it seemed somehow behind and separate from me. This time I experienced it obviously and directly as me. I began to cry and pray to all the Powers that be, "Oh, please, stay with me always, do not go, stay with me forever. Whither thou leadest I will follow." I lay there for quite some time in a twilight zone before falling asleep.

The next morning I awoke, immediately feeling the wound of my present experience and, almost simultaneously, noticing this new identification with Consciousness.

Throughout the day, at lunch with an old friend and during my participation in a trade show, I kept feeling myself simultaneously to be infinite Consciousness and this finite, mortal individuated being just as I am with all my desires, fears, strengths and weaknesses.

What a blessing! What gratitude I felt to have this awakening occur at last! The crucifixion of infinite Consciousness into finite form as a mortal human being had been stably re-cognized. The Core Wound had finally become conscious.

The occurrence of this most significant event evoked great relief and deep gratitude in the very core of my being. At last I knew myself to be infinite, unchanging eternal Consciousness simultaneously in and as a mortal, finite human form. All seeking on the level of spiritual attainment blessedly came to an end.

I became more ordinarily human than ever before. But also a profound connection to the Goddess came gracefully alive. I began to be blessed by wonderful encounters with people all over the world. Through all this I have been continually guided and instructed.

Saniel once said that this awakening, which he refers to as the "Second Birth," allows the Divine to infuse, inform and guide one more profoundly than ever before. It liberates one into life, not merely out of it. Then one has the potential to be an awakened servant of wellness and liberation for others.

For some, this starts with an irresistible impulse to teach, and for others, as in my case, it begins spontaneously when others recognize on some level what has happened and draw the awakened one into service directly.

My initiation into teaching began in Budapest, Hungary, in the year 2000. I was in Eastern Europe on business, and a Hungarian friend of mine put me in touch with a spiritually oriented group of her friends. Unexpectedly, they welcomed me as a kind of spiritual dignitary, and after initial introductions, the room became silent, and I spontaneously began to talk about my spiritual journey. This led to my doing a sacred empowerment dance ceremony and leading the group in a gazing meditation. I was quite surprised at the powerful response I received, and the profound effects my presence seemed to have on those who attended this event.

Since then I have returned to Hungary for other occasions with this same group of people. But, mostly, I am drawn to share my wisdom with those whom I meet in the ordinary course of life, and who show me signs that they are interested in such matters. When I meet such individuals, I am moved to serve them in all the ways I know how.

But I never forget that "those who teach much continue to learn." One never knows who one will encounter just around the next corner of life.

"Ruthlessness reaches IN to the inner being of the Other and taps that heart on the shoulder, so to speak, and says," Wake up. It's time to play in a way that makes you love yourself entirely and appreciate being alive."

Stevie

Nancy Stevie Peacock is a fine artist known for painting the spiritual energy essence of music as it comes through jazz musicians at work. Having grown up ballroom dancing to live jazz with her parents, later, as a teenager, she was taken by Rev. John Gensel, The Jazz Minister of New York, and his wife to all the great jazz clubs. First, she first sketched musicians playing live; then later in the studio, painted on canvas using her sketches for reference. Occasionally, Peacock is asked to set her easel on stage with the band and paint in concert. As "the jazz painter, Nancy Peacock," she is on the road half the year at jazz festivals and as Artist-in-Residence. She is mother to three grown sons, friend to her ex-husband, frequent hostess of meditations and celebratory neighborhood gatherings, and loves to dance. "Stevie," as her friends call her, a grateful beneficiary of the work of Saniel Bonder, is now an active colleague of Saniel Bonder and Linda Groves Bonder, in the further development of their work of "publishing Awakened Beings" in the world

RUTHLESS MERCY

My spiritual biography began in my parents' New York City apartment, watching boats passing by along the East River. "Boat" was the first word I spoke. At four, in a New Jersey apartment, my nighttime meditation was to watch the blinking red lights of three radio towers, focused on relaxing into knowing the pattern, from inside myself. At six, my parents and I moved into a house in Upper Montclair, on the side of Watchung Mountain, where into my bedroom flashed the light of the Empire State Building every sixty seconds. Another breathing exercise!

From late night radio I learned to recite the Hail Mary. My father, a Wall Street dealer in unlisted stocks and closely-held securities, visited a Roman Catholic Church workday mornings, and in the afternoons, a Greek Orthodox Church. I greatly admired him for making his quiet time a priority. At summer camp in New Hampshire, at eight, my joy and respite was to paddle a canoe across the lake to an outdoor chapel: a clearing in a birch forest, where I sat on hand-hewn birch-log benches. My forward-thinking mother gave me an out-of-print Yoga book when I was nine that held me in its thrall two hours each morning before school. The postures, breathing practices, and meditation were my joy, my Real Life; until at fourteen I attended Putney, the progressive mountaintop farm school in Vermont, where my schedule changed. There, running in the dark through the woods, as fast as I could, became my meditation. Once I ran into a fence, and collapsed into sweet, black mud until breath returned.

I knew I was in training for something that would later be revealed, and my life has been truly magical. Working in Tokyo as an assistant therapist in a Japanese clinic for autistic and retarded children at twenty-two, a Japanese neighbor brought me to a Temple for a ten-day retreat, which entailed wearing hakama, the huge divided indigo cotton pants (think: Kabuki actor) with white wrapped kimono-top, and chanting 13-hours a day: the Shinto cleansing breath practice, at times, quiet as a whisper, at others, loud as football cheers. Our infrequent meals were miso soup, rice with barley, and takwan (pickled daikon radish). There, sworn to secrecy, I was privately initiated into Shinto during a terrifyingly theatrical ceremony.

Not long afterwards, in a mountain monastery, I was introduced to Zen meditation, which fit well my appreciation of inner focus, simplicity, and early rising, during my three and a half year stay in Japan. In 1978, when Chogyam Trungpa Rinpoche presided at Naropa Institute in Boulder, I traded Zen for Tibetan Shambala Meditation, but by thirty-three, I was back to practicing Zen.

Meanwhile, Werner Erhardt cracked my act open for me to see in the est Training in San Francisco in 1973, and shortly following that, The Six Day in Tahoe. I was so tentative, trying so hard not to bother anyone, that I was really obnoxious! And so defended that my speech was too abstract to communicate clearly. I was the Watcher, continually practicing to live, but too scared to let myself just *be here*.

I practiced power exercises in Carlos Castenada's books and dream exercises in the Seth books. In what way was I "creating my own reality"? I felt anxious: I should know this already: what is the way to consciously create a balanced life, and enjoy being here? Mother of three young boys, wife to world-class acoustic bassist, Gary Peacock, I felt mystified as to how to get everything done and have any time for myself. I was running in the mornings, meditating, always striving for the perfect schedule, which life's demands seemed ever to alter. Plagued by self-criticism, I was still trying to "do life right."

I participated in the first Forum with Werner in the early '80s, and after he passed his technology on to some of his est trainers, in Landmark Education's bevy of trainings, communications and team leadership courses, where I gained a sense of competency and self-reliance. In 1983, grieving and handling the details of the passing-on of my parents and grandmother and clearing out their home across the country, I became exhausted. I was hungry for internal peace (and physical rest!) when I heard Bhagwan Shree Rajneesh speak one sentence on a recording—and recognized his voice, absolutely, as the voice of an old friend. It was time to go wherever he was. The prospect was inconvenient and terrifying. Who was I under all this "being polite"? What if I found out I was someone I couldn't stand?

After a month-long intense course there called "Primal," I was invited to move to the Ranch. From 1983-86 I lived there, at Rajneeshpuram in the eastern Oregon desert, where Dynamic Meditation commenced at 6 A.M., Kundalini at 6 P.M., and in the evenings "sitting at the feet of the Master." Bhagwan Shree Rajneesh ("Osho" since his passing), was still in silence that first year, and sitting in his presence felt powerfully revitalizing. I took seriously the commune practice: "Everything is a meditation." The cornerstones of Osho's work—meditation, catharsis, and celebration—made sense and were practices I welcomed into daily life. Buddha *and* Zorba–of course! "Zorba the Buddha!" Yet, still, I experienced a kind of pervasive angst in daily life: Would I ever get it (living) right?

In the early 90s, Pat Kalama trained me in Sweat Lodge with a few other women on the Nisqually Reservation. Following this, Wayne, a drum leader, invited me to join his Medicine Drum. I drummed and sang at practice on Friday nights, then Saturdays and Sundays, at pow-wows all over the state of Washington, as part of Shi-O-Ba-Ha (our drum group, laughingly named "Prairie Chicken" by our leader). When our group fell apart, after a year and a half, I joined a Native American women's study group that met weekends on Mt. Hood for several years, learning how to be in this world, "on earthwalk," in cooperation with our spirit helpers.

I "met" Saniel Bonder and his wife, Linda Groves-Bonder, in 2003 looking over my boyfriend's shoulder at three minutes of a video clip on Wakingdown.org and felt that imperative sense to immediately go *be* with them. Soon after, they came to Seattle! We did meet in person at their intro evening, where we did gazing meditation. Linda and I simultaneously burst into tears and, after some sobbing, laughter. The intensity of their transmission was powerfully grounding. Something in me came to a halt.

After the second intro evening, it was clear that the majority of human beings attracted there had long histories of commitment to spiritual seeking and finding. Being with them was so nourishing I returned for another intro evening and their Great Relief weekend, after which–laughingly—I really *did* feel a great sense of relief! I was strongly attracted to their transmission and to the ordinariness of the way they presented themselves. No "pomp and circumstance" here–Saniel and Linda were just being 100 % themselves. Suddenly, I felt my own true essence contacted like a small child awakening from a long sleep coming out to play. In their presence I could clearly see the wobble in my own alignment with my inner being. The company I kept showed it: I had let a man into my life whom I couldn't trust, who lied to me, and I didn't know what to do about it. I was allowing my well-being to be jeopardized. I felt disconnected from the Being I came here to be.

Saniel was pointing me to look inside and actually *feel* what was going on. It surfaced to meet me with the vengeance of the long-ignored. Acres of gooey pain, years of self-criticism and blame, regrets, grasped me horrifyingly. As I allowed myself, with Saniel and Linda's sacred cradling, to relax my hold on life as I was used to it, these feelings' grasping released, and I was able to let myself sink into the morass of despair. At their encouragement I allowed myself to plummet into utter darkness, lostness, hopelessness—and feel.

There was nothing to do. I had been doing too much for too long and not letting myself fully feel this pain. Saniel had warned that he pitied people who get into his Waking Down work because they go through so much hell. He was good to his word.

But I would never "go back." The more I allowed myself to be swallowed up by the fear and angst that had long been a part of daily life, the more that same anxiety, when welcomed and sunk into, became pleasurable. I was no longer fighting it. No longer trying to run away from it or fix it. Pain and pleasure simultaneously. This was a new way of experiencing life—checking in with my gut.

What am I feeling now? And now? And now? At first I may have become a bit preoccupied with my shadow side, but this practice allowed the habit of checking in with myself to become established. I was not always following my internal guidance system, but, at last, we had met and become allies, thanks to Saniel and Linda and that sacred holding replicated by Waking Down teachers.

In The Great Relief Saniel had introduced me to his concept of "green-lighting." What a door opener to freedom! Now, in lieu of blaming myself every time I did or said something I didn't like or didn't do or say something I thought I should have, I was able to simply "green-light" myself to be an asshole, a jerk, a wimp—the person who never gets it right. What a relief ! All these aspects I had up till then criticized soon became "so what!" I was moving forward, not clinging to my last bad opinion of myself and beating myself up for it, but, rather, welcoming life.

Newly, I was enjoying my own process: tuning into my body, feeling what was there to be felt, riding the crest of the wave of these feelings without opinion or preference. I was starting to perceive the sliding between positive pleasure and positive pain as naturally occurring shifts. For example, the pleasure of a hike may include processing some pain. Historically, I had been choosing one over the other, which had stopped that natural flow of sliding and resulted in my experiencing a frozenness with fear in myself. Over time I had ended up flat-lining. I'd get up, and my days would feel mechanical. I was living in managed fear, not aliveness, inside a bubble cut off from my own life force, running out of energy.

Through Waking Down I began to feel into what I really feared: tuned into my mistrust of pleasure and asked for that to be experienced more and as it was. The aliveness began to increase. I became curious to "go into"places in myself I had feared and qualities I had abhorred. My body-mind was now an exciting laboratory. I saw that by labeling pain as "bad," a repulsive energy had emerged to avoid pain. When I felt into my body, pain to the body became simply uncomfortable, which allowed me to stay with pain and truly feel it and not have to suffer.

According to societal patterns, suffering is necessary to "get somewhere," as in "noble suffering"; thus selflessness had become a kind of pleasure. With the dawning of unity of pleasure and pain together, unconditionally, a fearlessness emerged.

There was nothing to be afraid of as everything slides in the course of its natural unfolding process. Allowing what's present to be felt, I experienced feelings as moving and changing, evolving; and myself as at once the container, as well as what takes place inside it *and* outside it.

Now every action takes place within an awareness of structure. Oh, I wanted to be liked there. Oh, this person is speaking in a "loop," coming round and round in a hamster-wheel of practiced upset. How do I want to relate to this person now? On what level do I want to relate to this person? How can we access a cut deeper in this conversation? Now there are some options: I speak out of that commitment to unveil the Real in myself, and invite the Real in the other to come forth. So I tend to ask more questions, to listen more, and to listen from the place where you and I are the same.

And I am acting from curiosity about you, from "I don't know,"but here is what I sense, here is what I'm feeling right now in the body. We will be bringing this into the light together, as we are together here. This feels really bad right now–my gut feels tight and my breathing feels constricted. What's happening with you? How I want to relate with you is so we both feel good, and relaxed, and free to be ourselves fully.

Like a fish seeing the water, yet choosing *focus*, I began to see focus as a choice to feel what was there, then choose my focus of attention. Having become familiar with some main "broken places" in myself, I started to be able to see when I had fallen or thrown myself into what Saniel calls a Broken Zone, and I was able, while being IN it and *being* it, to communicate simultaneously with those around me: This is where I am, I'm fine, and I'll let you know when I'm back out of this emotional "hole"... or ... this is what I need: for you to check on me in 30 minutes and simply hold me from the back till I feel grounded again.

This freed me from fearing being emotionally triggered. Where previously I had used to run away, creating confusion, frustration and chaos, now I trusted myself to be able to speak from that lost place to alert others that I could not listen and "hear" them from that place of despair and set others at ease, in the knowledge that I would be willing and available to hear them upon my "return." I could even request how: If you let me lie down, and hold my head in your lap, you may communicate anything to me, and I will be able to listen and hear you, and respond.

INVOCATION AND SECOND BIRTH

The Waking Down Weekend was an innocuous little no-frills configuration of people talking about their lives in small groups of four, each with a teacher and interning teacher. The format seemed so simple—but add to that the transmission those teachers bring to the table, and—*whammo* !—all hell breaks loose inside.

I watched people unravel, felt myself go from rigid in life to rag doll laughing. The following day I made a strong invocation to *wake up*! The next morning a smile pulled me through the day like a helium balloon on a string. Standing out of doors, I felt enchanted–the bird songs seemed woven together; the land, the sea, the roots of everything had roots in each other and in me. Our connections were apparent. On the phone I told Ted Strauss, my teacher, that it seemed as though there was an enormous ball of yarn in the sky, but unlike the usual ball made of one single strand wound round and round, this one was made up of endless varied lengths, consecutively interwoven by agreement (each to keep its place), yet each one moving, writhing, like snakes, staying in this ball, remaining in relationship to one another.

Seeing-sensing this Divine inextricability of our being connected—all the people in my childhood, neighbors, people past, present, and future, in other countries—overwhelmed me with gratitude. For days I marveled at this vision, which stayed up in the sky, high above the tree-tops in front of my house. Much later, reading Ted's book, Your Endless Awakenings, I discovered he had written a chapter about a similar perception—his ball of string.

That evening I made another invocation for my own awakening—this time stronger: I yelled at Existence and demanded to wake up *now*! The next morning I woke up to the piercingly painful, yet mesmerizing, brilliance of sunlight playing through two rhododendron leaves. The sky was dark and cloudy. Yet the light showing through these leaves enchanted me with its strength and variety. They have spines, like us, those leaves. The leaves shifted and moved in what seemed a Divine dance I could not stop watching–for two hours. The rhododendron shadows on the opposite wall overtook my appreciative fascination. Gratefulness pulsed so hugely, my heart ached.

When finally I moved from bedroom into office, the sound of birds was so magnified it felt excruciating, as though each bird was miked to the max, and I had to cover my ears, even though I was smiling with new appreciation. I was equally fascinated as my ears were in intensely piercing pain.

Therein began a Second Birthing process that unfolded over a ten month period, divided into three-week sections. This first, one of sensory magnification: the intensification of colors, sights, and sounds. Three weeks of "double hearing": heightened ESP, hearing what was being said, while simultaneously hearing the inner conversations, hearing/ perceiving the motivations, the manipulations. People always wanted something from each other, and now I was perceiving what.

Then three weeks of hearing this in myself. Everything I said was a lie. I spoke some words, and underneath these words, there was ever a program running. Agendas blared so loud in their transparencies, I felt in constant alarm that everyone else could also see how false I was being. Then three weeks' remote viewing of those not physically in my view. Three weeks seeing people hurt each other. Three weeks of people loving each other sincerely. Followed by three weeks lying awake all night, seeing, smelling, and hearing my physical body crumble and disintegrate; while simultaneously present to feeling poignant sweet grief: Now that finally I appreciate being here and *want* to be here (in the physical body), this body itself is leaving. Profound gratitude wracked my being with intense sadness.

Ten months of three-week periods, each exposing a different "view" and understanding of this life, opened up to me. Throughout this, was a sense of my identity-as-personality becoming permeable, flexible, being shredded, leaving me open and vulnerable, without any buffer: rawly *here*. Fragilely being wide open, yet standing strong on my own behalf, and daring to say what's so for me, risking all with others, and growing deeper in our connection

Whereas previously I had experienced, the stress of being around a liar to be enormously painful and pervasive, now there was simply no "wiggle room" for lying to be in my space. Loving one's self is a primary responsibility, and now I could no longer allow myself to be near an oppressor. Around lying, everything hung as an unanswered question like stalactites dripping a paralyzing goo. Even one day generated too many loose ends to clear up: enervating, frustrating. How dare one not be straight with me? When one person is determined to fog, deflect and diffuse, diverting conversations from proceeding to a clearing, the swirl of frustration continues, uncleared, becoming despair. From there, anger is a step up.

I became present to a healthy impatience for bullshit; for anything that feels bad. I saw that opening to love of another doesn't necessarily look all lovey-dovey: sometimes it looks like going to the police. I no longer cared to "get to the bottom" of the lying I'd observed. I became an invitation for honest living. Through the body's wisdom, I had simply become unable to be with that which was clearly out of alignment. Mercy, at times, necessitates ruthlessness. I became a friend to and advocate for my Self, and now, through daring, I felt myself living in union with all of existence as experience in accordance with the rhythm of life, being connected with people where communication is clean and clear.

That's where mercy with myself can be ruthless—like cutting off my own head and watching it roll: "I was just being a real jerk. I'm sorry. That is not how I want to relate with you. The way I want to be with you is for both of us to be free to fully be and express ourselves, listening and coming from our hearts." Demanding that, or even inviting this level of relating, demands the ruthlessness of being more animal and being true to my animal self. Life as inquiry. Life as choosing to be clear—seeing through compassionate eyes and taking appropriate action to stay in synch with my Self.

Ruthless Mercy is speaking up when something is out of alignment such that the best of each person is appreciated and invited forward. When mercy is ruthless, the heart of hearts of people are contacted, not the surface, but contacted beyond the patterns. Ruthlessness reaches IN to the inner being of the Other and taps that heart on the shoulder, so to speak, and says, "Wake up. It's time to play in a way that makes you love yourself entirely and appreciate being alive."

"Presence continues to be more present."

Geoff

Geoffrey Oelsner born in Kansas City, Missouri, 1949. Premature birth with subsequent severe touch deprivation. Spontaneous psychic and kundalini awakenings in teenage bedroom. Meets Leslie Berman at Oberlin College, 1970. Attends first session of Chogyam Trungpa Rinpoche's Naropa Institute in Boulder, Colorado, 1974. Marries Leslie Berman in 1975. Adam Forest Oelsner born in 1981. Fixer-upper home purchased in Fayetteville, Arkansas. Begins clinical experience as psychotherapist and massage therapist (which continues to now). Second child, Amy Claire Oelsner, born 1985. Joyous family fullness! Begins decade of Buddhist meditation retreats; later forms local Buddhist meditation and spiritual support group. Works with Dzogchen teacher Lama Surya Das and several Tibetan teachers, including H.H. Chetsang Rinpoche. Four and a half years in Hakomi body-awareness-based therapy. Discovers Waking Down work in 2000. Special trust develops in relationship with WDM teacher Sandra Glickman. Leslie becomes involved with Waking Down work, 2001. Numinous early A.M. walks and sits replace "pre-meditated" meditations. A rock-hunting expedition to Missouri Ozarks profoundly grounds awareness. Second Birth recognition in September 2002 brings more freedom, resilience, contentment. Leslie awakens November 2002! Geoff releases a book of poetry, Native Joy, and a CD of songs, Morning Branches. He and Leslie attend Tantra of Trust weekend, WDM Deepening into Your Second Life retreat in Fairfield, Iowa, and later in 2004 an Advanced Mentoring Skills week in California. They become WDM mentors. Geoff resumes phone sessions with Sandra. His early Ozark morning walks and sits continue. Presence continues to be more present.

A COUNTRY WHERE ALL COLORS ARE SACRED AND ALIVE

RUMI

You let your prayer shawl fall at dawn and disappeared.
It's night again now and your shawl of stars is near,
wrapped 'round our shoulders, Rumi, though you seem to be
long gone. Your perfect absence sings and dances on.

Oh Rumi, you turn in circles in my heart.
You turn in circles in my heart.

When you met your final teacher you were well-prepared
for cooking in the oven of his self-consuming sun.
After many sacred days and night communing in that sun
with your teacher— baker— Shams, your fragrant heart-bread
was well done.

Oh Rumi, you turn in circles in my heart.
You turn in circles in my heart.

But when Shams was murdered by your envious students,
your grief tore your heart apart and broke its holy bread
for everyone, annihilating you in silent song.
Your perfect absence sings and dances on.

Oh Rumi, you turn in circles in my heart.
You turn in circles in my heart.

Listen to the words of the poet Rumi when he says:

"This we have now
is not imagination.

This is not
grief or joy,
not a judging state,
or an elation,
or sadness.
Those come
and go.
This is the presence
that doesn't.
It's dawn, my love,
here in the splendor of coral,
inside the Friend.
What else could human beings want?

When grapes turn to wine,
they're wanting this.
When the night sky pours by,
it's really a crowd of beggars
and they all want some of this!
This
that we are now
created the body, cell by cell,
like bees building a honeycomb.
The human body and the universe grew from this, not this
from the universe and the human body."*
Oh Rumi, you turn in circles in my heart.
You turn in circles in my heart.

**Poem by Jelaluddin Rumi (1207-1273), translated by Coleman Barks, in his book "The Essential Rumi," San Francisco, HarperCollins Publishers, 1995, pp. 261-262. Quoted in full with slight omissions and changes, with Mr. Bark's permission, on Geoff's CD, "Morning Branches," obtainable from him at* greenwaters@cox.net *or at* cdbaby.net. *Huge thanks go to Coleman for making Rumi's sublime poetry widely available to English-speaking readers.*

YOUR AUTUMN FACE

Now, there is no telling birds' curved shadows
from their crossing flights; the jeweled
antlers from winds that gorge them. Now all
flows in the veins of a darker rainbow
and motions couple in the dusk.

It is a time of coming together in the land.
Gelled sun bursts like a yolk on the
meadow-line; sky's violet eye deepens.
We lie scattered on the fading tapestry

of grass, looking upon ourselves with wonder.

One cannot own another (and I
could not lose you in this Mystery).

The leaf, the ground, the shadow meet
and fall into darkness together, as
the three of us— you, me, and all of us—
join ourselves with the fading shadows
and enter the smoky land coming together.

I ENTERED THE ANIMA'S GARDEN...

I entered the Anima's garden,
following the guardian through many doors.
There was a room of pastures,
one of dying stars,
a courtyard of stone
where water flowed from the living rock.

We emerged in a ruined temple
to the moon of this planet,
a place forgotten
on the torn mountain.
Making my way down an arduous slope,I stumbled and fell
perhaps a thousand feet
before the eyes of a pervasive goddess.
And when I came to,
tears of light fell on me
and a voice cried,
"Thank you. Thank you."
It was She who is glory,
giving thanks to me
who had so worshiped Her.

Now I have emerged and fallen,
leaving the desire for rooms
and desiring life without walls,
luxuriant with the leaves
and tides of change.

PRAYER IN THE NIGHT KITCHEN

Mother, you are living sapphire
and cool shade that spreads balm
over the naked gape of our wounds,
white jet of sea-rush, cherry petal,
and the feeding milk of stars.

I am your unquenchable child,
for from my pores well all the faces
of singing and crying beings.
We ache to be saturated.
Fill me, milky Mother. Into these
voices that roar pour your Grace.

THE CARAVAN

You came up over the last dune
in the caravan,
wind smacking the canvas,
and there was the sea.
You felt refreshed,
like there was no longer any trace
left of the circus.
All the paint had washed off
in the gradual rain,
and the two of you were now
truly nomads in the caravan,
not clowns or high-wire artists.
You then always got that
coming-upon-the-sea feeling
when you steered your caravan
into the crowded streets of cities,
down to low-lit districts
where faces doubled
by cobras of shadow
look up from their angst and anger.
Because that sea-feeling held,
when you came to town
you brought a gentle wind,
touching the screens;
seeming to question the watchers
on their stoops.
A questioning wind that leads out
somehow.

REMEMBERING

I get out of bed
still light with dreams.
Suddenly I'm there again
just above my head, remembering
everything is really THIS.
I could always feel
the way the mountains lean,
even against the wind,
but this solitude is lighter,
carries so much farther.

FINDING THE OLD NIGHT WAY HOME

I found a wakened way
to fly my slightest dream
across the prairie, wireless,
tree to tree. Then some trees
splintered into fence posts
in my dreams, and later
became phone poles. Barbed wire
and taut black talk-lines
sliced my flight. They stung
and nettled my dream-body,
just as they overhung and netted
this country. Encroaching suburbs
sometimes held me from
full span. Clenched fists
of smoke from factories;
dense inner cities pulled
on me. Yet I was willingly
drawn down to certain altars,
shrines, archways, parks,
side roads, homes, and human
gatherings where primal silence
reasserts itself. Then I could begin
to glide once more on amber
waves of light East-West
above the land. My being
sought sanctuary in mountains
and rivers, at estuaries of Spirit.
I rested in slow-breathing meadows far from men. Night
after night,
God moved me in vision-flight
beyond a life I had thought mine,
on through the gray where worlds meet,
into a country where all colors
are sacred and alive.

"It's what I had been missing and seeking my whole life. I was free, unlimited, pulsating with aliveness."

Ken

Ken Dvoren is a psychotherapist, mediator, and children's social worker living in Santa Monica, California, with his wife Joyce and two cats. He has two real children who are grown. Ken is a long-time seeker who is realizing that finding is more rewarding, and that even accepting and allowing can be sublime. He is currently deciding that though his trust in Being is increasing, the proposition that he creates his own reality is enticing, especially since he presumes he is already doing it. He is also concluding, with considerable excitement and anxiety, that encountering life's experiences fully and feeling them deeply is more satisfying than attempting to slide through life unscathed. His website: JourneyToOneSelf.com.

COMING HOME

I was being guided by Holly Springfield, then a Waking Down teacher, on a Witness Consciousness exercise. I had previously both struggled with and resisted this exercise. She began by asking me to pay attention to my breath. Fortunately, she gave me sufficient space in which to do this. I became aware that there were different aspects to the act of noticing. The first was locating the breath. The second was becoming the breath. I then needed to emerge from this convergence in order to witness it. Releasing myself from this identification has always been difficult. This time I was assisted by the recognition that being the noticer was one more aspect of the total act of noticing. From the point of observation, I moved toward the object, became it, and then returned to be the one who observes. When I settled back into this subjective state, the egoic "I" suddenly and naturally coincided completely with Consciousness. I uttered in amazement, "I am the Witness," and started to cry. It's what I had been missing and seeking my whole life. I was free, unlimited, pulsating with aliveness.

From this expanded, restful, exalted state, I simply observed all in my phenomena field, including Holly's verbalizations. After five or ten minutes, about half of which were spent in joyful tears of relief and gratitude, I was, without any ostensible precipitator, sucked down a funnel (diffuse at the top, focused at the bottom) directly into the third-eye area of my forehead. At first I was disappointed, assuming that this glorious experience had ended prematurely, as had other wondrous experiences of the past. But I quickly realized that Consciousness had traveled with me, as me, and had landed in my body. I started to gently cry from profound delight and gratitude. It was as if I was inhabiting my body for the first time, "coming home to a place I've never been before."

I wanted to honor this precious rebirth by not rushing to engage the outer world. I came very slowly and deliberately to a standing position and walked out to Holly's lovely patio, where a fresh breeze awaited me. I sat down and was immediately greeted by a neighbor's white cat, who nuzzled my toes, laid down, and got up to nuzzle some more, and couldn't stop. Neither can I.

RESULTS I NOTICE

I don't feel separate from something I think I need. The old quest to fill the emptiness inside of me is not present.

I feel as if I'm coming from myself rather than going outward to find myself or to get something. I feel whole and complete.

My sense of myself is less defined, more diffuse, more existing everywhere than just inside of this self.

I am both more accepting of whatever is and, at the same time, less tolerant of what does not please me. Paradoxes do not confuse or frustrate me, nor stimulate extensive efforts to comprehend them with my mind.

I am more comfortable around people. I am less anxious and less self-conscious. I perceive other's words and actions as about them, not as about me. I can get out of myself and listen non-defensively, and am curious about who they are, rather than taking things personally.

I have a bigger heart. I am more naturally compassionate. I'm more in balance between considering other people's needs and taking care of my own.

I have more energy. I feel like a grown up kid who wants to re-experience the world from a fresh perspective.

I'm happy. I laugh more. I find little things hilarious.

I experience the physical world with more sensual delight.

When my stuff comes up, it doesn't weigh me down or get stuck; it seems to pass more easily through me. I experience it from a broader context, a larger perspective.

I have more appreciation for and take greater pleasure in Being itself.

"An amazing healing has happened and still continues."

Pascal

Pascal Salesses was born and raised in the South of France. She came to the United States in 1983 and has been here since then. Besides being a Waking Down teacher, she is a Somatic Experiencing Practitioner. She is also finishing her Core Energetics training (body oriented psychotherapy). She left Northern California two years ago and now resides in Fairfield, Iowa.

WELCOME HOME

Once upon a time on August 6th of the year 1995 AD, I felt a pronounced energetic pressure inside my chest and with it I sank into a mild depression that kept drawing me deeper inwardly. I couldn't resist this inward pull. I felt more present in myself, reduced to a lower and more efficient level of energetic/physical presence and clarity. No thing, no one, could have gotten me out of this state, it seemed. I was pinned down to now and now and now, aware of what was happening to me. Although not understanding what was happening, I was at ease and trusting whatever it was. I abided in a quiet inner depth, simply feeling what was arising or not arising inside me.

My boyfriend at the time, James, who was also involved in the Waking Down work, complained about how self-absorbed I was. I couldn't bring myself to speak to him about what was going on inside me. We'd been arguing a lot recently, and our intimate connection seemed to be hanging by a thread. I explained that I needed to be real with myself and couldn't compromise myself for anyone. I stayed withdrawn from him, in protection of this new "thing" going on inside me. He wasn't happy with my answer and behavior, but I couldn't help him. I just couldn't try to please anyone else right then, and although in some part of me I felt selfish, I had to respect this inner impulse.

Throughout the whole of the next day a deep inner peace comforted me and freed me up. On a feeling level it felt like a continuation of what I had been going through for sometime, but more intensely now.

I was in a fast free fall. Mental, emotional, physical structures from my previous ideas about life seemed to fade away. The sensation was that of falling through an open sky, shedding old skins, feeling strangely lighter, while being held in a very subtle but still tangible trust but with nowhere to land. I felt as if I was flapping around in the unknown of it all and learning to get used to it. Over time I did get used to it although it was quite disorienting.

That night I had a powerful dream in which I felt myself completely free, omnipresent, blissful. Ardeliza, a spiritual teacher and colleague of Saniel Bonder at the time, was talking to me in a language of colors which I could understand clearly somehow. A pristine royal blue kept appearing as if somehow it meant something for me. Both of us were in an ancient Greek amphitheater. I walked down an aisle by myself and noticed many seats occupied mostly by men, only a few women, in a clear, almost transparent form. Many of them were looking at me. The place was filled with a powerful peacefulness, connectedness and love. It felt sweetly familiar being there. I could sense that everyone was silently welcoming me, welcoming me Home. What an uplifting and soothing experience that was!

The next day around noon I was at home alone preparing myself some lunch when suddenly and surprisingly the knife, the bread, the kitchen counter, the space in between objects and everything else I looked at, appeared vibrant, alive, eternal, full, free, conscious. As if it had always been that way and I had just noticed it. Next I could sense into an energetic channel inside my chest connecting to my head, and there was only consciousness there. My body was an object freely resting in the infinite ocean of Consciousness. WOOW!!!

My mind was small in size, and it either appeared to stand in the background of my awareness or to have become completely transparent so that all I could see, feel, sense was pure Consciousness. I sat down to eat my Consciousness sandwich filled with rapturous happiness, deeply released and present.

Later as I was blissfully washing the dishes, a swift and significant shift took over me, at my core, in my heart. In that instant I acquired a new identity, like a baptism. I was Consciousness! My true self was Consciousness! I am and had always been Consciousness before becoming anything else. It was all so obviously clear. This felt like a major stepping stone. I knew then that I was free. I was freedom itself—freedom, Consciousness, peace and eternity. Expanded Consciousness in and as me shone brightly for more than four days before subsiding.

At that same time my mind unleashed lengthy and terrifying doubts regarding what had happened and who I was. I had to dry my brow a few times before burning through them. I then figured out how to stay within the obviousness of Consciousness. All I had to do was stay relaxed and feel myself in the present moment, and so I did. This worked for some time, but then I grew tired of making the effort to relax for Consciousness to stay obvious, and I let myself embrace whatever arose instead of retreating into a serene state, and so I did.

Although there was a relief, the transition was bumpy. Part of me was so attached to having the Conscious Nature in the foreground all the time that I missed the confirmation and the clarity it brought. In time my Conscious Nature became an integrated part of the rest of me; it stayed quite obvious in a lower key way. Still I knew and owned that part of myself as me, too, and could choose to abide there more fully when I wanted to.

This recognition lasted a few months with different levels of intensity at different times. At some point, Saniel said to me, "Bravo! And you may want to notice now that there is still a very fine, very subtle separation going on. Take your time. Enjoy what you know of yourself now, but discriminate further."

Well, a few days later I started to recognize and feel how I had been keeping James at bay, and it hurt to feel what that was like. A wall crumbled between us, and I fell in love with him all over again with such passion and devotion that it took us both by surprise. There was a special moment over dinner when a veil lifted. I looked at him. I saw the utter beauty and deliciousness of his being. My heart exploded with joy. It was evident to me that there is absolutely no separation between us at the level of being. I saw the beauty and the beast. I am him. I am all. I sensed myself drop down inside my body somehow, more here than before, up close and personal, and that was new.

Consciousness is all that exists, inseparable from the doubts, the fear, the resistance, the effort, the clarity, the confusion, the tenderness, the expansion, the process, the forms, the space in between. I can rest or tremble. It doesn't really matter. It is all obviously the same. What an amazing mind and body-boggling revelation!

That was then. Now, here I am nine plus years later. Many shifts and integrations have happened since then. My journey now is much different from how it was at the beginning. During the first few years I went through long periods of disorientation at times, uncovering many skeletons in many closets. I revisited the confusion, the hurt, the defenses, the trauma of my childhood conditioning, but this time from a more complete perspective of being. Since I knew myself more fully, I could encounter all that I had disconnected from in my past and now came out the other side sobered, opened, stabilized, enlivened, compassionate toward myself and others. An amazing healing has happened and still continues.

It took some time to get better at riding the wild waters, but I did. Over time I learned to recognize and trust the intelligence of Being in and as the limited patterns coming up and follow their threads through new levels of feeling discomfort, containment, listening, liberation and transformation.

The split from our wholeness runs deep, at many layers of our make up and all locked up in our body. For a long time I have had a particular interest in how our bodies hold the energetic, emotional, mind patterns of separation, and so I have been studying Core Energetics and Somatic Experiencing. Both have been great gifts to help me broaden my understanding and help me resolve deep-seated issues.

At the core of my being I rest in more freedom, warmth, trust, compassion, pleasure, creativity. And, more importantly, I am here for all of it!

What this awakening has allowed me to do is dramatically change my understanding and my relationship to my human and divine nature.

In fact, it has changed my relationship to everything, especially to myself. What is truly amazing is not the "everything" aspect as much as the relationship in itself. Although it is hard to separate them, for me this coming back home, through this intimate relating to my many parts, opened the door to an amazing self-discovery and eventually owning my own feeling conscious-heart presence. I welcome and trust the continuous unfolding and mystery of myself, as human/divine together. The mystery keeps unfolding according to its own demands as the eternal Play of Being and my faith in Being is unshakable.

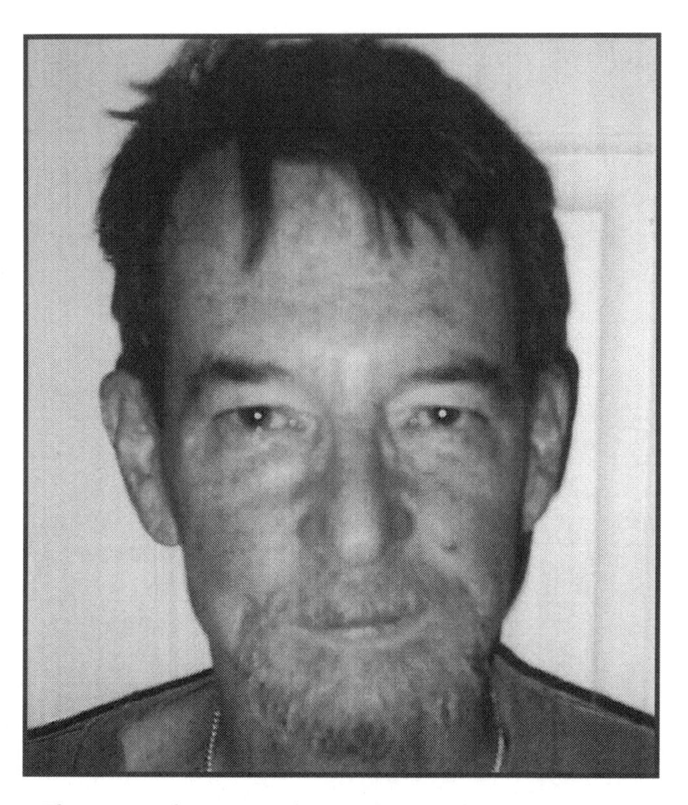

"Then, in my chest, I sensed, instead of burst-open compassion for my own form and for all form, an elliptical sphere of steel with a belt of titanium around it, so, as much as was humanly possible for me, I could be totally inured to all potentially painful feelings.."

Art

Art Pierce was born in San Francisco in 1937 to a U.S. Army Air Corps family, lived in seventeen different locations his first seventeen years, in twenty-six locations in his next thirty-seven years, and retired to California in 2006. Among many other things, he worked as a chemist and as an engineer. For ten years he volunteered for a not-for-profit which uses money from recycling and grants to distribute 2,100 bags of donated food per week to shut-in seniors. He was a prostate cancer survivor. He was married to his beloved Dee in 1967. Their children are: son, Allen Lee, daughter, Maleena-shuuum, and granddaughter, Violet Rae. Art was a Waking Down in Mutuality mentor who worked with many students in the Waking Down community. He passed away in 2007. We honor his contributions to our work.

PARADOX

As a child I was seeing colors around people which was pooh-poohed into subconsciousness by adults. Once, as a young teenager, I continued playing badminton while I was out-of-body about eight feet above my body. Frequently, when I had a fever, with my eyes closed I was a point of consciousness located in my heart, which was wonderful, and with each heartbeat that consciousness expanded to infinity, which was terrifying. There may have been more such events, but I don't remember them.

Also, I was forced to attend Sunday school and then church, wherever and whatever the nearest Protestant one was. Once out on my own, in my eighteenth location at Texas Tech, I became an atheist, then a few months later intellectually decided being an agnostic was more honest. In my first twenty-nine and a half years I never felt I was on a "spiritual path." Not at all.

In April of 1967 something happened that radically changed me. I had, as I learned much later, a spontaneous nirvikalpa samadhi. My experience was this: I felt my body was tiny in the midst of a very large and loud Niagara of upward energy. Here, not actually in location or form at all, without characteristics, was home: white intensity, infinite bliss, energy, love, all the same. Here (all this is only in retrospect) was no I or self or body, no form.

The formerly formless white intensity faded a little and, heartbrokenly, form just barely began, only, thankfully, to disappear into the white intensity. This (Dee told me) continued for another twenty minutes (her time) as the periods of white intensity became less long and the periods of form became longer. Heartbroken, I was infinite compassion for all form, myself included. Infinite compassion was the connector between form and white intensity. Each time form would come back, there was a psychic pain: this infinite compassion for my own form and all forms that I felt in my heart, especially at the sinoatrial node which, independent of heartbeat, simultaneously expanded everywhere. Finally, only form, no more transitionings as white intensity.

I was too stunned by this (non)experience to speak—words felt totally insufficient—even though people around me were asking me questions. I was asked to see an orange on a cushion on a stool for about thirty seconds, close my eyes for thirty seconds or so, and remember what I had seen, open my eyes again and see more qualities of the orange. This went on, more orange seen, more orange remembered, for about fifteen minutes, during which I realized that you could see additional qualities of the orange—or any form—forever. Then when I opened my eyes, the orange was gone. (The leader of the exercise had hid it to "eat later.") The disappearance shocked me and I was all the way back, capable of speaking, even though I chose not to.

Thus began a life of family support and, most importantly to me, a seeking to return to nothing but nirvikalpa samadhi, forever. Again, at almost thirty, I did not understand that all samadhis are temporary, so easy "translation" into permanent nirvikalpa samadhi became my spiritual quest for the next thirty years. My first teacher was the supreme Advaitist, Master Subramuniya, my beloved Guruji.

Guruji treated me with very kind and gentle (hyper)masculinity—asanas, meditations, yamas and niyamas, siddhi demonstrations—but I was not an heroically successful finder. I did become established in a stabilized "kaef" (Exclusive Consciousness/mere awareness Only) and was easily able to hear the different internal ringings in each ear as a two-toned chord, but was unable to ride the chord up above the top chakra into clear white light. I (more exactly, no-I) could only be moonglow inner light, not even golden, pink or blue light. My seeking for permanent (or any) clear white light was unsuccessful.

Although I continued these recommended meditation practices with Guruji, eventually, continuous in-person transmission was available only for monks and post-menopausal nuns; only pro forma distant occasions were there for married couples like Dee and myself.

Dee immediately dropped having anything to do with any "spiritual" practices: "Life will bring me enough to work with."

I, stunned by the famous photo of Ramana Maharshi, and similarly stunned by a photo of Franklin Jones, read some of what was written about Ramana, and everything Bubba Free John/Adi Da community produced, but the three times over ten years I tried to approach him, his "gate guardians" somehow, I felt, tacitly judged me and found me "wanting/lacking." The group felt very polite, but extremely standoffish. After tacit "dismissal" by Guruji, and finding nothing comparable to either Ramana (dead) or Da (socially shielded), I became bitter, more than a little cynical, and developed very sensitive antennae for the bogus and hypocritical. I gave up any hope of literal enlightenment or even any spiritual attainment in this lifetime, and even (possibly) any other potential lifetimes.

I had not only completely given up on, for me, the possibility of fully stabilized nirvikalpa samadhi, but had become totally subconsciously defended: willfully and purposely detached. After years of meditation practice, it's easy to hide in "Exclusive Consciousness Only" and feel all form as maya, illusion. At times, simply because I could, I would be unkind on purpose, just out of pure embittered meanness. And, as someone who was full-time very hyper-judgmental, cynical and *very* leery of spiritual exploitation, I became, over time, thoroughly rotted about life's "spiritual" possibilities.

At age sixty-one, Waking Down in Mutuality was recommended by Russell Swanson, my friend of thirty-two years from the Subramuniya group. I spent twenty-one months gingerly dipping my toe in the water ("due diligence") checking out this thing called "Waking Down in Mutuality (WDM)." Something new (and later realized as hopeful) from the start: For the very first time ever, spiritually, socially, personally or otherwise, I felt I wasn't being judged. After 21 months of careful peripheral association, I decided to give a Waking Down Weekend (WDW) a trial run on the Superbowl Weekend in 2001.

At the WDW workshop, in the small group, a repressed childhood memory surfaced. When I was seven, my best friend, Jerry, a cocker spaniel mutt, with whom I was deeply in love, had begun defending my next younger brother and me against people Jerry felt had the "wrong vibe," including an uncle and my father. Jerry was taken to the vet for a checkup. For the first time I was not allowed to come along. Jerry didn't come home because the vet wanted to "keep him overnight for a more thorough checkup." The next morning I pestered my mother for us to go pick up Jerry. Later in the afternoon, my constant requests were met with my mother saying, as she broke into tears, "Oh, honey, you don't understand. Jerry went to heaven." I quit eating and cried every moment possible for almost three days, even though on the second day my father promised, and he kept his promises, to give me a whipping if I continued crying over Jerry. I did continue and got two whippings before I was too hoarse to continue crying.

While I told all this, Holly Springfield, the teacher for our small group, was holding my feet and had tears running out of her eyes. Holly felt my pain more than I did—I wasn't *that* sad, I was just very tense. So, to break my tension, I went to a familiar defensive habit pattern, make a little joke. I said, "I guess I'm dog-boy." No one was even slightly amused. Then, in my chest, I sensed, instead of burst-open compassion for my own form and for all form, an elliptical sphere of steel with a belt of titanium around it, so, as much as was humanly possible for me, I could be totally inured to all potentially painful feelings.

At that moment I had a very conscious choice: Get up, walk out and run for the hills–I saw in my mind's eye my form getting ever smaller, with dust clouds coming from my footsteps as I raced away–like (here's that protective humor again) any normal, sensible, neurotic person or continue to investigate what might be able, over time, to surface in me. The choice was as hard as I had ever made. Because of the prior twenty-one months of continuing non-judgment and acceptance of me, and even in this terribly tense (underneath, protected from pain) moment, I chose the latter.

I didn't get the full import of that repressed childhood memory until nineteen months later, ten months after my Second Birth: Betrayed by my parents, I could no longer trust any other person. Guruji's retreat and Adi Da's up-front push away were just reconfirmations of that original wounding. In fact, every pain since age seven hurt so much that I couldn't allow myself to feel it "too much" or "at all."

WDM primarily recommends "tanking up"–you (gradually?) replicate the common characteristic (transmission) of the people you choose to hang out with. So, straining my resources and doing without some familiar material things, I began meeting with two teachers: February 7th, the next Wednesday, and Wednesdays weekly, with Sandra Glickman (only 128 miles round trip) and February 23rd, the last Friday, and last monthly Fridays, with Ted Strauss (226 miles round trip). I put the audio tape of *Waking Down* in my truck's tape player and listened to it every time I drove anywhere until late August. At which point I could almost tell you the words that would come next.

In early March 2001, just a month into "tanking up," and even though I felt no conscious change in myself, Dee, my wife of thirty-four years, mailed me from her work, something she'd not done before and hasn't since, a (somewhat saccharinely) card with a hand-written message: " Art, you're getting so much nicer I can hardly recognize you anymore! Love, Dee."

Effortlessly–it's not a switch anyone can turn on or off–I tanked up on Being this very Presence<=>Transmission. Also, Sandra and Ted, at every opportunity, gently and feelingly undermined my quest to look for an "improved" Art (whatever that imaginary construction might be) or to hope for a "different" Art–another defensive concoction to keep me from feeling myself as I now am.

As I began to really get ("grok") how any expectation for anything "improved" or "different" would just be holding me out of the present moment, I began, without any effort or practice of meditation, to spend more time Just Here. In retrospect, finally, that kind of looking for and hoping for was utterly gone. In retrospect, also, my habitual, protective, and formerly necessary defensive patterns were gently pointed out to me by Sandra and Ted as they began to see them repeated enough to be recognizable, or sometimes, even better, spontaneously discovered by me. Formerly necessary defensive habit patterns could surface because Sandra and Ted could listen and really hear, never judging, Being, fully trust able. To put it another way, before my "vasanas," my "subconscious habit patterns," my "governing sentimentalities" became conscious, they were running me without my noticing it.

Best of all, I didn't have to do a damn thing about the patterns except (recognition yoga) consciously notice them and just consciously allow myself to become and own them (yeah, I'm this, too). And, voila! (actually, way slower than that) they began to wither. It feels like very slowly letting air out of a tense balloon. In retrospect, the energy formerly used by the defensive patterns and used in the looking for, hoping for, "improved," "different" gradually became more always available. In retrospect, since it was now ever more obviously no longer necessary to control everything— including my feeling (a hopeless task that I had tried to do)—I began to feel more energy, more Presence. In retrospect, Being was, and continues to be, freed up for new exploration as and in and through me.

Just one time, in late August, I went out in a redwood tree grove and shouted, "I *want my second birth*." And sat back to wait for whatever that might turn out to be.

After thirty-four Wednesdays, on September 26, 2001, at the end of our mutual session, Sandra quietly said, "I'm outing you." At the time I thought, "That's odd. I'm not gay." I wondered what she meant.

On the drive home through the Coastal Range to the Pacific, I began to experience, instead of the usual me moving toward everything, everything was moving toward me. I was too afraid to go back and try to re-create the me moving toward everything. By the time I made it over the mountains, everything was moving toward me all the time. Within thirty more minutes, I began to fuse more and more with everything around me.

This fused-ness got stronger and stronger for twenty-six days. I acknowledged to myself this could really be: I guess I must be worthy because it has happened. Again: Along with my tentative acknowledgment came such an ever-increasingly strong sense of fusion with all ("Shakti rushes to embrace Siva") that by October 22nd I really didn't care what anyone else might or might not perceive in me. I knew the fusion was totally locked in; I couldn't be unfused anymore; I was unshakably fused.

Here is no longer the split of interior and exterior. What a relief. Home, at last.

"Exclusive Consciousness Only" had merged with everything and had become All-Inclusive Consciousness. And yet, I was still my ordinary self, plain old Art, in the midst of everything I could perceive. But I was (and am) self-confirmed, self-validated, totally, utterly, doubtlessly, merged with everything. Now, finally, I just quietly knew (and know). My old personal "me," the very limited Art that I had been afraid to go back to on that drive home from Sandra's on September 26, 2001, could now be gone back to without any pre-feeling of possible fragmentation. It's hard to reduce to words: I felt (and feel) like I (both impersonal Consciousness and embodied personal Art) am a "(life) spot in All (life)"—all together at once.

Four days later, on the drive up to Ted's on October 26th, I thought, "Hey, I'm unshakeably fused! What's the point in seeing Ted for transmission?"

Very shortly after I'd arrived and gazed with Ted for a little, he said, "Excuse me for a moment," and went over to his fireplace and lit a candle. He came back, sat down and moved the candle (in the sign of the cross!) in front of me and quietly said, "Welcome, Here." (What sweetness.) I said, "Thank you." (Any more words would have been, I felt, superfluous.) I feel, because Ted is primarily moved to bring people into Second Birth, when he asked if I felt any further need to see him monthly, I said, "No, not necessary anymore."

I, timeless and in time, have become non-exclusive Consciousness, one with everything and just myself, all united together. There is no separation, just this "Seamless Onlyness." For me, the initial bliss of fusion lasted fifteen months and then...but that's another story: Everything includes *Everything*. Let me just allude to how This feels by remarking I haven't become one with just what I had naively looked and hoped for and given up on: All the glorious, spiritual wonderfulness form(s). Here, all forms are more intensely felt, and some are excruciating.

What everything is and will be, what Being wants to explore as and in and through me and what can potentially happen next remains a familiar, strange, wondrous Mystery, both to myself and Being. Here is very paradoxical. Whatever This Here Is can't be understood. But, as I did, not as easily as a cold, you can, with much help, catch it. You can make it Your experience.

"My heart continues to stretch and grow each and every moment I am steeped in the alchemy of this community.

Lena

Lena O'Neill was born the youngest of thirteen children in Tacoma, Washington, in 1971. She resides in Seattle with her beloved partner, Tom, and daughter, Talia. She is a teacher in Waking Down in Mutuality. She loves to sing, dance, do yoga, write, and draw. She earned a B.A. with focus in psychology from The Evergreen State College in 2004. Her passion is to assist others through spiritual and emotional counseling, hands-on healing and shamanic initiation, including shamanic journeying for insight into current life issues, Soul Retrieval, and Sound Healing with her voice and drum. She also loves utilizing prayer and invocation ceremony to assist clarifying and manifesting the essence of their longings. Currently, she is earning an M.A. in counseling. If you would like to know more, see: www.lenabodywisdom.com. *Lena's email:* lenabodywisdom@me.com.

THE HEART OF WAKING DOWN

My life has been transformed and enriched in numerous ways since my first initiation into the Waking Down process, a little over two years ago. I would like to share with you some of the insights that have shown themselves to me through self-reflection, one-on-one work with Waking Down teachers, as well as attendance at Waking Down workshops and sittings.

Reparenting

The teachers and mentors' compassionate love has allowed my most broken, needy parts to be heard, felt, and seen in a way I have never experienced before. The more I am nurtured by this love, the more I am able to shine forth with my unique gifts, expose myself in vulnerable ways, and heal my wounds.

I am, and always have been, a Goddess. All that I needed was to have this reflected back to me in order to claim this as my identity, my destiny. With their unconditional love the teachers of Waking Down acknowledged me and called me forth as God-woman. Also, their confidence in Being gave me many unique living examples of this power in action, this divine presence in human form. And the wonderful part is that they say it feeds their hearts to commune with me, to assist me in shining forth.

As part of this process the teachers assist me in contacting this identity through my body, through my feeling sense. The feeling sense allows me to tap into the discomfort around being here in this body. As I drop more deeply into this discomfort, I am able to access the life force through cracks and crevices in my Being. These cracks and crevices have been created by the painful moments in which my needs were not met, due to unconscious behavior on the part of my parents, family, and community members. As an adult, I am triggered by seemingly small events in my daily life, which touch on these pains from my past. With adepts of this work to assist me, feeling into these painful memories creates gateways for the reclamation of bits of myself which have been frozen in time for years, sometimes even lifetimes.

The adepts have also helped me to realize that I needn't look any farther than the mirror to feel held and nurtured, because that which I've longed for to hold me has been holding me since the beginning of time—it is not separate from me, from my human body. My Second Birth awakening to myself as Consciousness has provided me with an enormous amount of stability and spaciousness with which to approach this unstable, ever-changing life on earth. Even in my darkest hours, I know that I am not bound by my pain, because I have traversed enough broken places within, and come out the other side stronger and more integrated. I need only have the courage to continue dropping deeply within myself and to feel the sensations connected to my personal woundedness in order to reveal my greatest source of sustenance. I find true freedom when I am willing to face into my own pain. Integration occurs when I welcome the shadow forward and heed its cry.

Mind/Heart Partnership

Previously, I had falsely perceived that this work was solely about being driven by my heart. However, I have discovered from my experience that my mind and heart inform one another as I listen within to what I want to do or say next. They must temper one another. This creates a balance, which is never fully realized, never fully grasped by my mind. I don't necessarily know why I act the way that I do. I must simply follow my impulses and pay attention to the impact I have on myself, and those I interact with. The feedback I receive from those I interact with tells me how I can fine-tune my sensitivity to others, while continuing to speak my truth. Each of my actions teaches me about myself—helping me become clearer about my motives, desires, faults, passions and priorities.

Shortly after I began the Waking Down process, I experienced a significant shift, called the Second Birth. This incredible, life-changing passage ignited a flame within me, which continues to burn with transformational power. The fire of this process unravels my emotional, mental, and physical wounding as I deepen into the knowledge of myself as more than a mere personality. Consciousness seeps into the deepest, darkest, most avoided corners of my being, sheds light there, and I merge with the uncomfortable sensations that accompany life as a human. As I am ready to feel and embody this pain, I am able to transmute it and utilize the energy for my own health, happiness, and well-being. The discomfort, sadness, confusion and heartbreak are intense while I am in the middle of them, but as time passes, and I breathe into them, an expanded awareness washes over me. Somehow, I end up more freed up and energized than I was when I started!

As a result of this healing, the way that I respond to the world around me is changing before my very eyes! I once held myself back when I disagreed with someone I considered an authority figure, and now I am finding myself speaking my truth, and stepping into life more than ever before. My old ways of being are brought into my consciousness with the help of my teachers, and I am able to feel the pain that these strategies cause me as I outgrow them.

It is absolutely fabulous to be living my life with the freedom to express myself in this way! I face each person I encounter with a new sense of myself, and his or her reaction to me does not define me anymore! My old identity was based on my conditioning and my response to it, and I am finding that my new identity is a fluid, ever-changing entity, based more and more over time, in my knowledge of myself as an indestructible, indefinable, vast expression of consciousness who just-so-happens to be in a destructible, definable, limited body. As I drop more deeply into this knowledge, there is more room for me to live my truth alongside others' truths without judging others' truths as being "wrong." There is, more and more, a place for everything in my world.

Reconfiguration

My ego continues to be shattered and reconfigured as I drink in the transmission of the awakened teachers. Prior to the Second Birth, my mind allowed me to function solely as a personality with strategies of higher/lower ego identity. My ego vacillated between, "You know best—you have the answers," and "They know best—you don't know what you're talking about!" This transmission brings forth these strategies until they are so "in my face" that I can't ignore them anymore. Eventually, the strategies are replaced one by one with the truth—I can't really claim to know anything about who I am, who another is, or what The Truth is. A fluid river of reception and expression emerges. This fluidity creates more and more gateways to the awareness all of Who I Am, out of which my true confidence is felt and experienced.

Due to the impact that this Confidence has had on me thus far, I find myself speaking and acting in spontaneous ways that are illogical. Unlike my old ways of being, I act in ways more connected to my life's purpose and the bigger picture of community. I now know myself as a fallible, imperfect human being simply fumbling around as best I can, *and* a powerful, love-filled woman with unstoppable gifts I must bring into the world.

An Invitation

In closing, there is no way to put into words the multitude of ways that this teaching has impacted my life and the lives of those close to me. My heart continues to stretch and grow each and every moment I am steeped in the alchemy of this community. I shine more and more every day because I am being loved forward by this sangha. This community inspires me to love and live with a great honesty and integrity. I am invited again and again to drop into my own body, my own heart. This invitation to be all of Who I Am is what keeps me coming back for more.

"I am deeply grateful for the profound silence which always resides in my heart, my body and my mind.."

Jean

Jean Marchand was born in Trois Rivieres, Quebec, and raised near Niagara Falls, Canada, where he has lived most of his life and still lives. He has two children from a previous marriage and a grandson. After graduating from the University of Windsor, he became a teacher of Transcendental Meditation which he taught for several years before becoming a stockbroker, a career he still practices. He also is an active teacher in the school of Waking Down in Mutuality which he practices out of his need to help mankind Awaken. He can be contacted at jeanmarchand@bellnet.ca.

QUI ES TU?

I was born in Trois Rivieres, Quebec, to parents that only spoke French. My parents moved to the primarily English-speaking part of the province of Ontario when I was less than a year old. Naturally French was my first spoken language; however, living in an English-speaking province I learned English from the neighbors and kids that I hung out with.

My mother, the third of ten children, was a devout Catholic who attended mass every day as she was growing up. She was only 17 when she married my Dad who was 23. She was 18 when I came along and 19 when my sister arrived a year later. Needless to say I was raised Catholic and attended Catholic school. I remember attending church on Sundays, having to be quiet during the service and hating the rigidity of the whole thing.

My home life as a young boy was very strict and I don't remember getting as much emotional nurturing as I needed. I know that my parents did the best that they could, given their young age and the stress of being in the equivalent of a foreign country and having to learn a new language. My father was an impatient man whose anger scared me to my core. It was his way or the highway and God knows his road was straight and narrow and I had better tow the line or else. Thankfully he mellowed with age and came to accept me and my way of being. I love my parents deeply.

However, before I get ahead of myself I need to digress and say more about the spiritual part of my early upbringing. The thing about being brought up Catholic is that religion is taught right from the start in elementary school. They give you this cute little book with a picture of an angel and baby Jesus on the cover. Inside the book are a great number of questions and answers which indoctrinate you into the beliefs of the church. However, there is one question that I will be forever thankful for and that is, as I recall the third question in the little book, which asks "Where is God?" The answer that they provide is, "God is everywhere."

As a young boy in second grade this question was very difficult to comprehend. I distinctly remember trying to wrap my head around this concept at the age of seven. From that moment on something inside me told me that I needed to really figure out what was meant by "God is everywhere." This was the beginning of my journey as a spiritual seeker.

I don't know if it was a French-Canadian thing or just a typical Catholic family expectation back when I was a young boy, but I distinctly remember that there was a desire on my mother's part for me to become a Catholic priest. The suggestion must have been strong enough on my impressionable young mind because I actually remember wanting to become a priest and considering the possibility. I really enjoyed the ritual that I experienced as an altar boy. I remember pretending to perform the Catholic mass, and as I raised the wafer representing the body of Christ, I remember ascending into blissful and ecstatic states of awareness. I would continue to seek these states in various forms throughout my life. I did the altar boy thing until I was eighteen, but I was more interested in music, sports, girls, and partying. The thoughts of becoming a priest and searching for God had abated for the time being.

In the fall of 1968 I left home to attend University to study pre-med. I thought I wanted to be a dentist. It was there that I was introduced to marijuana and experimented with this substance for a period of about four years. I experienced many different states under the influence of this plant. Most noticeably it brought me into the now and into my body. I became very present, in the moment, and in my body. I would only realize the familiarity of this after I experienced what we call in Waking Down the Second Birth.

In the summer of 1969 I traveled to British Columbia for a summer job at a paper mill managed by my uncle. This is where I met a couple of guys from Vancouver who also worked at the mill. At some point in time during that summer they asked me if I would be interested in taking an LSD trip with them. I was apprehensive, but they assured me that I would be OK. I was more than OK. I had a great trip. Every cell in my body became more alive. Music sounded celestial. It was what I would call "a good trip." Needless to say further experimentation with this psychedelic drug would not always produce such a wonderful result, and I do not recommend its use. However I would like to share two particular trips which stand out. I say that because they provided more of the experiential precursors or clues to my eventual awakening.

My third ingestion of LSD took place upon my return to University in the fall of 1969. I attended a live concert by the group Chicago. As I listened to the music my sense of self completely disappeared. I became one with the music, and then even the music disappeared in spite of the fact that I was sitting second row center. The subject-object disappeared and all that remained was Awareness. Awareness was aware of It's Self. It was only upon my return to self-consciousness that I could try to put words to this experience, and only years later that I realized what in fact had happened.

In February 1970 my college newspaper ran a small ad with a picture of Maharishi Mahesh Yogi advertising an introductory lecture on Transcendental Meditation. I had heard of the Maharishi because I was a big fan of the Beatles who had studied with him in India. Intuitively, I knew this was something that I had been looking for so I signed up. I remember going to my TM initiation with excitement and anticipation. The teacher took me through this ceremony and at the end of it he started saying this word (mantra) and asking me to repeat it. He asked me to close my eyes and to continue repeating the word quietly to myself. He said he would leave the room for a little bit and be back to get me. As I repeated the word to myself silently I felt myself dropping into spaciousness and vastness. I lost all sense of my body. The word disappeared and so did I. Nothing remained but empty Awareness. I have no idea how long I remained in this state.

Time stood still. When he came in and asked me to open my eyes I felt as if I had to come back from a very faraway place that I would prefer to stay in. I left his hotel room with a grin on my face that lasted for several days. I was ecstatic. I had found the source of inner peace that I had been looking for. I was hooked. This meditation thing was definitely for me. The inner silence beckoned me.

I stopped using drugs because I found it dulled the clarity of my meditation; however, in November of 1970 I decided to take what would be my last and most memorable LSD trip. A friend of mine had stored his LSD in a baggy outside and the tablets were wet. We assumed that the drug had been diluted and thought we needed to take more tablets to have the affect we wanted. So we each consumed several pills. This was to be both my worst, best, and last trip ever. Shortly after taking the acid we went for a walk and I began to lose my ability to support myself and even the ability to walk. My friends had to carry me back to my apartment. As my physical debilitation got progressively worse, my mental anguish became unbearable. The visions that I had were demonic and hellish. I saw the human cycle of birth and death happening instantaneously. I saw literally infinite numbers of bodies coming into existence and dying simultaneously. This was a bad trip and there was nothing I could do about it. Thankfully I eventually lost self-consciousness. I melted into the void of emptiness, which many traditions speak of, and I was relieved of my nightmare. I didn't know it at the time but the subject and object relationship of myself to my experience had completely merged. I recall awareness being aware. These are words trying to put a description on a knowing that cannot be described but only known. Fortunately for me I have been able to establish this knowing on a permanent basis without the use of drugs. In any case, approximately four hours after my bad trip began I came back to human consciousness in the arms of a friend that had been sent for to help me. I recall as I regained consciousness saying to him over and over again, "I love you, I love you, and I love you." I had no idea who I was or what I was. I observed my body and I thought to myself, "What is this?" As I looked at the different parts of my body I began to remember what a hand is, what an arm is, what a body is. I had a temporary type of amnesia whereby I had to look at an object, observe it as if I had never seen it before, and then the memory of what it was would come back. As I looked around the room, it was as if I was seeing everything for the first time. It was wonderful. I had never felt so alive. I knew without a doubt that everything was perfect. Everything was exactly as it should be. I had experienced both ends of the spectrum, beginning in Hell and ending up in Heaven all on the same trip.

I graduated from University in May of 1971 and, having become what my parents dreaded—a long-haired Hippie—I decided that dental school was not what I wanted to do so I got a job teaching high school and got married. After a year and a half of teaching, I resigned my position to go off to TM teacher training with the Maharishi in La Antilla, Spain. My wife and I landed in Spain on New Year's Day 1973 and spent the next five months training to become teachers. I won't bore you with the details, but it was one of the best five months of my life. It was like being on a retreat for five months. We meditated for several hours a day and I had many wonderful experiences but they didn't stick. We came back to Canada in May of 1973 and opened a TM center in St. Catharine's, Ontario, where I now live.

The whole concept of enlightenment as taught by the TM school and, as I was to learn in my later searches, taught by most schools was about a perfect state of whatever—Equanimity, Peace, Joy, Perfect Health, blah, blah, blah. Bah humbug. Most schools dangled the cosmic carrot in front of me, and like the compliant bunny rabbit I kept chasing it, one training or retreat after another with the promise that my awakening was just around the corner. I did the whole TM thing religiously for fourteen years. I am not complaining. All of my years of TM were grist for the mill of my eventual Self-Realization and I have no regrets.

In the summer of 1984 a TM teacher friend, Bruce, asked me if I would be interested in meeting his new Guru. Her name was Guru Mai. She and her brother had taken over the lineage of Swami Muktananda who had died two years earlier. So I drove to South Fallsburg, New York, to do a weekend workshop with her. Her technique is one whereby she transmits her Shakti. Even though my Kundalini had been awakened on the TM-siddhi course, I had no idea how powerful her Shakti could be. I sat in a hall with one hundred or so other people. She sat in front of the room, and we were asked to close our eyes and meditate. As I closed my eyes I began to feel the Kundalini rise along the back of my spine. The intensity was incredible. She walked around the room, and as she passed in front of me I thought the top of my head was going to explode. My spine felt as if it had an iron bar running through its entirety into the top of my head. The pressure was unbelievable. The top of my head felt as if it was opened to infinity. The empty awareness that I had experienced many times before was once again present.

That fall Bruce asked me to go to India with him on a business trip and said that we would spend a few days at the Muktanda ashram visiting with Guru Mai. We landed in Bombay and took taxis for a two-hour drive to the ashram. What I noticed the most about that visit was the intensity of the Shakti throughout the ashram. The intensity and strength of the Shakti was the greatest in the room where Muktanda's body was entombed. I walked into the room to meditate and I experienced the equivalent of my deepest states of meditation with my eyes still open. I didn't have to do anything. The room was meditating me. I disappeared into the vastness. The intensity of that experience was indescribable. As powerful as my experiences were at that school I never really had an interest in their teaching. However, I never stopped kicking tires. There had to be a Ferrari out there somewhere to get me out of this predicament called physical embodiment.

In the fall of 1994 another TM teacher friend, Richard, told me about a guru by the name of Arka who was visiting Toronto and asked me if I would be interested in meeting him. Since I was still chasing the cosmic carrot, I thought, "What the heck! What have I got to lose?" I spent the next two years in his entourage whenever he was in the Toronto area. I had many wonderful experiences during the time I spent with him, but the problem was I was dependent on his presence to have what I thought were elevated spiritual experiences. For me this was not at all practical. What I sought after was a spiritual awakening that would allow me to be eventually independent of the need for a teacher and his or her transmission.

In the summer of 1998 something began to shift in my consciousness. It was subtle but noticeable. I distinctly remember walking past the Buddha statue on my outdoor deck and feeling a transmission from the statue. I was not exactly clear or sure about the feeling, but it was soon to become clear. That August I attended yet another retreat weekend called "The Enlightenment Intensive." For those of you who have never heard of this retreat it is the closest thing to a military boot camp for spiritual seekers that you will find. The schedule is very strict and there is no messing around. Everyone is there to either get a taste of Enlightenment or in fact become enlightened. The premise is quite simple. The participants work in pairs for approximately 45 minutes before switching partners. During the entire 45 minute dyads, each partner asks the other partner, "Who are you?" This methodology is very effective for getting the mind out of the way, resulting in a state of "I Am," awareness. One keeps working with this question until reaching the state of "I Am." By Saturday afternoon I had achieved the state of "I Am." I recognized that I had experienced this knowing many times before. Then, it was onto the next question, "Who is other?" By Sunday afternoon, after being pounded with the question "Who is other?" I looked at the person across from me asking the question and realized through my waves of tears that there is no other.

Upon completion of the weekend I was definitely in an altered state of awareness. I knew then what it was that I had been looking for, but unfortunately this realization would only last for a few days. I knew that something had shifted, but I wasn't able to maintain it.

In October my friend Richard, who had introduced me to guru Arka, called and told me about a process called "Radical Awakening." He told me that his friend Charlie had taken him through the process and that he had had a profound awakening experience. He highly recommended that I try the process. So I made an appointment with Charlie. I remember the date because it changed my life forever. It was October 8, 1998. Charlie took me through a simple, one-hour process that he had learned from an advaitic teacher named Ramana. By the time we had finished I had awakened as Consciousness. I knew beyond the shadow of a doubt that I Am That, I Am always That, I have always been That and I will always be That. It was as if I had been looking for something that had always been there, and suddenly it was as clear as the nose on my face. I had always known this.

It was like waking up from sleep or recovering from amnesia. I could not have imagined ever getting something as abstract as what all the ancient and current philosophers describe as enlightenment, self-realization or being in the now, so easily. I was ecstatic. However, I was also afraid that I might lose this precious self-realization. It was blazing in its presence, yet delicate and tender. I did not want to ever lose it again. After a few months I became confident in the presence of I Am and lost the fear that I may lose this awareness. It, the awareness, was ever present as the observer to my every moment.

However, there was still something missing. This is where the Advaitans and I part company. They would say that there is nothing missing in this realization. I agree there is nothing missing because it includes everything. However, even in this realization of I AM the self, I still had (have) to deal with the mundane everyday problems of day-to-day life and relating to others. My buttons were and are still being pushed and I was (am) still triggered by others and events over which I have no control. I had a strong desire to withdraw and abide in the silence of the self, but who was going to look after my family and responsibilities? I still had feelings and desires that parts of me did not want to deny even though I Am Consciousness. This created a very real and uncomfortable dilemma for the human part of me. I was living in a paradox of being simultaneously infinite yet finite. It felt like something wasn't right, and I didn't know what it was or what to do about it. I felt frustrated and could not understand why after such a huge awakening I still had uncomfortable feelings which were difficult to ignore. I felt split.

Luckily for me, a friend whom I had led through the same advaitic process which I had learned to do, told me about Saniel Bonder and the Waking Down web site. Upon visiting the site on Feb. 23, 1999, I immediately felt that this teaching might provide the missing piece to my problem. I ordered Saniel's book, *Waking Down*, and immediately entered into contact with one of Saniel's teachers, Ted Strauss. Ted helped me to start feeling into what Saniel calls the Core Wound. This is the wound which every body on the planet carries, and I would venture to guess is the major cause of most problems that humans perpetrate on each other and the planet. Feeling into the Core Wound was very challenging, uncomfortable and frightening. I remember waking up in the middle of the night, shortly after starting to work with Ted on the phone, and I was sure I was going to die. I started hyperventilating and felt the starkness of Being here in a body. It was terrifying.

Two weeks after entering into contact with Saniel and Ted, I landed in San Francisco on March 12, 1999, to attend a Waking Down Weekend, a three-day intensive workshop. Just being with Saniel and the other teachers on Friday evening was very potent, but little did I know how potent. The next day as I gazed with Pascal, one of the teachers, I fell into a place that brought up an abundance of tears and sorrow. I didn't know what was going on, but I could sure feel my existential pain.

That afternoon when we broke up into small groups we each took turns feeling into what was going on inside and sharing with the group. As I felt into my pain, it was as if a dam of sorrow broke wide open and engulfed my entire being. Ted asked me, "Do you want to be here?" As I felt into the question, in the midst of overwhelming sorrow I realized that part of me did not want to be here in a human body because it was just too painful and limiting. Ted asked me again, "Do you want to be here?" I again felt into the question and this time I surrendered into the excruciating pain of being here in a body. I fell into the Core Wound. It was unbelievable. There I was, infinite, feeling trapped in a limited, finite body. I felt as if I was being crucified. I have never, ever felt such an intense and devastating pain. Yet the bizarre paradox was that interspersed throughout the pain was a bittersweet Joy, the Bliss of Consciousness. My heart was blown wide open. The Love I felt for the others in the room was unlimited. I looked into each of their eyes and felt their pain. I felt their pain of being here in a body. As I looked at them waves of sobbing overcame me. Their pain was my pain. There was no feeling of separation. I stayed in that tender vulnerable place in the heart for the rest of the weekend and several days after. As a matter of fact, I have never left that place of vulnerability in the heart. I am just more selective about who I am vulnerable with. Now I am more discriminative about being wide open in Love with everyone.

Two days later on March 17, I awoke in the middle of the night to realize that Being had landed here in my body. The feeling of being separate from my body and the world was gone. I now had permission to show up here on this planet as Being in a body, not separate from the body. What a relief. I had entered what Saniel calls my Second Birth. It was okay to be here. It was okay to feel the wound of being here now in all of its limitations. The Core Wound had become the Conscious Wound. What a "Great Relief," as Saniel calls it. I no longer want to escape to a cave in the Himalayas. Occasionally withdrawing into the silence of Being suffices. I am deeply grateful for the profound silence which always resides in my heart, my body and my mind. Life is more relaxed and enjoyable now than it's ever been. The moments of being vulnerable and feeling my own pain and another's pain are there more than ever, but I'm not trying to avoid it. Now my mission is to help my fellow humans to awaken to who they truly are, like I did, thus answering the question once and for all, "Qui es tu (Who are you)?" And by the way I did get the concept. "God is Everywhere."

"Intimate relationship challenges you to the core; that's why it is one of the most powerful paths to awakening, integration, love, and freedom."

Hillary and Ted

Hillary Davis was born in Brooklyn. After studying acting at Brandeis, she moved to California, where she studied with many spiritual teachers, including Osho, Jean Klein, and Poonja-ji. She met Saniel in 1994, Ted in 1995 and experienced her second birth shift in 19b 97. Her passion is to help people awaken to the truth of who they are and continue deepening. She feels blessed to be a Senior Teacher in the WDM work. Hillary also has a Jin Shin Jyutsu healing practice. She and Ted live in Marin County, CA where they help individuals and couples awaken and blossom. You can learn more at www.wholebeingawakening.com

Ted Strauss was born in 1956 in Hollywood, lived in Cape Canaveral for a few years while his father designed rockets for NASA, then grew up in New Jersey. During his teens, he bagan a long quest for spiritual awakening, which led him to become a teacher of Transcendental Meditation, then to Hillary and Saniel. Ted is an independent inventor and a Senior Teacher of Waking Down in Mutuality.

LOVE, AWAKENING, AND INTIMATE RELATIONSHIP

An interview by Bob Valine

You met before your Second Births and went through that experience together. So let's start at the beginning: What was your relationship like before your Second Birth?

TED: Hillary and I were inclined from the beginning to pursue our own truth and each other's truth at all costs. We were intent on being as real as we could be. In the past, being deeply honest was often problematic and didn't always bring the kind of intimacy we wanted, but in this relationship, it tended to bring us closer and closer together.

HILLARY: Awakening into the truth of who we are has been of prime importance to each of us. We always had a huge commitment here and we knew this when we began our relationship

So you both were together in wanting to awaken, and your relationship revolved around that in some way?

HILLARY: Right. I had an awakening into my conscious nature in 1991. Both of us wanted very much to have this shift into the Second Birth.

TED: In many ways, our relationship revolved around our awakening process, but also we were deeply in love with each other, so the relationship was bigger than that. Awakening will always be a big part of our lives and our work just because that's who we are.

What were the biggest challenges in your relationship before your Second Birth?

HILLARY: Before we got together Ted pursued me quite strongly. And I wasn't sure what I wanted. So I kind of felt "yes" and then "no," and it was constantly Yes. No. Yes. No. Back and forth. Ted held this really big space of unconditional love, trust and stability, which I'd never experienced before in any relationship. He held the space for me to come and go, to really explore myself, my needs, my confusion, to really honor myself in a way no one before him had ever given to me. I'd always given myself up in relationship–either giving up myself or giving up the relationship, but never having both myself and the relationship at the same time. I'd never had a template for that. And when I wanted to come back and be with him, he was there. He would let me go and he would welcome me back. Ted really won my heart by holding that space for me and allowing me to really be who I was. One thing that was a challenge was that Ted also wanted a commitment pretty early on in the relationship. I felt we really couldn't know who we are until we had this Second Birth shift. Ted agreed.

TED: Early on, I started asking Hillary for short-term commitments. I needed her to understand that I was making an investment in the relationship. We both were. I wanted to feel like she was really there with me in that investment. We made short commitments that were increasingly longer as we went along. We also decided that we wouldn't be ready to make the commitment of marriage until we at least had our Second Births because we needed to see who we really were.

Any other challenges?

TED: I think for Hillary there was a big challenge in her discovering that she could live her truth and be in relationship at the same time.

HILLARY: Yes, that was very, very strong for me because I always thought it had to be one or the other. That was always my experience in the past. So I tended to stay away from relationship because my truth was more important. Of course, I had other relationship issues that only became clearer to me after my Second Birth.

TED: I suspect it was Hillary's single-minded, warrior-like pursuit of her own truth outside of relationship that brought her into a somewhat detached style of awakening.

HILLARY: After awakening to my conscious nature I got more and more detached from everything, including my body, relationships and life force. It got to a point where it felt to me like my heart had hardened–I felt that maybe I needed to be in relationship. And that's when I met Ted. So there definitely had been that position of taking a step back from life, of feeling more removed from life. I thought I was becoming more awake by being able to be more detached, but really I was missing a huge piece about the totality of life; I didn't realize I was shutting out my own pain.

TED: Another challenge for me was my difficulty in being sensitive to Hillary's reality. So it was fairly often that Hillary would take me to Saniel and say, "Make him get me."

HILLARY: Well, I just want to preface that by saying that Ted was very much "in the sky" and in his head. He was much more transcendent. That was a big part of why I felt like I didn't know if he was really "my guy." He had more of a challenge feeling his feelings and being in his body. That was a challenge before the Second Birth.

Did your Second Births happen around the same time?

TED: Well, they happened within two weeks of each other. I had my Second Birth in early February '96 and Hillary took just another couple of weeks to clarify. We celebrate our Second Births on Valentine's Day.

HILLARY: There was also astonishment that he actually clarified his Second Birth before I did.

What do you mean "astonishment"?

HILLARY: Like–what a minute here! I had the Consciousness awakening. How could he do this before me? Still, the fact of his clarifying his Second Birth helped me drop into my own realization.

TED: Not long before we had our awakenings we realized that we had a subconscious competition going on that was tending to stop us from coming into the realization. We both wanted to get there first, so we weren't giving each other a full green light to land. When we talked about it, we realized that we both loved each other so much that we decided that it was OK for the other person to land first.

What changed in your relationship after the Second Birth?

TED: Well, what didn't change was the depth of the love between us. That only deepened. During the time of the shift, we both had a fair amount of fireworks. There was a lot of really powerful and exciting energy of liberation going on. Our lives were consumed in talking about this process and this amazing transformation that we and our friends were all going through. There were a lot of long walks, long talks, and sacred encounters with each other. It was a very remarkable time. But as we deepened, Hillary and I began to encounter our own and each other's conditioning at an even deeper and more troubling level than ever before. We were able to permit ourselves to feel things that previously we just didn't have the stability of wellness to deal with. And that wellness was not just in ourselves, but also more and more in the relationship.

HILLARY: But the container of our relationship got bigger and bigger as a result of our awakening shifts and the deepening and integrating that was happening in each of us. We had the ability to hold more and more discomfort and tension within ourselves, and so within the relationship. This is really the biggest issue for couples, because the point at which the discomfort gets more and more difficult to be in is the point where they say, "I'm out of here," because they can't hold the tension they feel. They interpret the feeling of tension as evidence that this must be the end of their relationship. They feel like something must be wrong or the relationship wouldn't feel so bad. Ted and I both learned that stuff will just keep coming up over and over again, you know? The fact of it being there doesn't mean there's anything wrong with the relationship. This is a really important point. For years and years after we were together my mind would come up with reasons why it didn't know for certain if this was really the right relationship or Ted was the right guy. Since then, we've worked as teachers for other couples in this process and we've seen how much this goes on for most relationships. They get afraid because their minds are telling them, "This can't be right. There must be something wrong here." We both learned to really hold that tension.

We also wanted total honesty with each other. Initially, it was total honesty even at the expense of the relationship because we had to be true to who we were. If that started to rock the boat, we learned more and more to just stand in our truth there. Sometimes we would have big fights –screaming, yelling, door slamming. That's just the way we've always been with each other–to permit what's there. I remember at one point we were having an argument—it was really strong—and my pattern had always been, "OK, I'm out of here. I want to leave the room." That day I made myself stay in the room and feel the immense discomfort that was contorting my body. And in just staying there and permitting it to be there some major alchemy happened. A new door opened for me and then for our relationship. These are the kind of doors that have been opening steadily in our relationship as we learned to permit pain and discomfort. Where we least expected to find an opening, if we stayed true to who we are and stood strong in ourselves, a door would always open, a new door, a new wave of love, a new wave of growth and understanding and maturity. It has totally influenced how we work with couples.

We have great faith in relationship lasting when two people want to awaken together. In our relationship after the Second Birth, we were able to really start seeing our patterning at much deeper levels–childhood patterning, the patterns of closing and putting up walls, barricades and defenses, and abandonment issues. All the issues had a chance to really come up! And we were just with them as much as we could allow and permit. Permitting the patterning to be seen, felt and experienced is a huge part of what happens in relationship after the Second Birth. It's a GOOD thing for patterning to come up strongly because that's what helps you become more and more free. It may sound contradictory, but it's not.

TED: We also learned that we didn't always have to be present with each other through the discomfort. We learned this through having arguments at night and both operating under the idea that you should never go to bed mad. Sometimes we stayed up till three or four in the morning trying to work things out, only to realize that it made things much worse because on top of being angry and feeling not gotten by each other, we were also exhausted. So we learned to have the faith that we could just go to bed and work it out in the morning.

It sounds like you've been talking about the Wakedown Shakedown. Was that a big challenge for your relationship?

TED: I'd say it was a huge challenge. So much stuff came up for the two of us individually and for us both about relationship. Everything, really. The relationship itself seemed to be shaking down. We both got triggered into our worst nightmares with each other. Relationship does that. We were forced to deal with what was coming up for ourselves and with each other. And if we hadn't had the kind of strength of commitment that had formed before the Second Birth, I don't know if we would have stuck together.

HILLARY: I agree with that because at that time in our work there was not as big a container to help couples go through the rocky times together in the same way that there is now. Saniel and Linda have become a container. Ted and I have become a container. Now that we've been through that, we love to support couples in helping them find their own container for the relationship. We want to help couples stay together if that is what they want.

Also, where an individual coming into the Second Birth has to go through greenlighting, the Rot, and the deepening phases, so it is with relationship after the two people have awakened. It seems to be that the relationship goes through its own awakening.

TED: The awakening of the relationship seems to be really triggered by the Rot in the relationship. Before the Second Birth, the Rot is essentially the discovery that the game of avoiding yourself is over. You may not like having been given the assignment of being you, but oh well. There doesn't appear to be any way out of being you, so you might as well stop resisting it and start really being you, even when you don't like it. Like that, the Rot in relationship is the discovery that, no matter how much you may resist the inevitable distress involved in this particular relationship, for some mysterious reason you can't help but keep choosing it, so you might as well stop resisting it and really be in it. Couples seem to go through some fairly predictable phases. First, it's like, "Oh, we love each other so much. We have so much in common. We both loved The Truman Show (or whatever)." That's the Honeymoon Phase, when everything is love and roses. You tend to look for and find things that you love together, things that you have in common. Then you hit the other side of that wave: all the things that you hate about each other and all the things you don't have in common and all the ways it's horrible to be together. Usually this is when couples assume something's wrong.

HILLARY: There's so much fantasy about the "perfect" relationship. Everybody wants the perfect relationship, the perfect fairytale. Really a lot of what real relationship is about is being willing to rot out of fantasy, being willing to face disappointment. You know, first he looks like your Prince Charming, and now you see all the warts, you see all the wrinkles–you see how he doesn't understand you, how conditional the "love" was initially. You see the patterning in the other, and how their childhood was so different from yours and what a totally different person they are. Because of that, they see the world differently than you do. When you live together and you do life together, you think, "No, we're supposed to do it this way!" And the other person feels, "No, we're supposed to do it this way!" You're both coming from your own ideals and fantasies and assumptions about what relationship is. I tell people one of the fastest ways to come into the Second Birth is to permit discomfort as much as you can. It's the same in relationship: to permit the discomfort, to permit the rot out of idealism and fantasy and to come into reality. It's so sobering and it's so humbling. It's very real.

TED: I think it's very difficult, especially for spiritually-orientated people, to let go of those fantasies and ideals because it seems like if you let go of all that you're going to be just an ordinary person, like your parents or like everyone else in the world. And in many ways, being an ordinary human being is one of the worst nightmares of spiritual people. After all, we're supposed to be more enlightened than all that, aren't we? Isn't being ordinary what we've been trying to get out of all this time? It feels like if we let ourselves be just ordinary, we'll lose all the "progress" we've made in our spiritual quest. But this is one of the great discoveries of our work—when you can let yourself be utterly ordinary, you discover your own Divinity.

I remember one of the times that Hillary and I were having a sort of a "rot" moment was when we realized that we could let ourselves have an intense screaming match and be OK with it. I remember in the earlier times of the relationship sometimes we'd get really mad at each other and we would try not to be expressing it. One or both of us would be trying to control it by either leaving the room or changing how we were expressing and trying to match some kind of New Age formula about how we were supposed to communicate. Eventually we realized that we could just be like the Honeymooners. We could just scream our brains out at each other if that's what we felt like. It actually felt incredibly freeing —but only when the other person was willing to receive the energy. You know, not perfectly or anything. Just basically receive it and feel the truth of where the other person was coming from. It brought a whole new awareness to the relationship that we could actually trust Being and each other enough to let ourselves be ordinary pissed-off reactive people when that's what was up. We started to realize that we didn't have to avoid anything.

HILLARY: It really feels like in the early days it was so important to just let go–in that way that Ted spoke about. That has shifted over the years of our being in relationship because we've deepened more and more and we're still deepening more and more. There's just more and more ability to hold tension. The need to scream and yell is not the same anymore.

TED: It seems to me that the reason screaming and yelling usually happens is that somebody is trying to express something and the other person doesn't want to hear it. So the person who's trying to express feels compelled to talk more loudly just to try to connect to the other through their resistance. Of course, sometimes the yelling is part of a need to compensate for a history of not being heard by parents and others. Or just a need to equalize a lot of internal pressure, and it feels like here finally is a chance to just let it fly. But I think what Hillary was just alluding to was that over time our resistance to hearing something that's uncomfortable or difficult has gone way down. Part of that is just our own capacity to be OK with whatever's happening. But there's another part.

In couples, there's usually a certain amount of unconscious fear that if you get into something uncomfortable it's going to spell the end of the relationship. That comes from our parents and almost all relationship role models we've ever encountered. Were your parents good at saying uncomfortable things to each other while being deeply present and truly receiving each other? When you speak something uncomfortable, there's often a feeling of a threat to yourself and to the relationship. Usually, it triggers a feeling of threat to your own physical survival when you were an infant or a child because the death of your parent's relationship felt like it could mean the end of your own life. So when you've investigated a lot of that material and found that you can actually stand and be present in the midst of it, it makes it much easier to be with the difficult stuff with each other and not feel nearly as threatened. So in a way, the essence of the container that holds a relationship of Mutual Onlyness is love, trust, and the willingness and ability to face whatever feels like death to you. So Hillary and I started to notice that when we could allow the dark material, it would inevitably open the gates to a lot of happiness together. I think most couples actually compromise by staying more flattened in order to stay more stable. The result of that is giving up your own truth and your own passion.

HILLARY: Which is also inevitable. It's not like everybody in every moment knows what their truth is. It can be very gray for a while until you come to know for yourself. Another thing I want to add to this is that when we would be in difficulty with each other, when you're in gridlock, somebody has to be willing to put themselves on hold and permit the other to move. Otherwise you're just tied up in gridlock. Whoever's the stronger in that moment needs to say, "OK, I feel what I feel but I'm willing to hear you out first. It creates a lot of stuckness when nobody's willing to hold the tension first and hear the other. But when somebody does that, things just start to flow. So Ted and I have traded off there a lot. It goes along with commitment.

TED: I think we were especially inclined to stick together because we'd both had so many relationships and we were both pretty sick of what it felt like to not stick in there through the tough times. We really wanted to find out what was on the other side of all that.

What was on the other side of that for you two?

TED: A really amazing discovery for us both. Saniel had always spoken about the importance of what he called "awakened mutuality," but through my relationship with Hillary, I was being forced into a recognition that totally blew my mind. I began to see that mutuality wasn't just a kind of relational capacity that was maturing among our awakened friends, it was actually another whole stage of awakening. It seemed to be a realization in its own right that goes beyond Consciousness realization, beyond the Second Birth, and beyond the ability to really feel others. I call it "Mutual Onlyness" because it's a shared awareness of Onlyness (Second Birth) that shifts your sense of self into something even bigger, where the previous sense of self is just part of a larger shared reality.

After years of extreme challenges mixed with intense love, we went through a kind of a transition that's hard to describe, but our relationship was full of love and light for about a month. At the time, it felt as if the relationship just had its own Second Birth. There was a real shift in the feeling of our "us-ness," a feeling of who we are together, that transcended our individual awakened selves. It seemed to signal the birth of a self that held our whole relationship in a much larger context. This has since appeared to me to be a transition that can only take place in a committed relationship between two or more beings who have awakened into what we call "Onlyness." The essence of it appeared to be a mutual surrender into what I call the Wound Of Relationship–the feeling of togetherness and separation, the feeling of intimate unity and apparent disunity at the same time. It's not a state of mutual bliss; it's a stage of realization that says we're absolutely committed to each other no matter what, because we've already found out what can go wrong, and we've discovered that the relationship is so big, it can include our worst nightmares.

It's very much like what happens in the Second Birth. You get that you're infinite Consciousness, and you get that you're a human person. For awhile, you feel like you have to choose sides—am I Divine? Or am I human? 'Cause I don't get how I can possibly be both at the same time. Being both feels like something is wrong. But when you get that nothing is wrong, and that the paradox and the feeling of a wound doesn't need to be resolved, you fall into Second Birth awareness. Like that, when you and your significant other get that the feeling of being intimate, it often has a quality of "wound." Yet nothing is wrong—it's a whole new revelation. Our love is not just Disney or Hell; it's both, and everything in between.

Does Mutual Onlyness fuse the relationship into a new whole?

TED: Yes and no. The realization is a kind of "third birth"–Mutual Onlyness is the birth of a third entity that has its own life and reality. Of course, all couples have some version of this, but I'm referring to a relationship entity that is awakened in its own right. Awake to the truth of who and what we are as a divinely human entity composed of us. But it's not like the individuals who make up that entity are merged or obliterated in the process; quite the opposite. Hillary and I have become more and more who we are as separate and totally unique individuals, and we've found the strength to grant ourselves and each other the total freedom to be true to ourselves, even when that appears to threaten the relationship. We found that strength because the relationship appeared to be threatened so many times, and each time it ended up bringing us closer together. After awhile we got the picture: this relationship gets to be true to itself when we're being most true to ourselves individually.

Is what you call Mutual Onlyness only available to sexually or romantically engaged couples?

TED: No, but deep commitment is a prerequisite. The commitment has to be so deep that it carries the relationship through the worst of times with each other. It seems to me that, at least most of the time, romantically engaged couples are more likely to endure this. But I'm not talking about commitment as an ideal to be achieved; I'm talking about commitment as a realization that dawns over time. You begin to notice that, time and time again, over a period of years, you find yourself having no intelligent alternative but to be with this person no matter what. Because they are just part of who you are.

HILLARY: And because you really know deep in your cells that your partner is part of who you are, when you are hurting the other you know you are hurting yourself. When you are walled up in yourself, you know you are affecting your partner. It's a very mature stage of being. You can only know it when you know it. It's not an intellectual knowing; it's a whole being knowing.

Can you say more about the role of commitment in your relationship?

TED: Commitment is something we found organically with each other over time. I don't think we would have said it at the beginning of the relationship, but I think we can look back at it now and say that, in a sense, our whole relationship has been the evolution of mutual commitment. It's not just the commitment to each other; it's also the commitment to being true to ourselves. I think if the relationship is right, those two turn out to be the same thing. It seems to me that if you're not willing to commit to living the Wound of Existence in your own Being, you're not capable of living the Wound of Relationship with another being. But even if you have committed to living the wound in yourself, that doesn't necessarily mean you're ready to make that level of commitment with another. A whole lot has to line up for that to happen.

HILLARY: I'll just add that for me I didn't really understand what commitment was. Ted really taught me about commitment and relationship because I had no template for it.

TED: I think I was always disposed toward commitment in the past, but I never had a reason to be as committed as I am with Hillary. My love for Hillary made me need to be with her no matter what. I think our organic need to be with each other no matter what is really what has carried us through the kinds of hard times that break most relationships.

HILLARY: I just want to say one more thing about commitment. In so many spiritual circles–you know, so many of us grew up with different spiritual teachers and in different spiritual communities–the word "commitment" was a "downer," something that would deny us our spiritual and physical freedom. A lot of spiritual seekers just want to feel the limitless part of their being. But life is also limited. You have to feel the limited parts of your being. Commitment is such an integral part of our work because life is both. It's the intersection of limitedness and limitlessness. And the more you can feel being limited, the more grounded, mature and truly wise you will be. Your relationships can get stronger and stronger if you're willing to feel and deal with the limited parts.

TED: Earlier, we mentioned that we decided to wait to marry each other until we'd gone through the Second Birth shift. As it turned out, after we had the awakening, we realized we should get at least part of the way through the Wakedown Shakedown before we got married, because there was still a lot to discover about ourselves and each other before we could make that kind of commitment. Later, I discovered that even the marriage commitment I made with Hillary was itself a sort of dress rehearsal. If I hadn't found myself going through my own worst nightmares, and then deciding that my relationship with Hillary was more important than holding onto my deepest survival strategies, I could never have known what true commitment was really about.

Can you say more about the tension between your individual truth and needs and the needs of the other and the relationship?

HILLARY: This is our strength as a couple–we've been told by people we work with and by different healing professionals that Ted and I model as a template for being together in relationship while being utter individuals at the same time. Both at the same time. Both of those have been really important for us–to keep our individuality and to be in very strong relationship with each other.

TED: I guess we could call that mutual individuation. We just discovered that, despite appearances, attending to our own needs was the same as nurturing the relationship. For example, when I first met Hillary, she had a big need for space and aloneness. I quickly learned that if I was to be in relationship with her, I had to spend more time alone than I was comfortable with. As it turned out, spending more time alone was just what I needed. I found out that I was using relationship to distract myself from some of the painful parts of my own journey.

Sometimes in these tense, difficult moments together your partner may feel that they're to blame for how you're feeling, that they've done something wrong. What do you do in that situation?

TED: This brings up a classic issue that Waking Down practitioners often struggle with. New Age thinking tends to suggest that you are solely responsible for how you're feeling, so if you feel bad, it's your fault, and therefore you're a bad person if you try to blame it on anyone else.

It's basically an extension of the "you create what you think/believe" philosophy. The problem with this idea is that it's only partly true. To make a point, I bring up an extreme example. You're standing in a room with another person. They whip out a gun and shoot you in the foot. You scream "Stop! You're killing me!" They reply, "Oh, yeah? Well, since the bullet is in your foot, you created it! Ha, ha!" So, who was "to blame"? Was it merely the recipient of the bullet? Was it the trigger-happy antagonist? There's no real answer here. Maybe the one who was shot had spent the last ten years tormenting the other person. Maybe the shooter was simply insane and didn't even know this person. Maybe someone else paid the shooter to do the deed. Most things can't be pinned down to simple causes.

Sometimes you're feeling bad–it's not your partner's fault, and it's not even your own fault. In fact, our whole notion of fault and blame assumes individual authorship of our feelings and our reality and tends to miss the fact that the whole universe has conspired to sponsor this moment. Shouldn't the universe get any credit for this event? So, having said all that, sometimes our partner IS to blame for how we're feeling. If someone said to me, "You're a worthless, good-for-nothing idiot," I'd feel pretty devastated even though I'd know that what they said was only two percent true. The idea that I'm supposed to be so cosmic that I am not affected by such things is drivel. We humans are extremely sensitive. If you're not affected, you're not embodied. But if I notice that I've said something that inappropriately hurt Hillary, it's my duty to myself, to her, and to our relationship to apologize. I'm not perfect; I make mistakes. We both do things that hurt each other. But we love each other enough to take responsibility for our humanness and to kiss and make up.

HILLARY: Which is why it's so important to communicate and find out what the truth really is here. You have to be willing to be with the difficult stuff and just keep trying to communicate. If you really love somebody and you really want to understand the other–if there's that kind of a commitment–then you have to go into these murky places and really find out what is going on here. What's going on in you? This is what's going on in me. What's going on in you? It's a way of really meeting and holding the other. It may be the first time they've ever experienced someone *Truly wanting* to know what their reality is, not just assigning motives to what they must be feeling. Maybe nobody's cared enough to really want to go in there and say, "Wait a minute! What is your truth? What's really happening here? Do you feel blamed? I wasn't blaming you." So it requires that kind of time and care.

Really *wanting* to get the other's reality is so important in relationship. You need to put yourself in their place. This is so healing for your partner because we never felt anyone really wanted to "get" us. When you do this for your partner they will start to be able to drop the feeling of needing to defend themselves from you because when someone really wants to get you, you no longer need to defend; it drops away and starts to free up energy and attention that has previously been held more tightly. Then love can bloom more fully.

TED: Time and care and the willingness to be uncomfortable again–that's what really drives the capacity to go into those murky places. It's not only the willingness to be uncomfortable, but the ability to be uncomfortable and stay present with what's happening, which Second Birth awakeness empowers like nothing else. If you're not willing to be uncomfortable, if you can't be OK in your own Core Wound, you sure as hell aren't going to be OK in the Wound of Relationship with somebody else. There's still going to be a tendency to run while convincing yourself that there's somewhere to go.

HILLARY: You start being willing and more able to actually speak what's going on for you instead of blaming it on the other person.

TED: A piece of this whole conversation has to do with the willingness to stand in your own imperfections and your own conditioning. I remember that Hillary and I used to have these fights in the earlier days where maybe she would blame me for something or she would say, "You're just being very defensive." I'd be saying, "No, I'm not." And then eventually I learned to say, "Right. I am being defensive because I feel attacked." And then she's like, "Oh, well, I don't feel like I'm attacking you." Then we could go into and analyze– "Well, when you came on with that energy, I wasn't even hearing your words. I just felt attacked by that energy." She's like, "I just had that energy because I'm frustrated. I wasn't attacking you." When you're able to stand present in the middle of the discomfort, you can actually investigate what's happening on stable ground and begin to literally untie all those sticky knots.

I remember a classic moment of this when we were standing in the kitchen of our first house. As was my inevitable experience in past relationships, sooner or later, my girlfriend would look at me in disbelief and say something like, "You need a mommy! I'm not going to be your mommy!" Now, in the past, I would have defended myself, saying, "I do not. You just need a daddy!"—all the while knowing I had been like totally busted. It was basically a defense against having to feel pain and admit that I'm imperfect. But this time was different. Hillary and I were deep in our awakening process, and a lot was cooking in us. We had a whole new disposition we were working with, and part of it was Greenlighting. We were learning to embrace whatever was happening without needing to push it away. So this time, I found myself taking a long pause, considering it, and then saying, "You're right. I DO need a mommy. And since no one else could do that for me, it has to be YOU." Hillary resisted this notion, but after awhile, she started to get that I was asking her to help me, so she agreed to do her best. As it turned out, this broke a big piece of my own code of personal enslavement. By simply accepting the fact that I am flawed, and by asking for the help I needed to heal this piece, I was able to actually get what I needed and then move beyond it.

HILLARY: So a lot of it has to do with how reactive two people are to each other. If there's only room for reactivity, it won't go very far. But if there's room to kind of pull the plug on reactivity and come down into feeling more of what your reality is–what was being reacted to–it can be amazing what can happen from that. Like unbelievable. Like you're never thought. There can be a huge shift in no time at all.

What are the benefits of being in Mutual Onlyness or a committed awakened relationship?

TED: There are many ways to answer that. One of them is that, for me, life has become much more simple and natural because I'm a very relationship orientated guy. It's like I need to be in an intimate, committed relationship just to feel happy. But I was never able to get how relationship could really work. Because no matter how hard I tried, it always seemed to go wrong. Something would come up. Something would be discovered. Some brick wall would be hit. It seemed like we could go no further. So for most of my life I was on this long journey of serial, monogamous relationships. Until eventually some part of me became cynical about the possibility of having an intimate relationship really work out long term. Another part of me never lost hope and was always investigating that.

What awakening has done for me, in a big way, is it's given me the capacity to hold the totality of what relationship is about–which is absolutely fantastic, wonderful stuff and really horrible, nasty stuff all together. In a way awakening has freed me to commit to the totality of what relationship is. Whereas before, as Hillary was saying, I was running from the parts I didn't like. Awakening has given me the capacity to stay present and realize that it's never going to be the way I ideally want it. My idealism about relationship and life and Being and the world was just idealism–reality is a different story. So I guess I can say that awakening has allowed me to choose reality and the reality of relationship with all its ups and downs. The ability to choose the totality of relationship allowed me to enjoy the greatest benefits of what relationship can be: deep intimacy and deep commitment and an abiding love that transcends any moment of difficulty or differences.

HILLARY: Well, on some level, in a committed relationship you almost have one heart. It's like the entity of your relationship is alive. You can't not take the other into account anymore. They're part of you in a way you haven't known before. There's also an incredible amount of support that you have in an awakened, committed relationship. It's very different than I ever, ever knew it could be.

TED: When Hillary was talking about the entity of the relationship, I realized that the essence of what takes place in the shift into what I'm calling Mutual Onlyness is that the sense of personal identity actually shifts into a sense of both personal identity and mutual identity at the same time. In other words, you become a bigger person because you're not just yourself. You're yourself and you're a member of the relationship entity. All of that is true. It's a paradox. This is why Hillary said you can no longer run from things in the same way. It's because you realize yourself to be not just this personal body/mind, but also the entity of this relationship. When you get that the relationship is also part of yourself, you can't run from yourself there. I can't run from the relationship because the relationship is part of who I am.

There's a kind of magic that takes place in all of this. There's a magic that doesn't look like the kind of Disneyland relationship magic we thought we were hoping for. It's really the magic of a kind of happiness that can permit you to be unhappy, and it can permit you to be ecstatic. It's a permission so big that it can allow for whatever can come up. With that kind of permission, you can completely relax and just be yourself spontaneously. That's the kind of a magic that none of us even knew was possible.

HILLARY: In reflecting back on all we've said, it may appear that we've mostly presented the darker, more negative aspects of relationship. But please don't get us wrong. We feel relationship is the most amazing path to awakening, deepening, and integration–if that's where you're drawn. Some people are alone, and that's perfect because they are following their own truth. But if you're drawn toward relationship, it becomes a cauldron for the transformation of everything that has not been seen, healed, or embraced in you. We just want to be real in talking about what couples actually go through. We want to bring all of that into the light of day, be honest about it, and let there be deep healing around it. Awakened, committed relationship can bring you more joy and healing than you ever imagined possible.

TED: If you're not allowing all of what's true for each of you, and what's true between you, if you're just going for the good parts, the hard parts will stalk the relationship until they succeed in getting your attention. If you're disposed toward avoiding all that, you'll end up miserable together, alone and bitter, or living in an endless series of relationships that never quite work.

For couples, the whole point of allowing yourselves to drop into the dark side is to free all the joy, love, and passion that's possible between you. It allows the relationship to awaken and blossom into its fullest and happiest expression. When you permit all of what's there, a whole new kind of relationship emerges. It's a relationship of spontaneous intimacy, respectful honesty, deep mutual honoring, and helpless commitment to serve each other. It's about real love.

"Each time I attended an event I would feel like I was in a subtle force field,
like feeling a soft current of water pushing against me.
Along with this came a continuous flow
of deepening insights about myself.."

Carl

Carl Klemaier was born in Springfield, Illinois, in 1947. Hehas worked as a teacher and a family therapist. He lives with his wife, Lucy, in rural Greene County, Illinois, and is presently opening a pub in Grafton, Illinois, on the Mississippi River where he will be the resident "Festivity Director."

PIECES OF AWAKENING

On November 16, 2004, while standing on a hill overlooking Tomales Bay, I simultaneously felt my body and the awareness of my body and, in an instant, realized that there was no separation in Consciousness. That instant marked the beginning of the realization that the most essential part of who "I" am is Consciousness itself—that part of us that registers everything before the mind starts to conceptualize and structure it into a "self."

This experience was a direct result of my involvement with Saniel Bonder and his teachers. Two years prior to this experience I had come across his work. I remembered him from his association with Adi Da, and, indeed, I had a book he had written about Adi Da. At this time in my life I was feeling that life had offered about as much as it could for me. I had money in the bank, a happy marriage and family. I worked as a therapist in a social service organization involved in the child welfare system and foster care. Because of this work, I had spent a lot of time with people, and especially children whose lives were very difficult, and I had often felt helpless to do much for them. During this time I also had a Buddhist meditation practice going which had, over the years, yielded some pearls of insight about the emptiness of the "self" which would be, as I will discuss later, very important in clarifying the opening experience at Tomales Bay. I also studied philosophical subjects having to do with existentialism and phenomenology, areas that also analyzed the nature of Consciousness and the experience of the "self." But despite all of this, I still felt like something was missing spiritually.

So after taking the introductory course called The Human Sun

Seminar, which explained basic concepts, I headed to the Waking Down Weekend in Boulder. I wanted an experience of transmission, an experience that would convince me that this teaching was more than just another weekend with nice people talking about a spiritual topic.

On that weekend I found what I had been looking for. While doing the open-eye gazing with Van, one of the teachers, I felt a ripple of energy in my body which drew my attention upward. My legs felt like they wanted to lift up as if they were trying to levitate and there was a feeling of euphoria. After the gazing finished we took a break. When we resumed, one of the teachers, Ben Hursh, stood up to speak. As he did I could feel an emotional intensity building in him and also in myself. It was like feeling an eruption about to happen. As he spoke very passionately, telling us that we all deserved to be awakened, I felt a jolt of energy hit me each time he made one of his three points.

The next day, as I drove the thousand miles back to Illinois, I felt myself go in and out of tearfulness as my feelings were somehow deeper. For a year and a half after that things were never quite the same. Each time I attended an event I would feel like I was in a subtle force field, like feeling a soft current of water pushing against me. Along with this came a continuous flow of deepening insights about myself. Some of these had to do with my family while others had to do with my personality defenses. But all of these involved an increasing sense of openness within myself.

Eventually this deepening led to some experiences of "witnessing," a sensation of being aware of yourself from outside, like feeling part of yourself watching from the outside. The first of these occurred on a trip to Chicago. As I was driving, I felt that my awareness was situated in front of me on the left side of the chest. From there I could sort of watch my mind working. The term "Great Relief" came to my mind. It was the name of another workshop that Saniel Bonder offered, but at that time I had only seen those words a time or two on the Waking Down web site. That term had meaning because there was a feeling of having been freed from the mental/emotional turning that always seems to be going on in the space called "mind." The experience of this Witnessing Awareness showed me that there was a "space" that could be free from the swirling mind. I even told my wife how amusing it was watching myself get irritated at other cars that were following too close. Experiences like that happened several times preceding the understanding on the Bay.

But it is very important to point out that even before I became involved in Waking Down, there had been, over the years, "spiritual" experiences similar to that—some lasting a few seconds, others a few or several moments. Indeed, like many others of my generation, I had become fascinated with spirituality through LSD. Thirty years ago during LSD experiences I had, on one occasion, merged for an instant into a white light. On another occasion, again after I had taken LSD, as I sank deeper and deeper into a meditative trance I suddenly felt like a spring had been released, and I merged for a second into what felt like the great space which contained me. For a few hours after, everyone I saw seemed like they were monks and all of us were on this spiritual journey together. These experiences showed me that Consciousness was a very strange thing and also started me on a serious spiritual quest.

A few years later, after I had quit using drugs and taken up meditation, I was planting onions in my garden. While I did so, I was repeating a mantra I had received from an Indian guru. Suddenly, my left hand felt disconnected from me until my sense of self seemed to be off in the distance. It felt like the onion and my hand were one thing or like the onion was using the hand to plant itself. It was not an out-of-body experience but, as I now recognize, a "witnessing." A few years later when I attended some Buddhists retreats, I again had similar experiences.

On my first retreat, which lasted seven days, as I sat in meditation a part of me was feeling tired and sore and a kind of whining voice started in my mind saying how tired and sore I was, and then another voice, which I called the "Master Sergeant" voice, popped in saying, "Stop your whining. You have been whining your whole life." And there was another detached part of "me" watching and listening to this go on. Then, a day later, as the meditation process deepened, something one of the teacher said flashed through my mind—"The known and the knower arise together." When that happened a sense of release occurred. And a few minutes later as I walked outside, I felt as though my body was an empty, little, rubber, robotic doll walking in this great Awareness.

On other retreats, I had similar experiences. Even though most lasted only a few seconds, they showed me that an opening beyond the limited and isolated sense of "self" existed. One occurred when I was naming the sensations as they arose in my body. If I felt my hand I silently said, "Hand." If I felt my foot I said, "Foot." The sensations arose so fast that the naming fell away, and there was just these ongoing sensations without an "I"—as though the sensations were arising like light bulbs going off and on. On another occasion, the sensations of my body merged into a feeling like a wave and the only sense of "I" was that wave and the awareness in which it was arising.

But in all these experiences, while there was a sense of losing the separate self, there was not an identification with the Consciousness that remained. I did not get the big *meaning* that "I" was also that transcendental Awareness. But in the moment at Tomales Bay there was the realization that Awareness was holding all aspects of the "I" together. Even the sensation of separateness itself was held in higher Awareness. Those other experiences lasted as memories, and I used them to extract their meaning about the illusoriness of the ego, but there would always be a falling back into separateness. After the experience on the bay, however, there always remained a sense of being connected to part of a space which contains all sensation, both physical and mental.

All of the above sets a context which explains how this experience was what might be called a basic Awakening 101. I often say I don't have myself confused with Ramana Maharshi. Saniel in his book, *The White-Hot Yoga of the Heart*, says that, "The noticing, witnessing conscious nature that you fall into identification with is so small, so work-a-day ordinary," but "this ordinary conscious nature is in fact not other than the thermonuclear source of the entire cosmic display." So it was with this first basic awakening, but it has changed me from a seeker to explorer.

Since that opening, it is interesting how, from this perspective, I can see that everyone has this wakefulness just at the tip of their fingers. But the difference seems to be understanding why this basic Awareness is a big deal. It is easy to say to someone, "Are you conscious?" and they say, "Yes, I can feel myself sitting here, talking." But it is not a big deal to them. They don't feel an awakening. Why? It seems to be because they see awareness as an extension of the egoic self. There is a self who is aware of consciousness, but that consciousness seems like a shadow —something that is obvious but not very relevant to the thoughts and feelings going on in the egoic mind/self.

In awakening, however, I realized just the reverse. Awareness becomes primary, the source from which the egoic body/mind is arising. This was the key thing that occurred in that moment. I felt the primariness of Consciousness as who "I" am. Furthermore, as the understanding matured, I saw that this egoic body/mind, that felt inner sense of thought and feelings knotted together which often creates a feeling of isolation and confusion is OK, that it itself is part of the process of reality. It is a primal process, a "Core Wound," as Saniel calls it. It is not an enemy as the Eastern traditions say. Awakening puts this egoic process into the correct context. Consequently, I have found that "understanding the experience" is an important part of the awakening process. As I said, it made all those earlier experiences make more sense

In the months since, there has been a persistent but gentle expansion of the sense of being part of a larger self. In part, this has been the result of an erosion of those identities that made up who "I" thought I was. My identities as a therapist, a teacher, an intellectual person, had to be released. Consequently, as these identities have become more amorphous, there has been a sense, a feeling, of being lived by a greater process, one in which the mind/ body arises. At times it feels like being surrounded by Consciousness. Also, the erosion of these identities has resulted in feeling more deeply into the "Core Wound." This is Saniel Bonder's term for that basic feeling of separateness and isolation. It is the feeling into this "wound" that, in part, makes up the "down" part of "Waking Down." This deepening involves letting those feelings of isolation, alienation, and anxiety that seem to underlie our separateness stand out. In doing this there has developed the understanding that these feelings are really the very basic core around which our "identities" are built.

When feeling into these places, the realization occurs that there is a oneness with all beings, a feeling that all of us are united by this basic fear—all those aging people in nursing homes, hospitals or prisons and all those who are feeling this fundamental alienation that freezes all us into fearful separateness. We all have this basic, ongoing, low grade, primal anxiety, a kind of emotional vigilance always sensing the next threat or, in a more positive tone, trying to expand itself to break out of its fearful limits.

But what is amazing is that this core feeling has become, dare I say, somewhat pleasurable as it occurs in the wider space of awareness. I might say it feels not like "my" fearfulness, but the fearfulness of existence. It has a generic quality. It seems to be the place where we must go to find the love that connects us to all beings.

"I explained to her that I could no longer orient myself to that place above and to the left of my head to observe myself. My whole Being was centered in my body. There was no separation!"

Tom

Tom Cain was born and raised in Seattle, Washington. Several years after graduating from college, he embarked on a career in apartment investment brokerage with a large company. Eight years later he started his own apartment investment brokerage with a partner. After 27 years he continues to operate this company but without the original partner. He started three other businesses with partners: one sold, one folded and one he continues to operate. After two marriages, he is in a long-term, committed relationship with Lena O'Neill, who is also in her Second Life. He enjoys collecting and listening to LP albums, gardening, cultivating his orchard, and watching professional basketball.

NON-SEPARATE CONSCIOUS EMBODIMENT

In the second grade my relationship with God took a turn for the worse. I was critically injured in a bicycle accident, and in order to save my life the doctors amputated my right arm. After a while my grief turned to anger, and I confronted Him, "Why me, God?" What did I do to deserve this? It wasn't fair. Eventually, God and I patched things up, and I went back to loving Him.

I went to Seattle Prep, a Jesuit high school for boys, where my father had gone before me. Overall, I received an excellent education there, but I became at odds with the religious dogma and its contradictions. How an all-knowing and all-loving God could send people's souls to hell for eternity for doing things like eating meat on Friday was beyond me.

After I graduated from Seattle University, I took a summer job in Alaska to earn money so I could travel in Europe. Growing up I had always loved nature. Where I worked was a vast expanse of land , water and mountains with very few people. I began to see that I was like all the living things—the plants, fish, birds, insects and other mammals—being born, living and dying. I was not greater or lesser than any other living thing. I gave up the notion of an afterlife. I concluded that God did not create man, but that man created God as an idea or concept and heaven as a strategy to overcome mortality. Atheism wasn't acceptable to me because the nonexistence of God was not provable. I concluded that I was an agnostic. I became quite comfortable with this and attained a level of peace that I had not experienced before. My agnosticism lasted seventeen years.

When I was thirty-six I began having extrasensory experiences. At work the phone would ring, I would think of a person's name, and that person would be on the line. On two other occasions at home I started thinking about a person that I would not normally think about, and several minutes later the person was knocking at my door. I could no longer limit existence to the physical. I went to Tower Books and purchased some mainstream books on ESP. I soon became convinced that life was not limited to the five senses. I immersed myself in learning about spirituality. I had this incredible hunger to know about existence, particularly my existence.

I continued to devour spiritual books. I began meditating daily. I knew that I was capable of attaining a greater level of peace and happiness, and I yearned for this. My earliest teachers were channeled entities whose love and wisdom were inspirational to me. I became immersed in the teachings of Paramahansa Yogananda. I wanted to become Enlightened. I also became very interested in spiritual healing and did work in this regard, especially around the pain I experienced in my family of origin

A friend who taught me in a meditation class introduced me to advaita vendanta, which I embraced. Some years later another friend showed me a videotape of a woman named Gangaji, an American spiritual teacher who met her teacher in India, a man named Poonjaji. This inspired me to attend a spiritual retreat in Northern California in the spring of 1998. Seated immediately in front of the seat where she was to sit, I waited for her to come into the room for the afternoon session. By the time she took her seat I was in a sublime state of indescribable bliss, peace and joy. I experienced myself as the vastness of Being, and yet I was still aware of my body. My eyes remained closed, tears streaming down my face from time to time. I wanted this to never end; it lasted for about four hours. My life was forever changed.

Later, sometime after I came home to Seattle, I learned that this had been a samadhi experience. My mind had stopped. I had never been so happy and peaceful. After about three weeks the thinking mind was back, an integral part of me again, with its tendency to worry about the future. Regardless, I knew that I was happier and more peaceful than I had been. I was fundamentally aware of my Being.

Through the years I continued to go to Gangaji retreats and to other retreats and events held by self-realized teachers. While I deeply appreciated the others, in a spiritual sense my heart belonged to Gangaji. When I was in her presence I experienced bhakti, the quality of heartfelt devotion that is described in Hindu tradition. As a Westerner I never dreamed of experiencing something that was so foreign to my culture.

Also, I began a journey of deepening into "Consciousness as the true nature of my Being." Oftentimes, as my thoughts arose, I would observe them as if from a distance, and then they would disappear into That from which they arose. More and more, I would watch my thoughts, emotions, body and circumstances as not really being who I am. I came to see that which comes and goes, that which appears and disappears, as not real, but only indescribable Being as real. I had identified as Witness Consciousness, seemingly existing in an area above and away from the back of the left side of my head.

Over time there developed a very high degree of non-attachment to my body, thoughts, emotions and circumstances. There was also greater space between my thoughts, and when they arose I was able to watch and let them go instead of identifying with and following them. I truly was in touch with a level of inner peace on a day-to-day basis that I hadn't experienced before. I was more aware, sensitive and compassionate. I had realized my true nature as Pure Consciousness. I believed that I was no longer seeking. But there was a longing that I felt that seemed at odds with myself as a non-seeker.

In early 2002 I went to my seventh Gangaji retreat and didn't get much out of it. In the past I had experienced such joy, nourishment and inspiration. In the fall I went to another retreat by a very gifted realizer I knew. I was very impressed with him and the energy he put into the retreat, but again it left me unfulfilled. The old ways of getting spiritual sustenance were failing me.

In January 2003 I went to check out Saniel Bonder at a Friday evening presentation in Seattle. A friend of mine, Krishna Gauci, whose spirituality I respected, brought him here. Krishna was a fellow advaitic, and I knew that Saniel was not of this tradition. I was curious.

During the sitting I was impressed by Saniel's aliveness, intellect and the way he engaged and related to the audience. I also liked his wife, Linda, who was presenting with Saniel. I bought *Waking Down in Mutuality* and left to go to my cabin for the weekend with my beloved, Lena, where I briefly read some of the book. After I got home and went to bed Sunday night something very unusual happened. During the night I woke up twice and then again in the morning. Each time I realized that in my dream I had been immersed in the Waking Down process, without really understanding what the process was. It was as if I had spent the whole night in a dream state in the Waking Down process! Nothing had ever happened to me like this before. I pay attention to my dreams, and I decided that this was something I was meant to pursue.

As part of the Waking Down work, one who is considering getting involved is encouraged to conduct an investigation or "due diligence" concerning the teaching and transmission. I talked to a few acquaintances I had met at past spiritual gatherings who were actively involved in the Waking Down process who encouraged me. Lena and I also attended a sitting that was open to people who had seen Saniel in January. We learned a bit about what the Waking Down work was and wasn't. Lena and I then attended the Human Sun Seminar which helped me understand the basic concepts and terms.

After that I began working with Krishna as my teacher and Michaela Kapilla as my mentor. Just a few weeks later in March, Lena and I went to the Waking Down Weekend in Seattle. What was amazing to me was the number of awakened teachers and mentors that came to facilitate the workshop. It was very interactive among the participants, teachers and mentors. We broke up into small groups, each with a mentor and teacher, for a number of sessions during the weekend. In each group the participants were given an allotted time to talk about what was going on in their life, particularly the hard and challenging aspects. The sharing was in confidence, and the teachers, mentors and even participants would give feedback.

Another part of the workshop was devoted to sitting and gazing. The teachers would sit at the front of the room and gaze into the eyes of the participants who were seated facing them. It is like a traditional meditation except people's eyes are open. As I recall, the participants had the option of keeping their eyes closed if they wished.

Over the next few months I experienced deep emotions relating to challenging situations in my everyday life. These were very difficult to experience, but I had Krishna and Michaela to help me through them. I am a mental type based on the Enneagram, not an emotional type. It was as if my emotions were exaggerated. I found that after these "oscillations" were over I would have low energy for a few days.

Gradually, I began experiencing my thoughts in a more comfortable, less dissociated way. Having awakened to Consciousness before this work, I could see that there was some kind of process that was bringing me more into my body. More and more I was experiencing thoughts as being part of who I am as opposed to observing them as the Witness. There was less alienation and separation from my thoughts. It was more like I used to experience the thinking process before I was awake except that now I was awake.

In May, Lena and I attended the Transfiguration Retreat in Estes Park, Colorado. During the first evening Saniel played one of his flutes. Listening I was moved to tears. Its tone and music was very Native American sounding. Saniel announced that he planned to do individual shamanic healings during the course of the retreat. I signed up for a morning session.

Lena and I arrived at the cabin where the healing sessions were being held that morning. About ten of us gathered around Saniel in a circle so the person he was working with could lie on the floor in the space in the middle. He told us that he wanted us to state what our intention would be at the beginning of our individual healing sessions. When my turn came, before Saniel even had a chance to raise his head up and look into my eyes, I blurted out, "I want my Second Birth!" He responded, "Easy enough." I stretched out on the floor. He specifically stated, "This is Conscious Embodiment," in referring to the Second Birth.

Saniel asked me about my arm and I told him about the accident. In addition to having my forearm crushed in the accident, I had four broken ribs and a collapsed lung. He asked if there was sensitivity on my right side and I told him that there was some numbness. With my permission he rubbed my chest area with his hands. He talked about the sorrow settling into the lower part of my heart. I gave permission to the people there to put their hands on me. Then Saniel asked which of his flutes I wanted him to play, and I asked him to play the one called The Wound. Soon after he began playing with the end of the flute aimed at my chest, I was flooded with profound grief and sorrow. I began wailing loudly, my chest heaving, the sound of the Indian music connecting me to a past Indian lifetime.

Afterward, Lena and I went to lunch at the common dining area. I shared with her a past lifetime that I had been aware of when I was a

Native American chief, head of a tribe and also a leader of many tribes. We were plains Indians. This is all I knew. I have never been able to have visions and I was always grateful to those who were able to have them to assist me. As I was telling this to Lena, she had a vision of my being a chief. She saw teepees. Fighting was in progress. Arrows were the weapons. In that lifetime at that time I was filled with heartbreak, grief and despair; my heart was experiencing excruciating physical pain. As Lena spoke, I began crying. She told me that my body was too old and worn out from fighting battles to fight, and that my people didn't want me to fight. I had been hidden in a teepee. I realized that my tribe was being massacred. The pain in my heart was so unbearable that I plunged my knife into my heart and died.

Lena revealed that in that lifetime she had been my wife and was visiting another tribe while this had occurred and her life was saved as a result. When she returned to the village she discovered that the entire tribe had been killed or were gone. The ground was covered with dead male bodies. I continued crying at lunch and sometime after when we were walking back to our cabins. My telling Lena that I used to run through Lincoln Park near where I live in Seattle in the early mornings in my buffalo skin moccasins seemed to lift my spirits.

At my small group meeting that afternoon, I explained my affinity to Native Americans and their culture—my books of Indian photos and stories, Indian prints and paintings on the walls of my home, miniature totem poles and my wolf drum. I told about a few sweat lodge experiences, including one alone by myself on the night I was initiated as a fire-walking instructor.

I told Hillary, our small group teacher, that I wanted to continue pressing this broken zone. She suggested that I lie on the floor, which I did, and she was able to get me in touch with that lifetime. I spent a while crying again. After I stopped crying, Hillary suggested that I focus my attention on my body. I tuned into the energetic sensations inside my body, becoming very aware of my body. After a while I felt very relaxed and got up. When I sat on the couch, she asked me how I felt, and I told her I felt very expanded and relaxed. She told me I looked very big. Jeff, who was the group's mentor, told me that he saw me as an Indian chief when I was on the floor. Hillary told me that when I was on the floor she saw this large energy come into my lower body. It was a very grounded energy that was associated with my lower chakras including my sexuality. I was sitting on the couch across from Hillary when she crawled over to me on the floor, held my feet with her hands and bowed to me.

The next day each of us in the small group had the option of meeting with Hillary in private for a session. I had clearly changed. I was very expanded and peaceful. I explained to her that I could no longer orient myself to that place above and to the left of my head to observe myself. My whole Being was centered in my body. There was no separation! She shared with me that when I was sitting on the couch the day before, after I got up from the floor, I appeared as an Indian, eight feet tall. This must have been why she told me that I looked big that day.

My relationship with Lena during the rest of the retreat deepened to a level I didn't think possible. I also realized that the feeling of longing that I had been trying to satisfy was no longer present. I had experienced my Second Birth.

Since then I have experienced life and myself with greater fullness and expression. I find that it is very difficult for me to keep thoughts and emotions inside when they want to be expressed, even when it's hard to do. Expressing what is true for me has become paramount and I have a deep appreciation for others who can do the same. I have a greater level of empathy and acceptance of others. I crave authenticity in relationships. My ability and willingness to experience emotions is greater, and yet I am more deeply grounded in Being. More and more I am bringing to life all that I am. I have more confidence in Being.

Also, through this work I have become very sensitive to others, and myself in relationship to others. I can experience other as my Self and other simultaneously. For instance, if I am having a conversation with someone I can experience us as non-separate and as separate individuals at the same time.

As an example, my relationship with Lena is one of the biggest beneficiaries of being in my Second Life. When her behavior is a problem for me, I can no longer really stuff my feelings, at least not for very long. I have this innate impulse to express how I am feeling that was not nearly as present before the Second Birth. Conversely, if Lena is upset with me for something I may have said or done, and verbalizes it, I am much less willing to react. I am able to hang in there and be with her with whatever it is that she is expressing. More and more I can feel what she has been experiencing around a particular issue and gain a real understanding of her perspective as we continue to talk. I have greater compassion and capacity for feeling. These conflicts ultimately most often result in experiencing the deep love I have for her. Before the Second Birth I was quicker to defend myself, less apt to work things through.

Waking Down is not easy. As I recall, Saniel has referred to it as a hero's journey. As I write this I have been in and am in what is described as a "shakedown." The way I am experiencing it is with low energy. At times my personal situation feels overwhelming with the significant tasks that are before me. I am experiencing very difficult personal challenges. I have periods of anxiety and there are times when I feel depressed. Generally, this is not the way I experience life. Yet, I persevere.

I am deeply grateful to Gangaji, and to her teachers, Poonjaji and Ramana Maharshi. Through their teachings, inspiration and transmission, and through grace, I realized my Self as Pure Consciousness. I realized that I was everything and nothing. But even in this deep realization, I can now see that there was a subtle split as I experienced it. As Witness Consciousness, observing my thoughts, emotions, body and circumstances as not real, or, as not real from the perspective of the Self, there was definitely an inferior quality given to anything other than the Infinite. As a Waking Down realizer, this is no longer the case.

I marvel at the map that Saniel and the early Waking Down realizers have put together to delineate this process. It seems that each person's process is unique, as each individual is unique. But there also seem to be stages that occur as one moves through this process. I am speaking as someone whose Second Birth happened fairly quickly. From what I can gather, this process seems to be accelerating for people who are newer to the work compared to those that have come before. I also do not want to give the impression that I know a lot about this teaching and transmission. I know more deeply who I am now, but I also know that as a human being I am a relative newborn in my Second Life. There are further levels of deepening that I have learned about but have not realized.

I am deeply grateful to Saniel and the others who have brought this teaching and transmission forward. I feel love and a reverence for those individuals who have been my teachers and mentors in this work. Sometimes I have been in awe of the way that they are. Yet, I have never put any of them on a pedestal as I have with many of my previous spiritual teachers. For me, this seems to be an aspect of mutuality that is inherent in this process. One of the most inspiring things for me is being with the teachers in this work. I have never been with a group of people who are so radiantly alive. It's contagious!

MY SECOND LIFE

Life began anew for me on May 22, 2003. For the first few months, I was in a state that was bordering on euphoria. I felt invincible and capable of achieving anything I put my mind to. At that time I owned an apartment investment brokerage that had been quite successful for twenty-five years but was in a state of decline. I had an opportunity to start a new business that would complement and support my brokerage business. With an out-of-state company that would provide a technological platform and support, I was to provide a database, my expertise and local support. I was confident that everything would fall into place. I had no idea of the enormity of what I was about to undertake.

I immediately began to experience staffing problems. The amount of additional data I had to accumulate to expand my existing database was overwhelming, and I had to hire many people to accomplish this. The time frame that I had set for completing this turned out to be unrealistic. I was working harder than I had ever worked before in my life; I rarely took a day off. I was extremely stressed out. My partner, Lena, injured her leg in an accident and couldn't walk without crutches and couldn't drive. On top of everything that was going on at work, I became her primary caregiver. The apparent neurological complications associated with her injury gave rise to the possibility that she would never walk again. My brokerage was losing money, I was investing money to get my new business going, and I was the sole means of support for Lena and her daughter who lived in a separate household. In addition to being under the stress of constantly working, I was suffering from anxiety about my financial situation. Lena was despondent about the possibility of never being able to walk again. Our relationship was in turmoil. My life was a nightmare.

The next year my brokerage made money, but the remaining agents left. This was the demise of a 28-year-old business that I had spent a lifetime building. I was devastated. The next few years of trying to make a go of my new business were extremely difficult. Eventually, I got to the point where the level of negative cash flow from the business was tolerable, and the work of creating my product was basically completed. There was a lengthy period of time when my partners and I had reached an impasse over operational issues. We eventually resolved our differences and began working together again.

Less than three months later I got sick. I lost my energy and my olfactory sense. I saw a variety of doctors and health care practitioners, none of whom could figure out what was wrong with me or help me get my energy back. It was like I had chronic fatigue. I didn't know if I would ever get my health back. Finally, after six months my energy returned. I was relieved. I still couldn't smell anything, though.

Four and a half years after my Second Birth, things began to look up. Recently, I have had some major breakthroughs in my new business. I can see the potential for profitability.

I have wondered from time to time what my life would have been like during the past five years if I had never had my Second Birth. I have no doubt that my main company would have gone out of business, as it did. In the midst of my agony during its demise, there was also a sense of relief. I had lost my enthusiasm for this business after so many years. I probably would have started the new business, although I don't know if I would have had the tenacity to work through the extreme hardships. As I write this I am OK with having gone through what I have written about here. What I am more than OK about is who I have become as a person. I wouldn't have traded this for anything.

Out of the pain and suffering have come integration, healing and wholeness. In the most difficult of times, as horrible as they were, I never forgot or doubted that I was Being, Onlyness, Consciousness, or God. There were times when I wished my life would be over, times when I wondered when my life would begin, but I never forgot who I Am.

I believe that the worst of what is referred to as the Wakedown Shakedown is over. I, as Being, or as the Life Force, whatever one may choose to call the universal, infinite part of one's self, together with the limited, finite "me," created circumstances and situations that allowed me to enter into those dark, wounded, broken places to fully experience them as an awakened man. This, the Wakedown Shakedown, was and is the catalyst for my integration and deep healing.

I am much more at peace with myself and life. Yes, my natural inclination is to avoid pain and suffering, but I am more able to accept its inevitability, as being part of life and not separate from me. As a result I am not struggling against the pain and suffering as I once was.

During this time I have become more aware of the impulse of Being alive in me, as me, and working through me, not separate. I have reached a point where my life is in service. Sometimes, when I am inspired to do things, the Buddhist term, Right Action, comes to mind. More and more I am able to feel into my body to help guide me in deciding what course to take, or sometimes to simply get information

I feel more; I am more aware and in the flow of life. I have never experienced this deep a level of compassion: loving the other as who I Am without judgment. As an example, before my Second Life I may have felt anger toward a perpetrator, sadness for a victim. Now, not always, but often I feel compassion for both.

I am less resisting, more accepting. When I am with someone, I have a greater capacity to take that person in and to hold him or her. There is a level of grace in being in relationship with another that I hadn't experienced before.

I still experience what are considered negative emotions, especially anger. Sometimes, when I might break something, spill something, or am unable to get something to work, I may explode in anger. At other times when I experience something that would normally trigger my anger, anger does not arise at all. I have no explanation for this; I just observe the absence of anger or experience the anger. When it comes to being angry at people's behavior, I am careful to treat others with respect when I express anger toward them. Mostly, my anger is directed at objects or myself.

I still experience fear, but it has eased. Not long ago I gave an hour lecture to an audience of around 150 people at the big annual apartment industry event where I live. I had spent most of my life being absolutely terrified about the thought of public speaking. The lecture was a big deal for me to do. It went well. I believe the process of speaking what is in my heart in Waking Down events has helped me in this regard.

I am 65 years old, and in some ways it seems like my life is just beginning. I am more alive. I have more energy for living. My life has never been so meaningful, the future so full of potential. Being a board member of the Institute of Awakened Mutuality is very fulfilling to me. Helping to make the world a better place gives me great satisfaction. I reflect on the deep fear of boredom that I used to have, especially around the prospects of getting older. This is no longer present. Opportunities for growth and fulfillment continue to materialize as I grow older.

I am extremely grateful for the support I have received from the Waking Down community. This includes my sessions with Krishna, sittings with Krishna and Lena, and the Second Life classes and the Transfiguration Retreats sponsored by the Institute of Awakened Mutuality. I am especially grateful for my relationship with Lena, my fiancé, who is currently an interning teacher in Waking Down. The love and trust we have for each other continues to deepen.

"This embodied Whole-Being awakening for the common folk is now very possible and very available..."

Van

Van Nguyen is a senior teacher of the Waking Down in Mutuality process. He is of Vietnamese ancestry and was born on March 5, 1951, in San Francisco, where he currently resides and works as a holistic dentist. As part of his search, Van was a long-time spiritual seeker (and "seminar junkie".) Among a variety of issues, he lives and dances with a version of obsessive-compulsive disorder. Van loves music and plays the shakuhachi, a Japanese bamboo flute. For recreation he enjoys surfing, snow-boarding, skiing, and hiking the Rockies. He currently surfs on a nine-foot Infinity surfboard at Santa Cruz's Pleasure Point beach.

IS IT WORTH IT?
A VIEW FROM 10 YEARS DOWN THE ROAD

Is it worth it? It's a hero's and heroine's journey, and it is worth it.

I feel that in having realized embodied awakening (that we are calling the Second Birth) and in living it day to day, I am living at the heart or core of existence. Although it's a workout to live in such raw vulnerability in the paradoxical whole spectrum of Being that each of us is, there is a fundamental wellness and inherent enjoyment of living in this embodied awakeness. Though it's a wild ride as we grow, evolve, and deepen in the Second Birth, this wellness and enjoyment magnify.

From the perspective of living this process for ten years in the Second Life, it definitely is worth it. Borrowing from the old Cream song that a friend recently reminded me of, "I'm so glad, I'm so glad. I'm glad, I'm glad, I'm glad." Let me sing some praises of the Second Birth and Second Life by sharing some personal experiences with you.

Very recently I experienced a graceful intensification that epitomizes and illustrates the further growth and integration that happen in the Second Life. I was doing some shopping at Whole Foods in San Rafael on a sunny Sunday afternoon. I had just been attending a three and a half-day Waking Down teachers' retreat and was feeling a satisfaction from all the hard work we did. I was also feeling some sadness from saying good-by to dear friends whom I may not see again in-person for another year. As I was walking around the crowded, hustling and bustling store, I was experiencing a magnification and intensification of embodied awakeness. What gracefully unfolded could be summarized as the following: the fullness and radiance of Being magnified, the human and divine became even more seamlessly interwoven, at home-ness in the body magnified, connectedness with others magnified, love magnified, and gladness or bliss magnified. Yet I was still being little, old "me" with all my neuroses and quirks as I was shopping.

To fully and truly describe this experience in words is not possible. Words are limited and conceptual symbols, and this Second Birth condition is so paradoxical. Only one side of the paradox can be spoken at a time, and the mind can't comprehend a paradox. In an attempt to use words to go beyond words, I will use a poetic form to convey a taste of what so wonderfully unfolded.

Shopping in the Continuum

The Continuum of Being is so intense! The rested resolution in my living core magnifies and spreads throughout the store.

The Heart is alive as all of this and me! Still I am the simple, ordinary human "me"–quirky and anxious.

I feel so at rest in this Continuum–the great paradoxical Continuum of Whole Being. I am unique, individuated–me–and I melt into the seamless totality that's me, too.

I'm so glad! At the same time, the whole variety of my feelings still goes up and down, comes and goes, arising and disappearing in Consciousness–the unchanging primordial Ground…

Paradoxically, the world is Consciousness. The world is alive as radiant Divine energy, manifested as this matter. The world is imbued and suffused by the all-pervading love-foundation of the Feminine Heart of Being.

The Continuum is so utter. I am It. It is "me." Everyone is This.

Everything is This.

My body is This. Everyone's body is This. The body is none other than this Continuum.

Strolling in the store, I feel so grounded in the body. This particular body–such solidity with feelings and sensations more raw. This store–such solidity with bright colors, smells, and sounds jumping out. This world–such solidity with hot and cold, big wow's and ow's–yet simultaneously, mysteriously seamless with the Transcendental Is-ness.

This is crazy, and blissful.

It's an extreme Continuum, yet I am at rest in the paradoxical seamlessness. Utter seamlessness and paradoxical multiplicity–simultaneous.

Alive non-dual multiplicity with heart. Heart-consciousness alive as all of this.

The bottomless well of seamlessness–gushing. The fire of seamlessness–blazing!

I'm still "me" within it. The seamlessness is pushing out of all things.

The new moment–complete, intense. Love-aliveness-bliss dancing in the stillness of unmoving Beingness. I'm reveling in the seamless This-ness.

Everyone is This. Every body is This.

In seamless now-ness, I am this naked body, more and more. I am this body more intensely than ever before. Ups and downs. Downs and ups. OK!

Yet, the Radiant Divine Mystery is intoxicating me now. I am It, as It is me. It is all of these people, all of these vegetables, all of these teas and nut butters.

My mind loves it, and reels in the inexplicability of it all.

How enjoyable. How absolute. And how ordinary.

Radiance and Consciousness–Divine Feminine and Divine Masculine. Shakti and Shiva are wedded and dancing everywhere. In the olive oil, in the zucchinis, and in the sweet little girl picking out bright Red Delicious apples with her father.

Love sings and dances as this.

The Heart of the Goddess underlies all these forms and becomes all forms.

We are Radiant Aliveness manifesting as all of this ordinariness and ordinary stuff. We are permeated by the Radiant Heart of the Divine Feminine–embracing, being all of us, all of this.

I'm just walking around picking out succulent vegetables and aromatic teas, with my heart swelling.

I'm deeper into this matter body. I'm deeper into the world. I'm deeper at home here. In this wild, ordinary moment.

And it's utter, paradoxical, simultaneous, seam-less-ness.

Paradox again, and again, and again.

Radiant Transcendental Divinity and limited matter—married forever—swirling and dancing as this mysterious Great Continuum of Being.

Blissful embodied "madness."

It's worth it!

Let's go shopping!

I want to now share some brief commentary about this experience. These kinds of intensifications have their own organic ebbs and flows in the Second Life. The bodily registration of the Second Birth condition moves from the "back burner" to the "front burner" and vice versa for a variety of factors. A large chapter could be written about this subject.

In addition, since this is embodied awakening for common ordinary folks, the ordinary personality with its core psychological issues continues to show up in the Second Life. I'd like to share a living example of this with you.

After I finished shopping at Whole Foods, I headed for home and parked at San Francisco's Ocean Beach. I watched the surf and the surfers, and I wrote notes about my intensification experience as I was continuing to enjoy it. I later took a short walk down the sidewalk bordering the beach and enjoyed the bliss of the Continuum I was resting in. As I strolled down the sidewalk, I happened to look down and notice a cluster of "oil spots" on the sidewalk as I walked on them. I then experienced a minor flare up of my obsessive-compulsive disorder and felt anxious. I thought to myself something like, "Yuck, argh...Is this some spilled hazardous chemical or is it just motor oil?" I was feeling the anxiety–youch–along with the underlying, inherent bliss of Being. Both/and.

This bliss of Being is a "paradoxical bliss." It is the inherent fundamental underlying bliss and wellness of embodied Consciousness. I was resting in this while, simultaneously, my body-mind was feeling the unpleasant anxiety state. In paradoxical simultaneity I was being the body, with its ups and downs, which was feeling anxious, and at the same time, I was abiding as the Consciousness in which the feeling was arising, and thus was not exclusively identifying with it. It was all happening in the mysterious Continuum of Being.

The increased capacity to hold myself and be with the primal craziness that may get triggered in the course of everyday living and relationships is something that deepened in my growth and on-going maturing in the Second Life. It's a process that I've seen happen for my friends and students in their Second Life development, too.

Speaking of the growth and evolution in the Second Life, you've read some personal accounts of what we call the Wakedown Shakedown or divinely human descent. I would like to say that even the Wakedown Shakedown is worth it. From this integration process, I end up having a greater capacity to embrace the whole spectrum of the body's reality.

This process enables me to claim, inhabit, and live the fullness and whole spectrum of myself and my Self. However, I still consider myself a work-in-progress even after ten years in the Second Life.

To further provide a balanced picture, I think it's important to say that in the course of my stressful, everyday life, I tend to reside more of the time in my human personality and its concerns, frets, and worries–all in the midst of being fundamentally established in the paradoxical Whole Being continuum that comes with embodied awakeness. The intensification that I enjoyed at Whole Foods is not an everyday event, though I believe it represents the evolutionary direction of the maturation process in the Second Life.

In moving towards concluding, let me return to the original question: "Is it worth it?"

You betcha!

In my own process, over time from the growth and evolution that has taken place since my Second Birth transition, I have experienced a number of benefits and positive shifts:

- more at home as this particular body-mind, Van
- more acceptance and increased ability to hold the whole gamut of my own human-ness and the human-ness of others
- a broader repertoire of creative self-expression
- more acceptance of and improved management of my wounded areas
- enhanced emotional-psychological healing and greater capacity to embrace my shadow areas
- my heart healing and opening, and deeper self-love and love of others unfolding
- improved quality and depth of interpersonal interactions and intimate relationships
- increased receptivity and flow with grace
- a deeper integration of my spiritual and Divine nature
- a magnification of the inherent wellness and the Heart-bliss of Being
- a deepened enjoyment of and magnified communion with the Divine Feminine, or Feminine Heart of Being
- an intensification of the fullness and seamlessness of the Whole Spectrum Continuum of Being

The miracle and grace of the Second Birth unfolding for a common folk person like me has definitely been worth it. At the same time, the living of the intensity of the process is a wild and sometimes bumpy ride that takes a brave heart. That's what makes it a hero's and heroine's journey.

I see the Second Birth process as the movement of Being in your being. It comes as a deep impulse in your being. Furthermore, I believe there is a big wave of awakened Being currently hitting the planet and acting as a catalytic evolutionary force. Therefore, this embodied Whole-Being awakening for the common folk is now very possible and very available.

If you are reading this book and are finding yourself mysteriously resonating with it, then very likely you are currently riding the wave of awakened Whole Being in your own unique fashion and unfolding.

The ride is worth it.

Surf's up! Ride on in.

I believe that the world needs our awakened hearts, minds, and bodies now more than ever before.

I wish for us all great grace, great blessings, great happiness, and great love in our divinely human full flowering process.

Happy surfing!

Learn More about Waking Down

If you're interested in learning more about Waking Down in Mutuality, there are a number of resources to help you. The many teachers of WDM offer personalized one-on-one and small-group support for your unique awakening process through private sessions (either in person or by phone), group sittings, workshops, and phone bridges (conference calls) of many kinds. Visit www.wakingdown.org for further information, schedules of activities available for your participation, and other resources such as books and tapes and related web sites. Or contact the Waking Down in Mutuality office toll-free at 888-741-5000 for personalized assistance with any questions.

The educational branch of this work is the Institute of Awakened Mutuality, which provides both experiential and conceptual education in the teachings of Waking Down in Mutuality. The Institute offers introductory, basic, and advanced courses, including mentor and teacher trainings. The curriculum fosters the continuous deepening and integration of the many aspects of an authentic, embodied, conscious life, as students awaken to the full spectrum of their nature, and bring compassion and integrity to themselves, one another, and our world. Please visit www.awakenedmutuality.org for further information.

And as you may have noticed, a number of the writers' biographies contain contact information. This book is an invitation to meet new people and perhaps make new friends, so please feel free to contact whomever you want. There is a growing community of people throughout the U.S., Canada, and Europe who are awakening in this manner, and your participation to whatever degree feels right to you will be most welcomed.

Welcome to Waking Down in Mutuality. If we can be of service to you, please let us know.

Glossary

Bob asked me to contribute definitions for some of the basic Waking Down terminology, which I'm happy to provide here. I just want to warn you that these are my own personal definitions, and other contributors to this book may or may not agree with them. I should also warn you that words (especially words that attempt to express grand concepts of Being and human unfoldment) are very tricky and can easily cause doubt and confusion. People often use the same words to mean very different things, and even if we think we're agreeing on definitions, it doesn't necessarily mean we'd still agree if we got into a long conversation about them. To minimize misunderstanding, please ask individual Waking Down Teachers, Mentors, or practitioners what they mean by these words. Please note that terms in italics are themselves defined elsewhere in this glossary.
Ted Strauss

Awakening: 1. (Verb) The endless process of including more and more of *Being* in one's sense of Self. 2. (Noun) In many traditions, awakening refers to the realization of Self as transcendental consciousness; here it refers to the *Second Birth.*

Being: The totality of existence and non-existence. Everything Absolute and everything Relative; everything manifest and everything unmanifest; everything infinite and everything finite. *Consciousness* together with form, spirit together with matter. Some might call this God, but here the meaning has no religious or theistic overtones.

Bodymind: The manifest aspects of ourselves: our bodies, minds, feelings, personality, and energies. The human, finite, limited, conditional, and conditioned dimension of our existence. The individuated personhood.

Consciousness: The dimension of *Being* that is Absolute, without manifest attributes. Because Consciousness is beyond space and time, it is birthless, deathless, universal, and not limited in any way by any form or condition of Relative existence. At the same time, it is not in any way separate from form. We humans have the ability to know Consciousness as the essence of our subject selfhood when it is recognized as the *Witness Consciousness*.

Conscious Embodiment: Consciously choosing to arrive into personal incarnation and relatedness.

Conscious Wound: The *Second Life* version of the *Core Wound*. Once the *Core Wound* has been realized as the fundamental, existential feeling of one's own *Being*, that feeling becomes much more conscious.

Core Wound: Prior to the *Second Birth*, the fundamental, existential irritation or discomfort human beings feel at the intersection of the Absolute and Relative sides of *Being*. It is an underlying whole-Being feeling that is felt differently by different individuals, but is often characterized by words like primal separation, confusion, incompleteness, insufficiency, anxiety, entrapment, pressure, or yearning. This feeling is good because it prompts us to discover the unity at the basis of our perception of separation and differences.

Embodied Feeling-Witness Consciousness: A stage in the awakening process in which the practitioner is aware of the paradox of being simultaneously infinite and finite, while still perceiving these aspects of *Being* to be somehow separate, at odds with either other, or needing to be reconciled.

First Birth: The physical birth of the bodymind organism.

First Life: The life that follows the first birth until the *Second Birth* occurs.

Freedom: The willingness to feel pain in order to embody your own truth.

Greenlighting: A disposition of radical self-blessing practiced by Waking Down initiates. By giving ourselves a green light to be exactly the way we are with all our human faults and limitations, energy and attention is freed up that was previously bound up in patterns of self negation. The freed energy and attention permits a deepening recognition of our true and total nature.

Hypermasculine: Natural masculine qualities of detachment and mind-based analytical reasoning taken to out-of-balance extremes. Hypermasculine also refers to all the ways we are conditioned to fix, transcend, negate, reject, or numb out to life, rather than simply embrace it and let ourselves be affected.

Mutuality: 1. A disposition practiced by Waking Down initiates that basically says "my truth is true, your truth is true, our truths are often uncomfortably different, but we'll honor those differences and lean into that discomfort because we need and honor each other as part of ourselves." 2. A realization that matures through years of post *Second Birth* work in awakened relationship in which you increasingly discover that others are indeed part of yourself. 3. A capacity to get others' reality along with a willingness to be deeply affected by others and to be truly vulnerable in relationship. 4. The willingness to remain in direct communication and feeling contact with another, whether that brings joy or pain.

Onlyness: The *Second Life* perception of *Being* as a single, seamless reality that excludes nothing.

Rot: The Rot is a pre-*Second Birth* period of transition during which one loses faith in and fascination with in-the-world-conditioning and whole-Being beliefs that suggest there is a way to fix, escape, or transcend existential discomfort. It is a period of decay out of the natural, defensive, hypermasculine strategies for avoiding What Is that permits an increasingly stark encounter with the *Core Wound.*

Second Birth: The (sometimes very extended) moment in the awakening process when a person registers that his or her sense of self is no longer limited either to the *bodymind* or *Consciousness* (or both, as in the *Embodied Feeling-Witness Consciousness*), but seems to include All of Being. It is a shift in perception that permits the sense of self to include both unity and duality as a single, seamless reality that needs no reconciliation. It is often felt as a "landing"; a feeling of fundamental arrival into self, life, here, and now in a way that was previously unimaginable no matter how much we may have imagined it.

Second Life: The stage of life that follows the *Second Birth.*

Wakedown Shakedown: A period (usually spanning many years) of sometimes intense purification that spontaneously follows the *Second Birth.* The Shakedown brings every hidden wound, split, and pattern in your Being into the light of realized *Onlyness* for investigation and healing.

Waking Down In Mutuality: Consciously inviting awakened or awakening consciousness to enter the personal, bodily, and relational dimensions of existence in *mutuality* with others who are doing the same.

Witness Consciousness: Conscious recognition of the aspect of *Being* that is unmanifest, and is registering experience and form. For awhile, the witness can appear to be somewhat detached from life. As the awakening process matures, the witness is recognized as simultaneous with the *bodymind* reality (see, *Embodied Feeling-Witness Consciousness*). After that, the witness appears to be identical to the *bodymind* and experience. Years after the *Second Birth*, any sense of there being a witness that is separate from form disappears.